Black Scholars in White Space

Black Scholars in White Space

New Vistas in African American Studies
from the Christian Academy

edited by
Anthony B. Bradley

PICKWICK *Publications* · Eugene, Oregon

BLACK SCHOLARS IN WHITE SPACE
New Vistas in African American Studies from the Christian Academy

Copyright © 2015 Wipf and Stock Publishers. All rights reserved. Except for brief quotations in critical publications or reviews, no part of this book may be reproduced in any manner without prior written permission from the publisher. Write: Permissions. Wipf and Stock Publishers, 199 W. 8th Ave., Suite 3, Eugene, OR 97401.

Pickwick Publications
An Imprint of Wipf and Stock Publishers
199 W. 8th Ave., Suite 3
Eugene, OR 97401

www.wipfandstock.com

ISBN 13: 978-1-62032-995-5

Cataloguing-in-Publication Data

Black scholars in white space : new vistas in African American studies from the Christian academy / edited by Anthony B. Bradley.

xx + [209] p. ; 23 cm. —Includes bibliographical references and index(es).

ISBN 13: 978-1-62032-995-5

1. Christian universities and colleges—United States. 2. African Americans—Education (Higher)—United States. I. Title.

LC3727 B65 2014

Manufactured in the U.S.A.   01/14/2015

To Mom, Kim, Tanya, Madison, San, and Amy Kristina

Contents

Religious, Historical, and Cultural Studies

Preface

Where are the African American scholars?

ON AN AMTRAK TRAIN from Philadelphia to New York I was having one of those reflective moments watching the landscape whisk by. In the long journey that culminated in this book's production I reflected on the two experiences that were critical to the idea for this book. First, I was recently speaking at a conference comprised of real "movers and shakers" in the evangelical Protestant world and I noticed that I was the only African American scholar on the roster who teaches at an evangelical college. At first I thought it was odd, given the content and context of a conference that dealt with many issues involving the black community. I left wondering why the conference organizers did not know about the long list of black scholars who could have addressed those issues. The conventional wisdom is that black scholars simply do not exist in high numbers in American evangelical Protestant academic circles. While it is true that black scholars are in low numbers overall in the academy and at religious schools this does not warrant the assumption that these scholars do not exist at all. This book is a way for me to identify some of them. The second experience that launched this project came while taking a feminist theology course with Professor Jeannine Hill Fletcher at Fordham University. I was sitting in class one day when I thought, "What African American women are making history by being the first to hold faculty positions at America's Protestant evangelical colleges and universities, who are making good contributions to the scholarship in their respective fields, especially those addressing issues related to women flourishing?" It was the intersection of these two experiences that led to the creation of this book. By extension, it means that this book is somewhat historic. Never before in American history has there been an opportunity for one book to showcase the research of leading and emerging African American scholars who are also teaching at historically Protestant evangelical colleges. Moreover, these scholars are asking new questions about the black experience in America and, in the process, making significant contributions to their respective disciplines. These authors are all seasoned or emerging scholars but few people in the broader Protestant and non-religious academy know about them or the historic positions they hold.

It is extremely difficult being African American scholars working at Protestant evangelical institutions. On the one hand, many of us have to deal with being called "sell-outs" for not working in more traditional black church and black academic circles. On the other hand, black scholars have this profound sense of otherness knowing that when they walk in a classroom of predominantly white students on the first day of class their first job is to dispel whatever stereotypes these students might have about their temperament or intelligence. Additionally, many scholars of color with Protestant evangelical convictions would be politically and theologically disqualified from many non-religious public universities and private colleges. To add salt to the wound, I have noticed that when Protestant evangelicals look for insight into issues in the humanities and social sciences, such as are addressed in the chapters in this volume, White evangelicals will tap scholars of color who are in progressive Protestant mainline communities. The consequence of these currents is that African American scholars teach, research, and write with a type of double-consciousness that leaves many of us isolated. African American scholars at Protestant evangelical institutions are sidelined, by those inside and outside of their tribes. My hope is that this book is the beginning of the end of these assumptions and trends.

Being an African American scholar teaching at a predominantly White evangelical space is difficult for many reasons that are covered in my book *Aliens in the Promised Land: Why Minority Leadership Is Overlooked in White Christian Churches and Institutions*. Among the limitations of that book, *Aliens in the Promised Land* primarily focused on issues of race as it relates to questions of ministry and theological education among Protestant evangelicals. It was while sitting in Professor's Hill Fletcher's course that I realized what I owed to my sisters who are laboring in the shadows and on the margins at evangelical institutions. These sisters have the double burden of being people of color *and* female. I aim to showcase their work as much as possible because these women are making important contributions to understanding the black experience in America. The contributions by the brothers in this volume are equally important, as these friends and colleagues are doing work that often goes unnoticed.

One of the challenges of this book is that to discuss the black experience in America, it crosses multiple disciplines in the humanities and social sciences, including psychology, sociology, political science, education theory, history, and theology. By design, the book does not have a central narrative from beginning to end. The project's overarching purpose is to suggest that these kinds of issues that need to be on the table when we discuss race and the black experience in twenty-first century America, not only in the Protestant evangelical world, but the academy at large. There are of course many more issues worthy of exploration, but the academic research present in this volume reveals the necessary scope of issues facing African American Christians and African Americans in general in the decades to come. I am also aware that there are more scholars who could have been added in this book. There were many whom I contacted who were not able to contribute, as they were tied up with other projects and commitments. There were also a few that I discovered later in the writing process and were not able to be included.

The book is divided into two parts. The first covers research in the social sciences and the second covers research in the humanities. Readers will notice that such a division created a split between the women and the men. The gender split is representative of the current debate among evangelicals regarding the role of the theology professor. That is, are theology professors functioning in the role of a teaching pastoral office, or in a role that is purely academic in nature? Given this dispute, many Protestant evangelical theology professors come from ministry positions in denominations that tend to reserve the teaching office of pastor to men. Depending on the particular school's denominational affiliation, if one exists, these types of divisions may or may not change significantly.

In chapter 1, Larycia Hawkins offers creative insights into the framing of the black church tradition's relationship with politics. This research focuses on black churches outside what is traditionally defined as the black church milieu (e.g., black Baptists, AME, CME and COGIC). Specifically, this research hypothesizes that black churches in non-black denominations are more likely to possess characteristics of what scholars term "political churches" than churches in historically black denominations. Political churches deem "political awareness and [political] activity as salient pieces of their identity" by McClerking and McDaniel. The tendency of scholars of black religion and politics to focus on historically black denominations in defining black political churches is logical, but leaves black church prophets in non-black denominations in scholarly limbo.

Since scholars typically speak of the black church monolithically, their failure to distinguish between types of black churches may obscure important differences between churches in the black church milieu, namely those in non-black denominations. First, black churches in non-black denominations may have *different theological motivations* for political participation than those in black denominations. Specifically, Hawkins expects black churches in non-black denominations to be more likely to espouse black liberation theology as an explicit aspect of church identity than churches in historically black denominations. Second, given different historical trajectories of black denominations and non-black denominations, political mobilization strategies may differ in kind and in frequency of application. Third, in large urban areas, a number of black churches in non-black denominations are megachurches. Including these black megachurches will help answer whether they represent a countervailing trend in black political activism (Harris et al., 2005), enervating levels of activism rather than increasing levels of activism.

Since pastors of black churches are prophets in the black community, this research examines how scholarly failure to comprehend prophets in non-black denominations and the different dynamics of black churches in non-black denominations contributes to a tendency to underestimate the role of black liberation theology in black politics and to a tendency to discount the role that these black political churches play in a supposed post-racial era.

In chapter 2, Hawkins examines how members of the Congressional Black Caucus, as well as non-black members, speak about one domestic policy—welfare reform and one international policy—aid to Haiti. My expectation is that black members of Congress are more likely than non-black members of Congress to frame policy issues with reference to religion. In addition to uttering more religious referents than non-black members of Congress, Hawkins anticipates that the religious referents uttered by black members will tend to be of a particular theological stripe—culturally steeped in a black Christian tradition that emphasizes bondage in Egypt and deliverance from Pharaoh alongside the deliverance from sin provided by Christ on the cross. Specifically, African American religionists are more likely to emphasize liberation from injustice for the oppressed and judgment for society and government where injustices remain unrectified. If and when non-black members express religious referents in their policy images, I expect them to be less likely than black to emphasize themes of liberation theology. This research will enhance our understanding both of black religion and of black politics, but also of policy framing by political elites more generally.

In chapter 3, Rhiana Mason raises important concerns about literacy rates in the black community. For decades, the literacy levels of Caucasians have outpaced those of African Americans creating a persistent gap. This literacy gap is not limited to common everyday reading materials but it also extends over into health-related genres. This chapter provides an account of two experiments which examine the role of vocabulary in the comprehension of different health and non-health literacy texts by African American adolescents and adults. In Experiment 1, forty-eight African American adolescents of either moderate or low vocabulary proficiency were randomly assigned to read experimenter-designed texts about both health (i.e., asthma, cancer, etc.) and non-health (i.e., crime, albinism in animals, etc.) topics. In Experiment 2, forty-two African American and Caucasian adults with similar vocabulary levels were administered widely used measures of health literacy and analogous non-health literacy. Across the two studies the current findings demonstrate that one's facility with the English language and the format of the text influences the appearance of the literacy gap. Since literacy level is linked with language and culture, future directions for literacy assessment are proposed.

In chapter 4, Yvonne RB-Banks explains that African American women are not new to being pioneers or groundbreaking leaders in the overall context of society. However, as their numbers increase in the Christian academy, they are facing new and less-explored challenges. This chapter seeks to unravel the experiences, puzzlements, demands and often unspoken struggles faced by African American women as scholars in Christian Higher Education. The ethos of the Christian academy sets it apart from other institutions of higher education, and many of women enter into the Christian academy unsuspecting of the dilemmas they will face. In general the Christian academy has been progressive in the acknowledgement of the barriers women face, as well as the unequal access to the academy that blacks experience. Yet, there appears to be some disconnect as to what it means to enter the academy as an African American and a woman.

Women of faith from the African American experience are united by social and cultural concepts of sisterhood. They often bring with them embedded messages that tell them to support, guide, share, sacrifice, mother-others, and stand in the face of overwhelming odds for the bet-terment of the community. They find to their dismay that even though there are overarching themes in the Christian academy related to service and sacrifice, there is a lack of balance. During the evaluation or promo-tion process in the academic context there is no cultural reciprocal re-lated to sisterhood. The lack of such reciprocity as it relates to the notion that the Christian academy will give back what has been given creates a matrix of complexities for African American women. Grasping, from the perspective of African American women scholars, what "sisterhood" means in the context of the Christian academy experience is essential to achieving a perceived balance for their contributions.

In chapter 5, Michelle Loyd-Paige utilizes an autoethographic re-search method to weave a contextualized self-narrative, exploring the multiple and varied mentoring experiences of an African American college administrator. This autoethnography analyzes how relationships have (or have not) contributed to her leadership development and ad-vancement to the dean for multicultural affairs at a predominantly White college campus. Working from a critical race-gender-intersectionality framework, Loyd-Paige examines the meaning of a scarcity of profes-sional mentors within her higher-education context. Specifically, Loyd-Paige begins this chapter with an introduction to autoethnography as concept and process. Next, Loyd-Paige provides a theoretical context for examining the mentoring experiences of professionals-of-color (with special attention to African Americans) within predominately white institution of higher education. Loyd-Paige includes self-narrative data associated with her journey from an undergraduate student to the dean for multicultural affairs at the same Midwest private Christian liberal arts college. The chapter concludes with a framework for situating mentoring strategies and processes that she used to negotiate the challenges of being an African American learning and working at a predominantly White academic institution of higher education.

Chapter 6, Deshonna Collier-Goubil explores how students of color on predominately white Christian college campuses find themselves in a unique, at times difficult, and at other times life-changing intersection. They have purposefully chosen to attend a university that will place a large emphasis on the integration of spirituality with their academic dis-cipline. Millennials, being the first generation of student to hear language of diversity and racial tolerance from attending K–12, are often quite surprised when they encounter racial and gender micro-aggressions on these campuses. Millennials of all races and ethnicities often lack the social skills needed to manage cross-race interactions. In addition, this generation's students of color have been shielded from the harsh realities of marginalization in U.S. society; they often lack the needed skills and resources to respond to micro-aggressive encounters. This chapter seeks to identify and discuss the unique experiences of black female college students on these campuses and propose possible programmatic solutions that faculty, administrators, and student development leaders can take to improve their experience, boost student success and university retention of this population. The chapter also includes a discussion of the millennial generation and what it means to be a black female millennial. Three programmatic pillars of a proposed leadership development program are outlined with suggested program components provided.

Chapter 7 moves the book from the social sciences into the humanities. Vincent Bacote asks, "How has the construction of race ground the lenses of our perception so that we 'see' others yet also fail to truly see them?" "Race" exists as a virtual fiction that has often played a role greater than divine revelation in our understanding of human identity. This chapter considers how the doctrine of theological anthropology leads us toward a greater and more properly complex understanding of human persons. If we can "erase" race in the sense of removing its characteristics that blind us and disable our capacity observe and celebrate ethnic particularity, then Christians (if no one else) can better see each other and model a life together that is a foretaste of the diversity found in Revelation 5:9 and 7:9. Our doctrine rather than a cultural fiction should be primary in our understanding of human identity.

In chapter 8, Eric Washington uncovers an important aspect of black history as it relates to the growth of Christianity around the world. It turns that African Americans had have a long tenure in world missions that needs to be recovered. Many African American Protestants during the nineteenth century understood this prophetic narrative to mean that God had decreed a resurgence of African civilizations through the acceptance of Christianity, commerce, and civilization. These thinkers also believed that God had planned providentially that millions of West Africans would be enslaved by Europeans, brought to North America, Christianized, emancipated, and would return to Africa to establish Christian colonies. Lewis G. Jordan who served as corresponding secretary of the Foreign Mission Board of the National Baptist Convention, USA from 1896–1921 articulated a similar belief in his published works

and in his editorials in the *Mission Herald*, the monthly organ of the
Foreign Mission Board. This chapter will focus on Jordan's Ethiopian vision for African American missionary work in Africa during this period,
and the prospects of renewed emigration to Liberia during the 1910s.
Its argument is that Jordan's thought served as both an expansion and
continuation of nineteenth-century Ethiopianism articulated by African
American Protestants such as Alexander Crummell and Edward Blyden
while maintaining a robust evangelical motive for engaging in African
missions.

In chapter 9, Todd Allen reasons that one of the most powerful
means for engaging sites of public memory is to visit them—to walk on
sacred ground. Historian James Horton believes that "few experiences
can connect us with our past more completely than walking the ground
where our history happened." Adds Edward Linenthal, "The conviction
is that somehow places speak." Thus it is through the public's engagement
with the rhetoric of the commemorative landscape that one can come to
understand the past. Commemorative practices related to the civil rights
movement of the 1950s–60s have been gaining popularity over the past
decade. Despite this increase in commemorative activity, knowledge of
the civil rights movement and its relevance for today's generation appears
to be on a decline.

This chapter will address the implications and relevance of commemorative practices related to the civil rights movement. While exploring the civil rights movement in general, particular emphasis will be
given to forms of commemorative practice which incorporate Christian
symbolism into their design. Remembering these old landmarks of
the African American freedom struggle reveals their pedagogical and
spiritual role in teaching lessons on the importance of honestly confronting the past, while promoting healing, forgiveness, and reconciliation
in the present.

In the last chapter, I revisit the controversial issue of affirmative action. Preferential policies as a way to redress past social injustice continue
to stir much emotion and debate in the United States and around the
world. The African American experience of both formal and informal racial oppression has encouraged lawmakers to seek ways to level the playing field given the fact that Whites have enjoyed hegemonic advantages.
Affirmative action emerged a few decades ago as an intervention into
the systemic realities of white privilege. With few exceptions, the debate
about affirmative action developed with great controversy because of the

complexities and uncertainties about the effectiveness of these programs as a remedy for previous injustice. One central question is this context to consider is this: "Is affirmative action fair?" There are two ways apply this question. First, is affirmative action fair with respect to African Americans and secondly, is it fair with respect to Whites with preferential policies potentially limiting the opportunities for Whites as individuals? This chapter seeks to explore the contours of these questions. What is missing in the debate is the realization that those on both sides of this issue are relying on different moral foundations to make their respective cases. In the end, there will be little to no progress in the discourse about affirmative action until there is a substantive debate about the definition of fairness.

As a way to frame the discussion, this paper uses the Moral Foundations Theory of Jonathan Haidt to provide a conceptual starting point for the philosophical roots of the disagreement over affirmative action policy. Haidt's research can provide needed tools to advance the discussion of racial justice. With an understanding of the competing conceptions of fairness, this paper seeks to propose a more effective approach to the discourse that encourages listening beyond the prevailing tribalism and confirmation bias on all sides of the debate.

Despite the efforts of so many and what I intended to accomplish, this volume is not without its limitations, for which I take full responsibility. There are more scholars to include and more topics to discuss. One of overarching goals is to tell the Protestant world that there are many African American scholars doing important work, who often are the only person of color on their faculty, and we need to do a better job soliciting their perspectives and intellect. Doing so makes us all better off and shows the world that diversity is more than merely cosmetic.

Acknowledgments

THIS PROJECT WOULD NOT have been completed without the insightful editing and formatting work of Rebecca Au. Her joyful attention to detail, high standards, and professionalism made the process of editing this book a delight. The King's College is a much better community because of people like Rebecca. I am very fortunate to have had her as a teaching assistant. I must give a special thanks to Jeannine Hill Fletcher, professor of theology at Fordham University, for helping me see the need to celebrate the contributions of my female colleagues in ways that have not yet been normalized in American Protestant evangelical circles. A significant portion of the vision for this book emerged as a student in one of her courses. I am blessed to have had the opportunity to be also inspired by dynamic Fordham professors like Barbara Andolsen, Celia B. Fisher, and Ann Higgins-D'Alessandro during the process of creating this book. Attending Fordham University continues to be one of the best decisions I have ever made. The influence of my professors helped me ask the right kinds of questions in my search for contributors for this book. My colleagues at the King's College continue to be extremely supportive as co-celebrators of my work and I am extremely fortunate to have them. And finally, it continues to be a pleasure to work with the great team at Pickwick Publications, an imprint of Wipf and Stock Publishers. Christian Amondson and Chris Spinks were invaluable from the start to finish.

1

Prophetic and Priestly:
The Politics of a Black Catholic Parish

Dr. Larycia A. Hawkins, Wheaton College

Introduction

THE BLACK CHURCH HAS been defined almost exclusively in terms of historic black Protestantism (Lincoln and Mamiya 1990; Raboteau 1995). While this definition certainly squares with the thrust of black religious activity since slavery, it fails to inculcate the reality of mainline black churches outside the ambit of the historic black church and black Catholic parishes. These churches remain a puzzle because as political scientists have sought to understand how black Christianity provides micro and macro resources for black politics, they have focused solely upon the historic black church.

Black political churches are typified by the messages that flow from the pulpit as much as they are by actual political activity. As leaders of the central institution of black life, pastors of black churches exert an enormous influence upon the political and civic views of black congregants. Indeed, black congregants expect, as a matter of course, that pastors utilize their pulpits to express views on issues of social and political import (Pew 2009). Pastors, then, are important political elites in the black community, affecting African American public opinion, whether or not that opinion is translated into direct political action or civic activity.

Of course, much scholarship indicates that the black church does indeed serve as an incubator of civic skills and as a venue for the translation of civic messages into civic action. Much of this evidence comes from aggregate level data rather than church-level statistics, but it is reasonable to conclude that pastoral civic and political messages matter for black politics, both in terms of opinion formation and in terms of political mobilization (Harris 1999).

To understand religion and politics, we need to understand how race mediates this relationship. For example, scholars who study Catholics and politics have noted the importance of distinguishing the politics of Latino Catholics from those of white Catholics (Wilson, 2008). Furthermore, we need to ascertain how understudied denominations and institutions of black religion, like black Catholic churches and black churches in historically white mainline denominations differ from or converge upon the black church. The current study examines the dynamics of one black Catholic parish and asks: 1) how does the black Catholic experience compare to the black church experience in terms of theology, worship, and polity, 2) what types of civic and political messages are proffered from the priestly pulpit and promulgated in parish level activities, and 3) what role does the priest play in promulgating civic and political activity?

Methodology

The current study primarily utilizes the participant observer method. As I sought to gain an in-depth knowledge of racial and political dynamics at the parish level, a single case, St. Sabina Catholic Church, was selected for study. I attended services over the course of three years, from June 2009 to February 2012. During this time, I observed two different priests presiding over mass. After my first visit in June 2009, I decided to attend mass on the first Sunday of the month, termed Unity Sunday, because Unity Sunday is the only Sunday where the entire parish attends one service. On other Sundays, mass is offered twice a day.

One scholar notes the importance of understanding Christianity in local context (Howell 2008). Only by disaggregating religionists can scholars behold the unique dynamics of faith as affected by context. The location of St. Sabina in the economically-depressed, South side Chicago neighborhood of Auburn Gresham, therefore, is assumed to affect the tone and tenor of congregational politics. Furthermore, the universal nature of the Catholic Church is presumed to matter for parish politics, but the nature, extent, and efficacy of top-down dictates is observed best at the parish level.

Finally, it is important to note that I have sought in previous scholarly work to understand the unique dynamics of the historic black denominations in their complexity. In previous work, I have attended the services of black Baptist churches, the African Methodist Episcopal church, and the Church of God in Christ, which all range in their theology, worship and polity. Thus, the current study builds upon previous participant observation and study of the black church writ large, as it seeks to understand the dynamics of black Catholicism as they relate to the politics of black Catholics.

Come to Black Jesus: Black Church Message with Catholic Church Vessel

If you visit a handful of Catholic churches, you would likely notice a pattern—holy water at the entrances and a crucifix prominently displayed in the front of the church. Catholic faithful kneeling in prayer and crossing in reverence. At St. Sabina, however, this is not the case. Ethnic African print adorns banners and African flags hang from the rafters. Praise dancers follow the traditional processional where the cross and the sword of the spirit are the most prominent elements. Standing and shouting to gospel music, as opposed to kneeling and genuflecting silently, is the congregational norm. Holy water flows through the serendipitous style and flow of the service rather than as a purification ritual at the beginning of mass. Shouting and raising of hands in affirmation of the priest's sermon replaces crossing during liturgy.

The dynamic of St. Sabina can only be explained by its geographic, and thus its cultural, location. St. Sabina Catholic Church is situated in the Auburn Gresham neighborhood of Chicago, a neighborhood which is over 95 percent black and where 32 percent of the population is below the poverty line, compared to 24 percent of the population of Chicago families and 12.38 percent of the U.S. population (City Data 2013). Parishes are purposefully local institutions. Thus, Catholics, unlike Protestants, are deprived of choice in church—they are assigned to the most proximate local congregation. Given patterns of racial and ethnic segregation in the United States, it should come as little surprise that ethnically and racially homogenous parishes persist in the United States. Thus, even if the color of the parish changes—St. Sabina was originally founded in 1916 as an Irish-American parish and became increasingly black with the Great

Migration of the 1940s (McGreevy, 1996, 25–26)—the fact of racial ho-
mogeneity may be one of the most enduring factors of parish life. Of 356
Catholic parishes in the city of Chicago, thirty-seven are predominantly
black (Chicago Archdiocese 2011; National Catholic Register 2012). Of
course, the priest and laity can take pains to counter parish ethnic exclu-
sivity and anyone who visits St. Sabina Catholic Church realizes quickly
that whether black or white, no one is a stranger at St. Sabina. Visitors
are greeted and hugged, and invited to sit with regular members when
sitting alone. As evidence of Catholic universalism, the church broadcasts
to seventy countries around the world.

St. Sabina reflects the contours of the local, racialized context. Inside the church, a portrait of a lively black Jesus hangs where a bloody
crucified Christ would normally be ensconced, signifying immediately
that this is not a traditional Catholic church. If the black Christ does not
signal the uniqueness of the place, perhaps the neon Jesus sign hanging
prominently over the choir loft and lectern bespeaks the gospel-centric,
liberation-laden moments to come. Of course, some facets of the mass
at St. Sabina are thoroughly Catholic in cast and tone—the priestly vest-
ments, the processional where incense is diffused and the cross is lifted
high, the presentation of the gospel where congregants bow in deference
to the living word, and the Eucharist where individuals cross themselves
after partaking of the body and blood of Jesus. Very few icons are present
and those that exist, including a statue of the Virgin Mary, are relegated
to an ancillary position in the church decor. Despite these elements of
Catholicism, one familiar with the traditional black church would feel
rather at home during a St. Sabina service. St. Sabina's thorough fusion
of a black worship style, a liberation theology approach, and a Catholic
sensibility render its religion as well as its politics of particular interest.

Despite the fact that 51 percent of Chicago Catholics are non-white,
including 3 percent who are black and Catholics, diversity among Catholic priests is more rare (Archdiocese of Chicago 2011). There are 40,000
priests in the United States, but only 250 are African American (USCCB
2012). While there are sixteen African American bishops, only six dio-
ceses in the United States are headed by an African American bishop
(USCCB 2012). Perhaps, then, it comes as little surprise that a white
priest has presided at the helm of St. Sabina Catholic Church since 1981.
Father Michael Pfleger, a baby boomer ordained in 1975, came of age
in the civil rights era and was enamored with black preaching and had
mentors in the black church despite his seminary training in Catholic

institutions. Father Pfleger is a charismatic figure to whom congregants respond with marked and visible enthusiasm. His charisma does not emanate from a cult-of-personality, but rather flows from congregational loyalty to a white priest who has displayed deep devotion to the predominantly black, Auburn Gresham community over the years. Father Pfleger has adopted three black sons (one of whom died due to stray gunfire). He has been disciplined by the Chicago Archdiocese both for adopting children and for remarks he made about Hillary Clinton during the 2008 presidential primaries. Most recently, Pfleger said that he would leave the Catholic Church if the Diocese decided to reassign him to the helm of a nearby Catholic school, St. Leo's. The fact that Pfleger has served as parish priest for over 30 years is remarkable given that the average tenure of a parish priest is estimated to be one to two terms (six to twelve years). Priests serve at the will of the Archdiocese, although there is a designation of "irremovable" pastor in Canon Law, and even a movable pastor can challenge his revocation of tenure (Papi 1911). I have found no evidence that Pfleger is of the irremovable designation and he has certainly challenged every attempt to silence or move him.

Father Pfleger's sermons simultaneously evoke an evangelical sensibility and bespeak a black liberation strain. Ten-minute homilies are waylaid for two-hour sermons. In the evangelical vein, Pfleger states:

> God is passionate about being in relationship with us. He came
> to restore the breach caused by the sin of Adam. The cross is a
> bridge so we wouldn't have to have a high priest. But the irony is,
> we run after other relationships. You can't know *what* love is until
> you know *who* love is. (Emphasis in original, October 4, 2009)

This statement is not remarkable from an evangelical point of view. Evangelicals emphasize the priesthood of the believer, whereby an individual chooses to enter into a relationship with Christ by his free will and continues to pursue that relationship with Christ via prayer, Bible study, fellowship with other believers, and personal piety. Come-to-Jesus religious conversions are common in historic black Protestant churches as they comport with the evangelical sensibility, but altar calls of the come-to-Jesus ilk are in conflict with the Catholic norm of conversion—infant baptism, catechism, and confirmation.

Of course, one not born into the Catholic Church can become a Catholic convert, but the relationship between humankind and God is not an individualistic one, but a mediated one. The notion of the priesthood of the individual believer is an idea born of Martin Luther and the Reformation. Per Luther and those Protestants who followed, an earthly priest is not the key mediator between God and man, but rather, the resurrected Christ who mediates on the Christian's behalf. The believer in Christ has confidence herself to enter the heavenly throne room to intercede on her own behalf, independent of a priest. That Father Pfleger elevates the spiritual autonomy of the individual Christian over the spiritual authority of the parish priest is contrary to the dominant thrust of Catholic teaching and to the preponderance of Catholic theology.

St. Sabina feels less hierarchical in nature and less constrained by dogma than most Catholic churches. Father Pfleger is accessible and down to earth. While his position of priestly authority is clearly revered, he preaches at the level of the parishioner, walking across the front of the church and up the aisle. There is no elevated platform or lectern separating him from his flock. This democratic demeanor is evocative of black Baptist churches. The church is emblematic of Pentecostal and charismatic black churches in that the structure of the service is open—Father Pfleger bursts into song at times during the sermon. The Holy Spirit, not a rote liturgy, directs the service.

Father Pfleger, a non-conformist who eschews hierarchy, spiritual and otherwise, ironically uses the power of his lofty, priestly position to promote his prophetic politics. The priest is revered as above the laity, a mediator between Christ and the faithful. And while St. Sabina encourages Scripture literacy and personal prayer without the mediation of the priest, Pfleger's revered status is perhaps his greatest asset in promulgating a patently political message and in propelling a lively civic and political activism rooted in religious faith.

Consonant with a black church dialectic between personal piety a la evangelicals and fundamentalists, and social consciousness a la Mainline Protestants and Catholics, Pfleger mixes messages. He excoriates the *individual behavior* of those congregants who would find the joy of Christ "on a shelf at the liquor store" or "in a blunt" (October 4, 2009). But he also calls congregants to *change societal structures* via "eagles' strength— the kind of strength that will help you fly alone" since the black church has too many "turkeys . . . chickens . . . and buzzards who fly in groups" and prey on people, rather than changing structures. Pfleger serves at the will of the *Catholic Church*, but identifies St. Sabina, both in mode and message, as a *black church*. St. Sabina is Catholic in term of church polity and black in worship style and sensibility. Given the fluid blend of

black and Catholic, what types of civic and political messages are proffered from the priestly pulpit and promulgated in parish level activities?

Data and Findings

At St. Sabina, congregants are implored weekly during the sermon to
pursue social justice. Father Pfleger personally invites them to join
marches against gun violence in the Auburn Gresham neighborhood
and in other neighborhoods across the city. Black intellectuals, activists,
and entertainers are invited to church to promote black history and black
empowerment—Cornel West and Maya Angelou are among the digni-
taries invited to speak. Local politicians and public officials attend mass
and are invited to give impromptu speeches, including former Chicago
Police Superintendent Jody Weis who spoke at length about community
partnerships in policing at the conclusion of one sermon. Pastors from
other prominent political churches in Chicago show up for mass unan-
nounced, including Rev. Jeremiah Wright of Trinity United Church of
Christ on one occasion.

Political churches deem "political awareness and [political] activity
as salient pieces of their identity" (McClerking and McDaniel 2005, 723).
The tendency of scholars of black religion and politics to focus on historically black denominations in defining black political churches is logical,
but leaves black church prophets in historically non-black denominations in scholarly limbo. Father Pfleger's sermons promote black power
politics—that is, black Christ as liberator energizes black power in the
political and civic realms.

Beyond Parish Boundaries: Protest and Pay Your Tithes

At St. Sabina Father Pfleger demands that *faithful congregants* be *active
citizens*. One morning, Pfleger stated, "The last thing Jesus said was 'go
to the ends of the world.' *It's not what you do in here but what you do out
there.* You are in here to get the word to go out. I got you in here to get
you pregnant [with the word of God]" (emphasis added, August 2, 2009).
One of the most remarkable features of St. Sabina is the active nature of
implorations to extend advocacy beyond the confines of church walls to
the Chicago community, to the United States, and to the world.

On one Sunday morning in August 2009, an announcement encouraged parishioners to attend the Citizens of Action Rally for Real Healthcare Reform. All announcements are approved by the church hierarchy and thus when delivered can be deemed "official." Thus, while one cannot infer that an announcement equals an endorsement, it is safe to say that the clergy are not opposed to the expression of the sentiment that healthcare reform is not only necessary, but also that a particular version of healthcare reform beyond the status quo is preferred. In this church, even seemingly incidental announcements are tantamount to an endorsement by Father Pfleger given his unabashed expression of political and policy content from the pulpit.

Pfleger has commanded national attention for his anti-gun violence campaign, appearing regularly in the Chicago media, national network news programs, and on CNN to name a few. On one Sunday at the conclusion of a sermon, he announced that the city was accepting guns during an amnesty period for the surrender of firearms. Father Pfleger also announced an upcoming press conference where he, with the support of the church, planned to offer a $5,000 award for information about the shooter of a teenager struck down while leaving a church picnic. Recently, Pfleger has spearheaded a petition to press for passage of H.B. 5831 which requires titles for handguns and bans assault weapons altogether. The anti-violence efforts of St. Sabina are not limited to the Auburn Gresham neighborhood—the city's infamous leader in violent crime in 2009 according to police district crime statistics (Loury 2010). Indeed, concern about violence, its causes and effects, extends to Congress and the President. In the name of justice, Pfleger states, an interfaith, countrywide effort must be sustained to "end this epidemic of violence" (Archdiocese of Chicago 2012).

Whose Side are You on Anyway?
Beyond Beer Summits to a Black Agenda

While Father Pfleger espouses an agenda consistent with the most liberal visions of the black polity, including radical structural reform, he minces no words when he speaks of his disdain for politics and politicians as usual. His effort to enact gun control legislation is evidence of Pfleger's willingness to utilize the political tools and institutions at his disposal. Yet, in the spirit of the prophets of Scripture and the prophetic voice of the black church, Pfleger has little patience for the proverbial Pharaoh's complicity with societal injustice. No one, including the first black president of the United States, is immune from his ire.

For example, in the wake of the erroneous arrest of black Harvard professor Skip Gates at his own home, President Obama condemned the discriminatory treatment that blacks receive at the hands of police, but nevertheless invited the white arresting officer, Sgt. Crawley (along with Dr. Gates) to the White House for some brews. The event was dubbed the Beer Summit by the media and represented Obama's first presidential foray into the issue of race. Father Pfleger critiqued President Obama for hosting the Beer Summit, sarcastically stating: "I thought instead of having service today dealing with issues [of importance to the black community], we'd have a beer summit" (August 2, 2009). He went on to recount those issues of importance to the black community that he believed the first black President was symbolically neglecting by neutralizing the racial discrimination inherent in Professor Gates arrest—"508 children shot in eigt 18 months, 43 Chicago Public School children shot last school year, 150 Chicago Pubic School children shot in the last 3 years" (August 2, 2009). As children in Chicago Public Schools are predominantly poor and minority, Pfleger expected that a black President should concern himself with these issues of import to his community rather than toasting white officers who arrest black men for no apparent reason. Descriptive representation, a black man in the White House, means nothing without substantive representation, black issues on the national agenda.

In addition to Obama's neglect of policy of significance to African Americans, Pfleger questioned Obama's judgment for meeting with Sgt. Crawley at all given that the act served to minimize black anger at discrimination. Pfleger, invoking the persona of the victim, Dr. Gates, as he protested the injustice of his arrest, stated: "I'm not arrogant. I'm in my house. I won't be intimidated" (August 2, 2009). He then questioned the President's motive for inviting Crawley to the White House—"How dare you (Obama) invite that man (Crawley) to the White House?" The Beer Summit, for Pfleger, was a photo opportunity for the post-racial President to promulgate racial transcendence and a veneer of racial reconciliation (*see* Clayton 2010).

For Pfleger, the scenario represents a typical one in the black experience—the black oppressed continue to bear the brunt of societal racism and discrimination in a purportedly post-racial era. But even in the midst of oppression, God offers hope for the oppressed. The black liberation themed sermon du jour emphasized the special relationship between black people and God: "If you understand you are chosen by God, you don't walk around like you don't belong" (August 2, 2009). This theme of black empowerment and chosenness is consonant with black liberation theology's emphasis upon God's favor for the oppressed and consistent with Catholic Social Teaching's emphasis upon the preferential option for the poor. Black liberation emphasizes Jesus' solidarity with the least and the last and the lost. Jesus' ministry was on behalf of the most vulnerable in society. While God is on the side of the black oppressed, President Obama's Beer Summit sidelined the agenda of the black oppressed for political gain.

Suffering Christian Community Not Cotton Candy Church

If black interests will not be promulgated by a black president, who will do the difficult work of advancing black interests? The black Christian herself must pick up the political mantle. Father Pfleger maintains that the calling of the Christian is a difficult one, requiring the bearing of crosses as burdens—not only spiritual crosses, but also crosses for justice via the political realm. Pfleger chastises congregants against a shiny, bubble-gum Christianity: "We want the cotton candy church. We want Joel Osteen" (August 9, 2009). To the contrary, Pfleger describes the call of the Christian as a difficult road where God "calls you by messing up your plans. . .he bothers you. The question is, what will your answer be? Shallow people want to wear the crown of resurrection but will you wear the nails of crucifixion because if you do not die with him you will not rise with him" (August 9, 2009). Pfleger, consonant with black liberation theology, calls the oppressed to suffer, and even die, for what is just and right, as Jesus did. Father Pfleger elevates the call of the Christian in the political realm to that of movement soldiers, fighting for a communal cause (justice a la liberation theology) not for an individual cause (well-being a la the prosperity gospel).

Catholic Communitarian Personalism radically challenges ideas consonant with the dominant cultural thrust of individualism. "While the Catholic vision shares certain commitments of a democracy like the United States, it radically challenges a culture that prioritizes economic efficiency over solidarity with the weak and marginalized, or narrow national interest over global concern" (Heyer 2008, 63). Just as Catholic theology's preferential option for the poor and solidarity with labor cut against a resurgent Social Darwinism, St. Sabina emphasizes the communal responsibility of its members to the parish and to the world beyond parish boundaries. In this regard, Pfleger's teaching and preaching cut against the grain of a countervailing trend in black churches—the prosperity gospel (*see* Smith and Harris 2005). Father Pfleger refuses to proffer a vision of Jesus as the route to health and wealth, but rather persists in challenging members to pour themselves out in solidarity with the least, the last, and the lost, consonant with Jesus' earthly ministry of liberation. How might this calling beyond cotton candy, self-aggrandizing religion to self-sacrificial communal welfare affect the political views of the congregants at St. Sabina?

One scholar notes that political ideology for the Catholic faithful may be a function of *how* each Catholic perceives religion to matter as opposed to a function of *whether* religion matters at all (Leege 1988). Of particular significance to political ideology is whether or not a Catholic deems herself a religious individualist or a religious communitarian (Leege 1988, 725–726). Religious communitarians focus on societal conflict and collective well-being and are more likely than noncommunitarian Catholics to be socially liberal. Religious individualists focus primarily upon individual conflict and personal well-being and are more likely than non-individualist Catholics to be socially conservative. Of course, some people integrate these two views and likely lean toward one pole or another or classify themselves as ideologically moderate. For our purposes herein, this is instructive for two interrelated reasons: 1) African Americans gauge their own welfare by the welfare of the black community and 2) black Catholics at St. Sabina are taught that the Catholic faith emphasizes communal solidarity over individualism.

Fight the Man—Even if He's Black Like You

Along with the theme of communal solidarity with the poor and oppressed in black liberation theology is the call to fight the oppressor. But what if the oppressor of blacks happens to be black himself?

The task of taking on President Obama is complicated by black public shows of solidarity with the race. Tavis Smiley, a black political pundit and media mogul, and Cornel West, a prominent black intellectual, have

both been lambasted in the black community for daring to publicly criticize President Obama (Harris-Perry 2011). The unspoken cultural rule
is to support fellow African Americans in public and to oppose fellow
African Americans only in private. Thus, Clarence Thomas, while clearly
a conservative, had black public opinion on his side during his bid for
the Supreme Court. The fact that Father Pfleger regularly and publicly
denounces the President in Obama's hometown and in front of Obama's
racial kin illustrates the legitimization of Pfleger's prophetic role in the
eyes of his congregants. The fact that Pfleger is a white pastor of a black
church and is critiquing the President so boldly is interesting and potentially dangerous given the rule that no one critiques a black man in public,
not even members of his own race. Father Pfleger has been legitimized as
a member of the black community and can thus critique the President in
the context of the black Catholic Church. Plus, fighting Pharaoh is what
prophets do. Where prophets are concerned, racial bets are off—whether
Pharaoh is black or white is of little consequence. Where prophets are
concerned, political does not dictate the voice—whether Pharaoh is a
Democrat or a Republican matters not. Prophets call rulers to task for
injustice in the kingdom.

Father Pfleger, the prophet, not only rails against injustice, but also
teaches his parishioners to combat injustice themselves—whatever their
station, and whatever the source of the injustice. Elites must counter the
plans of fellow elites, just as the ruler Jairus followed Jesus, in opposition to his fellow synagogue leaders who were planning to assassinate
Jesus. The black masses must have courage to combat injustice despite
their low standing, just as the woman with the issue of blood pressed
her way through a throng of people to touch Jesus, the source of justice
and truth and healing. She had courage to aver that she had touched him
and the power of all power healed her predicament. Pfleger likened the
courage of these biblical figures to the courage that parishioners need
to combat injustice on the streets of Chicago: "There is power to heal
the blood flowing in our street" (June 28, 2009). Jesus provides succor
for regular people's problems, but he also provides courage for political battle. Christianity is not an opiate of the masses, but rather acts a
catalyst for societal change.

For example, Father Pfleger encourages his congregants to be agi-
tated not only about the President's policy failures, but also about a black
President's intransigence on behalf of black people. Pfleger stated "It's
okay to be angry at bad stuff" (August 2, 2009). This form of righteous

anger, Pfleger believes, is precisely what propels real change in communities like Auburn Gresham and in the city of Chicago writ large. If the first black President refuses to prophesy against injustice, a predominantly black parish should stand in the gap. Precisely what role does the priest play in promulgating civic and political activity?

Rebel without a Cause or On a Mission from God?

On what basis might we analyze Father Pfleger? His outspoken positions, his oppositional tactics, and his priestly presence render him difficult to typify. Some label him a firebrand. Others label him a sycophant. Still others call him a rebellious priest with no commitment to the Catholic Church. Since Pfleger has uttered threats to leave the Catholic hierarchy but keep preaching at St. Sabina or elsewhere, perhaps the rebellious moniker is not off the mark. But the cause of Pfleger's flamboyance seems clear: he views himself as on a mission from God—and so do his congregants.

Pfleger may be radical in style and in tone, but his emphasis on social justice is not unprecedented in the Catholic milieu. One researcher developed a typology of priests according to the types of topics that they cover in their sermons. Priests are termed social justice priests if they discuss themes related to poverty and justice often. Priests are termed personal morality priests if they discuss abortion most often. Finally, priests who take pains to mention both are termed mixed-emphasis priests (Smith 2008, 46–47). During the three years of the St. Sabina study, Father Pfleger mentioned abortion only once, and even then it was mentioned in an analogous fashion—e.g., they want to abort your ability to fight for justice. Father Pfleger would best be typified as a social justice priest given the emphases of his sermons. Table 1 illustrates themes and issues with civic and political content covered over the three years of the study. The chart divides the issues into domestic related issues and international related issues. A sample phrase or quote, where available, reveals a bit of the context of the issues.

Table 1. Sermon Themes & Issues with Civic and Political Content

Domestic Issues	International Issues
Healthcare	Sudan
Gun Violence	Iraq War
Education	Afghanistan
Prisoners	War
Racism	Taliban/Al Quaeda
Gun Control—National Rifle Association and IL Rifle Association	
Gender roles—"real men cook"	
Black empowerment—I'm beautiful, beloved, the apple of God's eye/world lies about beauty	
Black history—You know more about Jay-Z and Rhianna than you do about Malcolm and Martin	
Young people—realizes the demographic shift "young people, you are the best of us, the fruit of this church"	
Independence Day—"I need a real independence. I need a spiritual independence."	
Jobs	

Religious elites matter, yet, in the black Catholic context they are vastly understudied as a source of political mobilization and meaning. The messages from parish priests may or may not reflect the statements of the church hierarchy—whether the diocese, the United States Conference of Catholic Bishops or the Vatican. Indeed, in none of my visits did Father Pfleger reify a dictate of the local, national, or international church body. He never references papal encyclicals and rarely, if ever, references church doctrine and teaching. On one occasion, he quoted St. Augustine, but rarely if ever does one sense that St. Sabina is ruled from afar. The tenor of the local context matters for the types of political and civic messages that emanate from pastors (Smith 2008, 56–57).

If black politicians and some black pastors in the historic black church have assumed a more pragmatic stance toward political progress (Glaude 2008; Hawkins 2009) Father Pfleger represents a different type of prophet. A *prophetic pragmatist* like President Obama is willing, in Pfleger's words, to accept healthcare reform as evidence of progress, even though it represents a band aid on a more systemic problem:

> We've bailed out the banks but people on 79th [Street] are still suffering. The current administration goes to the white community and says we're going to get you healthcare and to the black community they say be a good parent. We've got to change the whole structure. (August 9, 2009)

Pfleger is unwilling to compromise on the need for total reform of society from the streets to the schools to the systems of power. He demands change at all levels, from the White House in Washington D.C. to the crack house around the corner. His message of change is in the tone of the prophets of old and in the key of the historic black church, but he refuses to settle for surface level solutions that fail to touch the heart of problems that plague the black community. Father Pfleger is a *prophetic radical* who wants to "change the whole structure" (August 2, 2009). Indeed, a documentary about Pfleger is called *Radical Disciple*.

Pfleger's prophetic style is exemplified weekly, but a sermon problematizing the death of a young black honor student at the hands of other young black high school students epitomizes Pfleger's prophetic style. The brutal beating drew national attention, in part because a bystander videotaped the entire incident. Pfleger leaves no room for question—we are all guilty of the death of Derrion Albert. Pfleger avers:

> Derrion Albert's blood is like the blood of Cain when he was murdered by his brother. And God said to Cain: "Where is your brother?" Cain said: "Am I my brother's keeper?" God said: "His blood cries out to me from the ground."

Derrion's blood cries out from the ground. Few people knew about him when he was alive. But his blood cries out. . .they heard about him in Asia, in Africa, in Europe, in North Shore. Derrion's mouth as an honor student wouldn't be listened to, but his blood cries out from the ground.

I told CNN that Derrion's murder is an Emmett Till wound. August 28, 1955, Emmett Till was murdered. And his mother said, "Leave the casket open" so the world could see the face of racism. Pictures from JET Magazine and The [Chicago] Defender allowed the world to see it. In 2009, it's not JET or The Defender. I believe God used the person videotaping and the videotape became the face of violence.

Chicago, you have failed.

Illinois, you have failed.

America, you have failed.

We provide counseling for soldiers coming back from war with PTSD but we do not provide counseling for children living in war every day.

Rosa Parks said she thought about Emmett Till on the bus. MLK said Emmett Till kept them marching. Emmett Till changed the country in 1955. Will the face of violence change us or will we go on with business as usual in two weeks?

God says: "Where is your brother?" Am I my brother's keeper? Yes. Hear me brothers and sisters, we lost the Olympics [bid] . . . we cannot lose our children. The gold medal I want is for education, for feeding them well. . . .I want the gold medal for our children.

If we do not act, I speak prophetically to this country and to this city, the wrath of God will fall upon us. The worst has not been imagined as to what will be loosed. Racism doesn't have to exist. Our children don't have to die. (October 4, 2009)

This portion of Father Pfleger's sermon is rife with language emblematic of prophets and evocative of black liberation and civil rights themes. No individual or group is immune from prophetic critique. Indeed, Pfleger excoriates the very community to which he ministers—the African American community, a move tantamount to biting the hand that feeds you. This is especially dangerous since Father Pfleger is a white man who could be viewed as paternalistic and patronizing toward the black community for his remarks. But Pfleger is unflappable in his prophetic fury—toward blacks and whites and plumbers and Presidents. African Americans are guilty of the death of Derrion Albert because he was murdered by his proverbial black brothers. Pfleger demands that "we are our brother's keeper," but blacks must especially be the keepers of their own—if the oppressed do not care for one another, who will?

Furthermore, Pfleger asserts that the broader Chicago community must take responsibility for the acts of oppression inflicted upon children of the South side who are among the most vulnerable groups in society given their moral and economic dependence upon adults. When Pfleger references the reach of Derrion Albert's voice, he decries the fact that Albert's murder in the structurally depressed South side neighborhood of Roseland, where economic oppression and educational inequality is the norm, seemingly had to become international news for people in North Shore Chicago neighborhoods, where economic opulence and educational opportunity, to care to listen. Poor black children, Pfleger declares, live in war zones, yet they lack societal salve to heal their wounds. Metaphorically and realistically, children on the North and South sides of Chicago die from very different diseases. Honor students on the North side of Chicago reap accolades while honor students on the South side of Chicago reap the whirlwind. Chicago has failed its children indeed.

Prophets not only rail against societal sin, they also call society to stand with the oppressed. Akin to the prophets, Pfleger paints this particular act of societal oppression as an important opportunity for societal redemption. Emmett Till's death served as a fulcrum for the civil rights movement. The memory of Till's senseless death evoked righteous anger which regular people transformed into purposeful protest. The death of Derrion Albert, Pfleger asserts, represents a moment that can propel a movement—a movement to counter the violence that plagues poor communities and that robs children of their natural vitality. All children are vulnerable, but children in war zones are doubly vulnerable—vulnerable to the guns that riddle holes in their innocence and vulnerable to the specter of death that deprives them of their hope.

Prophets portend doom if society does not mend her ways. The viral nature of the grueling death video represents a blessing in disguise—a moment like the one where Mamie Till broadcasted the brutality of racism to the world and galvanized the sleeping giant of public opinion and mass protest. If Derrion Albert's death does not wake up the world, Pfleger wonders, what will? If conscience-pricked people fail to act now, Pfleger warns, the worst is yet to come. Prophets' messages are time- and context-specific—the time is now to end violence. Of course, this prophet had been prophesying against gun violence for many years. In fact, one of Pfleger's adopted sons died at the hands of gun violence. Thus, the diatribe about Derrion Albert's death was not a convenient sermon vignette culled from the nightly news, but rather represented an issue of grave import to the Auburn Gresham community where St. Sabina is located, to the city of Chicago, and to Pfleger himself.

Prophets are doomed to stand alone—alienated and exiled due to the critical nature of their voice. Their role is not a revered one. They are without honor. They are banished from cities. They are crucified. They are reviled. They ate locusts long before sustainable diets were in vogue. And sometimes, they wonder as Moses and Jonah did, whether God cannot appoint someone else to do the job or do it himself!

On one Sunday, Rev. Jeremiah Wright, President Obama's former pastor at Trinity United Church of Christ whose sermon inspired the title of Obama's book, *The Audacity of Hope*, attended mass, sitting in the balcony unnoticed until a church official alerted Pfleger that Wright was present. Pfleger opined that since Rev. Wright had retired, he was the only "fool" left in town: "There used to be two fools [preaching in Chicago]. Now there's just one" (August 2, 2009). President Obama left Wright's church during his 2008 bid for the presidency amid claims that Wright's prophetic rhetoric, "God damn America," in a sermon both inflamed racial tension in certain sectors of society and rankled the patriotic sensibilities of some Americans. The man who led the President to the cross was left at the altar. Pfleger, however, spins the narrative differently—"Jeremiah [Wright] is the *real* patriot. . . . You [Rev. Wright] aren't the crazy one. Stop trying to fit into the clique. Walk your own way—to hell with them [President Obama and his aides]" (emphasis in original, August 2, 2009). Father Pfleger encourages Rev. Wright, despite his framing by the media and President Obama as a brash, anti-American, black liberationist, to maintain his prophetic stance—which is always defined against, not in accordance with, the political status quo.

Prophets are lonely indeed. Not unlike Wright, Pfleger has encountered opposition as well—mostly from the Chicago Archiocese which has force-placed Pfleger on administrative leave on two occasions for reasons largely related to his exercise of the prophetic voice. But Pfleger remains nonplussed and undeterred, a prophetic radical to the end. And he is white. Pfleger's race, however, does not serve as an impediment to his leadership of his black parish. Prophets come in all colors. The irony of his whiteness is not lost on Pfleger himself, who told the congregants one Sunday, "You don't know what God has in store for you! You never thought you would be in a black church led by a white man!" The congregation laughed up-roariously. The prophetic radical has spoken the truth again.

Conclusion

Since scholars typically speak of the black church monolithically, their failure to distinguish between types of black churches may obscure important differences between churches in the black church milieu, namely those like black Catholic parishes that exist outside the ambit of the historically black church. Since pastors of black churches often operate in the prophetic mode by calling society, government, and individuals to account for injustice, this study has also highlighted how scholarly failure to comprehend prophets in other church sectors may cause us to underestimate the role that religious messages play in black politics. If these churches outside the historic black church turn out to be more radical in their messages of black empowerment than those of the historic black church, we cannot discount the role that these black political churches play in a supposed post-racial era.

Black churches in non-black denominations may have *different theological motivations* for political participation than those in black denominations. Specifically, I believe that black churches in non-black denominations to be more likely to espouse black liberation theology as an explicit aspect of church identity than churches in historically black denominations. The reason is this: African Americans in non-black denominations represent a beleaguered minority within a majority church whereas African Americans in the historic black church represent a majority within a minority church. Minorities within white majority denominations are more likely to espouse black empowerment themes and more likely to be marginalized within their own denominations. Black churches in non-black denominations may be more wedded to black liberation theology than churches in historical black denominations.

If theology motivates politics, black Catholic parishes like St. Sabina may evince more radical politics than black Protestant churches that are less explicitly wedded to liberation themes. Eddie Glaude (2008) claims that the black church is dead because it is no longer on the front lines of politics and community change. St. Sabina seems to prove otherwise, with an active Social Services Center that provides financial and resource assistance to local residents of a sufficiently low income, a Senior Citizen's

Center with eighty units of housing as well as services and activities for se-
niors, two Safe Homes that provide residence to children in the foster care
system, a Business Development Program, and a medical clinic in Ghana.
Each of these ministries has both civic and political significance, and
some ministries are operated only with monetary and program support
from government. The Senior Center was enabled in part by a grant from
the U.S. Department of Housing and Urban Development and the Safe
Homes program began as a part of a policy initiative of Richard M. Daley's
administration in partnership with the Department of Children and Family Services of Chicago (The Faith Community of St. Sabina 2012).

Most African Americans embrace a view of linked fate whereby the
individual African American links his personal well-being to the well-
being of the group (Dawson 1994). That said, perhaps the presence of a
communitarian mentality at St. Sabina is not surprising given what we
know about African American politics, but neither is it axiomatic given
that some components of Catholic theology and Social Teaching might
also easily comport with the individualist orientation. For example, the
Catholic teaching "Forming Consciences for Faithful Citizenship" actually identifies the individual as the locus of decision-making about political and policy matters. Of course, Catholic teaching should guide the
individual decision maker, but the document leaves it up to the prudence
of the individual Catholic to decide how to vote, reifying the religious
individualist perspective and potentially marginalizing the communal
perspective. Obviously, the parish priest can be a countervailing force
against individualism by highlighting the communal aspects of Catholic
teaching and the needs of the oppressed in local, national, and international communities. This study indicates that *linked fate is defined locally
as much as it is defined nationally*. Father Pfleger promotes stories and
statistics of Auburn Gresham and Chicago so that the plight of black
Americans is not defined merely by Department of Labor statistics.
Linked fate begins at the local parish.

Prophetic radicals proffer civic messages in their parish sermons,
but they also *set local and national political agendas*. Father Michael
Pfleger seeks to propel parish politics beyond the confines of the Auburn
Gresham neighborhood of Chicago. St. Sabina emphasizes the univer-
sality of the Catholic Church by highlighting themes like the preferential option for the poor and universal healthcare. St. Sabina has led the
Archdiocese of Chicago in a campaign to license guns in the manner of
licensing cars. Father Pfleger is a national mouthpiece for ending gang

and gun violence. The zeal of one parish priest is setting agendas in the city of Chicago and in Congress.

Priestly pulpit messages in this black parish are both practical and political. One is bombarded both with messages to be civic, but also to eat well, to exercise, and to get flu shots. The church speaks to the whole person, not merely to the spiritual and political person.

Table 2. Announcement Themes with Civic and Political Content

Domestic Themes	International Themes
African American History Tour	DNA Test for African Roots
DNA	Fund Raiser for Haiti
Community Bridge with Police	
Rally for Healthcare Reform	
Hispanic Heritage Month	
HIV Prevention Study	
Flu Shots	
Marriage Preparation classes	
BP (British Petroleum) Protest	
Cook County Taxes	
Census Forms 2010	
Burr Oaks Cemetery	

This is consistent with studies that indicate that black churches have become important venues for County and City health initiatives concerning medical issues that plague the black community, like Type-II Diabetes (e.g., Campbell et al. 2007).

Black liberation theology as explicated by Father Pfleger serves as a foil to the rise of the prosperity gospel. Pfleger stated "I am sick of churches and church people trying to pimp God (October 2, 2011)." He mentioned T. D. Jakes in the same sermon. The gospel, Pfleger warns, requires Christians to take up their crosses and suffer for what is just. Christianity is less about rewards than about relationship with God and humankind.

Catholicism continues to thrive because racially particular parishes like St. Sabina are vehicles for reform. High levels of tension within the Catholic Church ultimately lead to revival and reform (Finke and Wittberg 2000) both in the church writ large and at the parish level, where all politics is local, and sometimes, that politics is racialized *and* local. Albert J. Raboteau argues that "African American religious narratives have functioned as rhetorical challenges to the conscience of whites, as well as rhetorical strategies for the survival and flourishing of black communities" (2009, 10). Ultimately, there can be no unity sans particularity. "Universalism [of the Catholic sort] needs to include all; otherwise it simply means the hegemony of the dominant group. On the other hand, particularity, with no reference to a universal dimension of cross-cultural and interethnic community, becomes . . . a race religion" (Raboteau 2009, 17).

St. Sabina emphasizes black particularity in form and substance by emphasizing prophecy and an evangelical sensibility. This unique melding of Catholic universalism and black Protestant particularity render the priest in a unique position to influence politics via the power of his hierarchical position and via the prophetic style of black church sermons. Father Pfleger's prophetic radicalism spurs his congregants on to good deeds, spiritual, civic, and political, but also reflects the realities of life on Chicago's South side. All parish politics are local—and sometimes, parish politics are racialized too.

2

Jesus and Justice: The Moral Framing of the Black Policy Agenda

Dr. Larycia A. Hawkins, Wheaton College

THE CONGRESSIONAL BLACK CAUCUS motto succinctly summarizes the face of public solidarity among African Americans: "Black people have no permanent friends; no permanent enemies; just permanent interests." If the black faces in Congress represent black interests writ large (Tate 2004) they also define the boundaries of blackness (Cohen 1999). Nevertheless, there is a dearth of literature on the language that frames black policy visions and putatively defines the black public interest. In the black political milieu, the black church represents a significant cultural variable, providing resources for political mobilization (Harris 1999) but beyond voting and civic skills, the church provides rhetoric for political battle.

I hypothesize that the language that frames black politics is steeped in liberation theological themes emanating from the black church. The research examines how members of the Congressional Black Caucus, as well as non-black members with similar ADA ratings,[1] speak about one domestic policy—welfare reform and one international policy—aid to Haiti. My expectation is that black members of Congress are more likely than non-black members of Congress to frame policy issues with reference to religion. In addition to uttering more religious referents than non-black members of Congress, I anticipate that the religious referents uttered by black members will tend to be of a particular theological stripe—culturally steeped in a black Christian tradition that emphasizes

---

1. ADA ratings are maintained by Americans for Democratic Action and represent a composite score based upon a member's voting record on twenty social and economic issues during a year.

bondage in Egypt and deliverance from Pharaoh alongside the deliverance from sin provided by Christ on the cross. Specifically, African American religionists are more likely to emphasize liberation from injustice for the oppressed and judgment for society and government where injustices remain unrectified. If and when non-black members express religious referents in their policy images,[2] I expect them to be less likely than black to emphasize themes of liberation theology. This research will enhance our understanding both of black religion and of black politics, but also of policy framing by political elites more generally.

Additionally, this work has implications for the intersection of theology and praxis in the public square. Historically, black liberation theology framed slave freedom narratives and the black freedom movement. This work posits that black religious themes continue to frame black politics today. Similarly, some evangelicals, especially since the late 1970s, frame politics in religious terms. While generic references to God and providence are deemed acceptable per the American civil religion, scholars and cultural critics (e.g., Rawls 1996) have been vociferous in their critiques of evangelicals' invocation of religion in the public square. This paper illustrates that while evangelicals and African American Christians honor the same God, they emphasize different aspects of the biblical text. These differing Scriptural emphases generally result in divergent political perspectives in the black church and evangelical milieus.

Literature Review

The black church represents an essential repository of civic and electoral resources (Verba, Sclozman, and Brady 1995; Rosenstone and Hansen 1993). For example, studies indicate that African American parishioners receive general and specific messages from black pastors about politics and other civic activities. Additionally, the black church serves as a venue where black politicians, and politicians generally, can reach and mobilize the black constituency. Beyond the provision of sacred and civic space and the promulgation of social networks for political activity, the black church provides policy images (Baumgartner and Jones 1993) for black politics. Frederick C. Harris' work on the black church and politics (1999)

2. Policy images are shared images of public policies. In this case, we might expect similarly liberal democrats to have shared images of policies, for example, a policy concerning comparable worth might be spoken of as shattering the glass ceiling or leveling the playing field (see Baumgartner and Jones 1993).

illustrates that beyond the historical importance of the black church in fomenting protest via the utilization of black sacred symbols in protest language, these symbols provide resources for present day politics. Melissa Harris-Lacewell (2004) demonstrates that the black church is a venue where everyday black talk contributes to African Americans' collective understanding of the political realm. Despite these important works, few scholars probe the salience and impact of theology in the framing of contemporary black politics.

African American Christians, not unlike many evangelicals, hold Scripture as both inspired by God and the literal word of God. One recent study indicates that while such biblical literalism influences partisanship, biblical literalism is filtered through cultural lenses: "even those who believe that the Bible is the literal word of God still infuse aspects of their culture into its interpretation (McDaniel and Ellison 2008, 180)." Non-black Christians (e.g., white evangelicals) who interpret Scripture literally tend to stress personal piety and moral conduct by emphasizing individualism and inequalities of outcome consonant with white framing of American culture. Black Christians, on the other hand, emphasize moral responsibility by stressing communalism and radical equality grounded in the imperative to impart justice and mercy to all, regardless of circumstance. While it is interesting to note that most African Americans are Democrats and most evangelicals are Republicans, what is important for the purpose of this research is that differential theological emphases matters not merely for partisanship, but matters also for political expression.

Black liberation theology (Cone 1969) asserts that non-black theology, largely Western and conducted by white males, is a tool of the oppressive state. Per Cone (1969) white theologies encouraged black compliance with the status quo of an unjust social order via scriptural injunctions for slaves to "obey masters" and "work as for the Lord." Conversely, black liberation theology takes seriously Yahweh's admonition in the prophetic books that Christians are called to care for the oppressed and to pursue justice in society by imploring oppressive governments to act justly toward the least of society. In the book of Isaiah, the righteous city/government is defined as the one that pursues justice on behalf of the oppressed. Many black churches, pastors and denominations ascribe to this prophetic emphasis upon social justice[3]—described in the Hebrew

---

3. Of course, some non-black religionists do as well; namely, Catholics who ascribe to liberation theology and/or emphasize aspects of Catholic Social Teaching like the preferential option for the poor.

Scripture as seeking justice for orphans, widows, aliens, and the poor and oppressed of all stripes. In addition to the evangelical emphasis upon being born again, Jesus Christ identified his earthly ministry as synonymous with the pursuit of justice for the oppressed, consonant with the prophetic call of Hebrew Scripture:

> The Spirit of the Lord is upon me,
> because he has anointed me
> to proclaim good news to the poor.
> He has sent me to proclaim liberty to the captives
> and recovering of sight to the blind,
> to set at liberty those who are oppressed,
> to proclaim the year of the Lord's favor. (Luke 4:18–19)

Per black liberation theology, Jesus is positioned not only as liberator of the black soul, but also as liberator of the black predicament. *Through the lenses of black liberation, the Jesus who stands in solidarity with the oppressed is black and prefers the poor and oppressed.*

Black liberation theology's call to pursue justice is reflected in the policy priorities of African American Protestants who evince the highest levels of support for issues salient to social justice when compared to other Christian religionists. For example, on domestic politics, 82 percent of black Protestants are quite interested in aid to the poor compared to 58 percent of evangelical Protestants, 56 percent of mainline Protestants, and 62 percent of Roman Catholics. On the world front, 41 percent of black Protestants are interested in developing world relief compared to 25 percent of evangelical Protestants, 23 percent of mainline Protestants, and 29 percent of Roman Catholics (*see* Wilson 2007, 43).[4] African Americans' concern for the last and the least extends beyond the borders of the United States to the world.

Given the imprint of black theology on black culture and the ubiquity of religion in the black community—88 percent of African Americans believe in God and 85 percent of African Americans in historically black churches deem religion very important to their lives (Pew Forum, 2008, the expectation that some sacred symbols *frame* secular politics is not unfounded (Harris 1999). Framing represents "the conscious strategic efforts by groups of people to fashion shared understandings of the world and of themselves that legitimate and motivate collective

---

4. Data from the Religion and Politics 2000 survey, Princeton University, as cited in J. Matthew Wilson, *From Pews to Polling Place: Faith and Politics in the American Religious Mosaic.*

action" (McAdam, McCarthy, and Zald 1996, 6). In the black community, politicians and pastors often frame politics and create policy images to engender group solidarity around policies of import to the entire African American community. Individuals may employ multiple frames simultaneously.[5] Among other frames, I expect black political frames and policy images to be rooted in black cultural experiences, including religious experience. Certainly, they are expected to invoke American values as well, but non-black members of Congress are expected to rely upon reference to American values more than black members given differential historical experience of black and non-black Americans.

African Americans view their individual political and economic fortunes as intimately linked to the collective political and economic fortunes of African Americans as a whole. This sense of linked fate (Dawson 1994) in the African American community may increase the propensity of black members of Congress to utilize black cultural frames, including those grounded in black liberation theology and emanating from the black church. Civil rights or protest-oriented frames are also likely to be salient in black political rhetoric and on black policy agendas (Hawkins 2009).

Data and Findings

I assume that black members of Congress will use black religious referents in their justifications for policy in one of two places—in the presence of predominantly black audiences (whether in the district or otherwise) or in venues to which black constituents would be likely to be attentive to black members of Congress' speech—like the floor of Congress. Thus, I explored the floor speeches of members of Congress since these are televised, publicized by the members themselves, and entered into the Congressional Record. Prior to conducting the search, I chose to focus upon one domestic policy issue, welfare reform of 1996, and one international issue, the Haiti earthquake of 2010. I assumed that both issues would generate a significant number of floor speeches given the controversial nature of welfare reform on the one hand and the catastrophic nature of the Haiti earthquake on the other hand. The reason for the divergence of years was the need to choose an international issue on which members of the Congressional Black Caucus would have had the opportunity to

---

5. Charles Tilly (1999, 345–346) terms this use of multiple frames polyvalent performance.

make significant floor speeches. Given that a preponderance of the Sub-committee on African Affairs were members of the CBC and the salience of the Haiti earthquake, I choose the floor speeches on Haiti relief.

To determine whether black members of Congress frame politics differently than non-black members of Congress, I decided to compare Congressional Black Caucus members to non-CBC members with similar ADA ratings. The Americans for Democratic Action (ADA) rates every member of Congress is based on how he/she votes on issues of concern to the group. For example, the focus of the 2008–2010 agenda of the ADA included broad issues like poverty, health care reform, and tax reform with concordant specific commitments to establishing a living wage, implementing a single-payer health care system, and ending the Bush tax cuts (Americans for Democratic Action 2012). An ADA score of one hundred reflects high commitment to the liberal ideals of the ADA and reflects low commitment to the liberal ideals of the ADA.

Since CBC members are the most liberal members of Congress, I chose to compare their speeches to non-CBC members who are similarly liberal. In doing so, I controlled for the effects of ideology on the framing of policy issues. If liberation theological themes rooted in black religion do appear in the policy rhetoric of black members of Congress, we would not expect non-black members of Congress who are similarly liberal but not similarly rooted in black culture to express policy in the same manner.[6] Controlling for ideology is imperative methodologically as it leaves open the possibility that we might find the alternative hypothesis that there is no difference between how black and non-black members of Congress frame issues. An incidental side effect of comparing the most liberal members of Congress is that the sample includes only Demo-crats—imposing an additional control for political party.

I obtained the floor speeches from the Congressional Record. I con-ducted a search at thomas.loc.gov/home/crquery.html for all the floor speeches in the sample. A search of articles about the Haiti earthquake in the 111th Congress generated a sample size of 100 speeches and a search for floor speeches concerning welfare reform in the 104th Congress gen-erated a sample size of 142 speeches.

In terms of the content analysis, words and phrases within paragraphs were the primary unit of analysis. Within the text of the speeches, I coded for the presence of expected themes relating to religion generally (e.g.,

6. Unless of course, they are rooted in the black church or in institutions where liberation theology is prevalent, like some Catholic venues.

God, prayer, etc.) and black liberation theology specifically (e.g., the last and the least, the oppressed). I also coded for additional themes related to liberal and American ideals—such as language indicative of humanitarian values like human rights, human dignity, etc. and language indicative of American values like equality, liberty, rule of law, and the like. Since the manner in which members of Congress frame policy problems affects the policy solutions that they employ (Stone 2001) I also coded for the policy options that members of Congress discussed relative to the issue of welfare and the Haiti disaster. Finally, I coded so as to allow emergent themes to develop that might have been unanticipated by me.

The imposition of ideological control limited the relevant documents to black members of Congress and non-black members with similar ADA scores. The Haiti sample includes sixteen speeches (16 percent of the total sample) including eleven from members of the Congressional Black Caucus and five from non-black members of Congress with similar ADA ratings. There were 132 total paragraphs in the Haiti sample. The welfare reform sample includes two speeches (2 percent of the total sample) including one from a member of the Congressional Black Caucus and one from a non-black member of Congress with a similar ADA rating to the selected member of Congress. There were nineteen total paragraphs in the welfare reform sample. I employed line by line, focused coding for this study. Open coding allowed for the emergence of both expected and emergent themes. As framing concepts emerged from the speeches, I listed discrete words and concepts, noting patterns and conceptual connections across documents. I counted each reference to expected and themes. For example, if there are two distinct instances of the phrase "the least and the last" in one sentence, each instance is counted. In the next stage, I grouped concepts into analytical categories on the basis of shared themes or subject matter. The context of the words within the speech served as key indicators of the theme and category labels were established to be broad enough to include multiple frames, yet specific enough to be distinguishable from other categories. The two instances to "the least and the last" would be and placed under the category of *Black Liberation* because this phrase is synonymous with the oppressed in black liberation theology.

As much as possible, I placed themes in categories on the basis of theoretical expectations, but open coding leaves open the possibility of new and nuanced framing of issues along unexplored dimensions. Thus, despite my theoretical grounding in black liberation and black church literatures, I could not anticipate the precise manner in which frames would be employed or the nuance with which they would be employed. For example, black members of Congress did not use generic liberation language of "the oppressed" and "the oppressor," but explicitly defined the oppressed in terms of populations or constituencies and oppressors as systems or institutions. Similarly, for themes unrelated to religion, I counted and coded into categories on the basis of shared or similar properties and/or subject matter.

There exists both variation and precision in the broader categories that emerged (Strauss and Corbin 1998). The *Black Liberation Theology* category includes references to themes of black liberation and to specific religious practices and themes, including prayer, the Good Samaritan, and the like. While the expectation is that black members of Congress are more likely to use religious language rooted in black theology than their non-black liberal counterparts, it is entirely possible that *non-black members* of Congress utilize similar themes in their political rhetoric and as frequently. The *American Political Values* category includes references to civil religion, the founding documents, the American Dream, capitalism, and bootstrapping. It is expected that both black and non-black members utilize such language, but my hypothesis indicates black members will rely on this framing less often given the cultural salience of religious framing. The *Politics/Policy* category embodies references to policy nuance and detail, ranging from welfare time limits to debt forgiveness, that emerged as viable policy options in Congressional discussion of legislation related to welfare reform and Haiti earthquake. to the political and policy issues explored herein. The *Global Humanity* category reflects a commitment to broader creeds like human dignity which do not necessarily have a religious rootedness.[7] Condolences are more generic than prayers. For some members of Congress, the justification for help will not be wrapped in sacralized reasons, but rather in secular humanitarian appeals.

Are members of the Congressional Black Caucus more likely than their non-black liberal counterparts to use culturally-rooted religious frames? In addition to the presence and frequency of religious framing, the data indicate whether members of the Congressional Black Caucus frame policies differently than their non-black counterparts

---

7. Of course, this indicates the precise difficulty in coding certain phrases. Some Judeo-Christian religionists might speak of human dignity and actually mean the *imago Dei*, but for the purpose of this study, only explicitly religious referents are counted as religious.

along dimensions generally salient to liberal Democrats. For example, given the role of government as oppressor in liberation theology and in African American history, members of the CBC may be less likely than their non-black peers to justify policy according to American Political Values. The findings of the data will be explored below by reference to Table 1 and Table 2.

Table 1. Haiti Earthquake.

Category Key Words	CBC Members	Non-black Members	Total
Black Liberation Theology (n=39)	*79% (31)*	*21% (8)*	*39*
Faith	2		2
Prayers/Pray	8	3	11
Prayer Breakfast/Day	2		2
Good Samaritan	1		1
God Bless	1		1
Solidarity	5	1	6
Oppressed/Suffering/Victims	1	4	5
Orphans	9		9
Least/Last	2		2
Global Humanity (n=33)	*48% (16)*	*52% (17)*	*33*
Condolences	2	3	5
Moment of Silence	1		1
Moral Responsibility		1	1
Neighbor		1	1
Haitian People	13	12	25
American Political Values (n=8)	*37.5% (3)*	*62.5% (5)*	*8*

Category Key Words	CBC Members	Non-black Members	Total
U.S. Independence	1		1
U.S. National Security		3	3
Democracy		2	2
Work	1		1
Opportunity	1		1
Politics/Policy (n=137)	*60% (82)*	*40% (55)*	*137*
CBC Leadership	17		17
International Community	8	3	11
Charities/NGOS	3		3
Bipartisan Response	2		2
Swift Response	7	2	9
Temporary Protected Status	3	2	5
Aid/Assistance/Resources	24	26	50
Humanitarian Relief	3	3	6
Rebuild	4	1	5
Recovery	5	3	8
Accountability/Transparency		3	3
Stability		5	5
Security (Haitian)		3	3
Self-Determination	3	3	6
Debt Cancellation	2		2
End Poverty	1	1	2

Table 1 shows coding for key words that emerged relevant to the Haiti earthquake. As explained previously, concepts were categorized together if and when dimensions of the concept seemed akin to other concepts in terms of textual analysis. In the Black Liberation Theology category, 79 percent (thirty-one) of all text units were uttered by members of the Congressional Black Caucus. The most prevalent dimensions for CBC members were "orphans" (nine text units) and "prayers" (eight text units) whereas non-black members emphasized the "oppressed" (four text units) and "prayers" (three text units). It is not only of note that explicitly liberation refrains stating solidarity with the oppressed in Haiti were uttered primarily by black members of Congress, but also significant that 82 percent of *all* religious language in the Haiti sample was uttered by CBC members.

In the Global Humanity category, the most prevalent dimensions were similar for both CBC members and non-black members of Congress. General "condolences" and expressions of sadness on behalf of the "Haitian people" were equally salient. There appears to be no difference between CBC members and non-black members on this front. While condolences may be expressed in a religious manner and/or context, whether or not help is apparently *rooted* in religious sensibilities rather than religious ones is less important than the whether the appeal itself includes identifiable religious referents or is in the context of a paragraph with religious sentiment.

In the American Political Values category, the total text units for the various dimensions of the variable are so small as to make comparison difficult. Of note, however, is the differential emphasis along the dimensions of the category. Non-black members made the majority of references and emphasized themes like "democracy" (two text units) and "national security" (three text units) whereas CBC members who mentioned American political values emphasized themes like "opportunity" and the quest for "independence."

In terms of Politics/Policy, members of the CBC and non-black members of Congress evinced largely similar preferences for "aid." Yet, the manner in which they did so differed. Black members were twice as likely as their non-black counterparts to emphasize engaging the "international community" in the provision of aid (eight text units for black members versus three text units for others). Whereas non-black members emphasized "accountability" (three text units) in the delivery of assistance, black members did not mention this theme at all. Black members emphasized "CBC leadership" (seventeen text units) which indicates racial solidarity of black Americans with black Haitians, but they also applauded "bipartisan" support of Haiti relief (two text units). The theme of black solidarity with the black oppressed is a theme of black liberation theology.

Table 2. Welfare Reform.

Category Key Words	CBC Members	Non-black Members	Total
Black Liberation Theology (n=28)	82% (23)	8% (5)	28
Left behind/Cut-off	1		1
Rich	3		3
Least/Poor	4		4
Orphans/Children	15	5	20
American Political Values (n=18)	17% (3)	83% (15)	18
Market incentives		2	2
Personal responsibility		3	3
Self-sufficiency		1	1
Public dole	2		2
Nuclear family		2	2
Parental responsibility		3	3
Work	1	3	4
Working families		1	1
Politics/Policy (n=37)	14% (5)	86% (32)	37
Robin Hood	1		1
Job provision	4		4
Welfare rolls		2	2
Welfare recipients		6	6

Category Key Words	CBC Members	Non-black Members	Total
Teen mothers		1	1
Able bodied		3	3
Safety Net		3	3
Time limits		2	2
Welfare fraud		1	1
States		9	9
Waivers/Experimenting		4	4
Flexibility		1	1

Table 2 indicates coding for variables relevant to welfare reform. In the Black Liberation Theology category, both members of the CBC and non-black members of Congress honed in on the theme of "children" as oppressed victims of poverty and the welfare system generally. However, black members of Congress emphasized aspects of black liberation theology, such as the tension between poor (four text units) and rich (three text units) whereas non-black members did not mention the class dynamic at all.

In terms of American Political Values, the analysis revealed a differential framing between non-black and black members of Congress. The "public dole" (two text units) perhaps seems out of place, but the code emerged as a black member of Congress explained that this type of reckless welfare use was not consonant with American values. The non-black member of Congress revealed a plethora of dimensions of the American Dream, including the "nuclear family" (two text units) "personal responsibility" (three text units) and work (three text units).

For Politics/Policy, there is a divergence between how non-black and black members frame welfare reform. While this particular set of articles was limited by the search criteria, the dimensions that emerged are consonant with the tenor of debate (*see* Hancock 2004). A liberal non-black member of Congress framed welfare as a "safety net" (three text units) for the *deserving* poor, but not for the *undeserving* poor. This liberal non-black member, consonant with the notion that poor people do not deserve welfare, framed welfare recipients (six text units) as "able bodied" (three text units) as engaged in "welfare fraud" (one text unit) and as "teen mothers" (one text unit). In terms of policy options, federalism was emphasized with references to the "states" (nine text units) occurring frequently in the discussion of policy options and "waivers" (four text units) from federal regulations regarding welfare. Framing welfare recipients (six text units) as undeserving certainly contributes to a tendency to impose time limits (two text units). Black liberation theology does not distinguish between the deserving and undeserving poor since Jesus prefers the poor in black liberation theology. The black members of Congress emphasized job provision (four text units) as a policy option for those welfare recipients who reach their time limit. Consonant with the theme of rich and poor in black liberation theology, welfare is described positively as a "Robin Hood" (one text unit) policy by a black member of Congress.

Analysis

Black Liberation Theology: Alive and Kicking?

The current work explores whether African American legislators differ from non-black members of Congress on an important dimension, the language they use to frame politics. The Haiti documents were derived from a special Congressional Black Caucus Haiti Hour. In the 111th Congress, five of eight members of the Subcommittee on Africa and Global Affairs were members of the Congressional Black Caucus. This special emphasis on issues related to Africa is consonant with literature that indicates that black legislators tend to serve on committees of particular interest to black communities (Haynie 2001; Tate 2004). In addition to service on "black committees," black members of Congress pass more symbolic policies related to African American constituencies than substantive policies (Tate 2004). If we consider symbolic policies as an opportunity for position-taking (Mayhew 1974) by black members of Congress, it is reasonable to expect floor speeches to reflect the racial substance of the symbolic policies proffered by Congress. Indeed, if symbolic policies are targeted to activate black constituents, language should be sufficiently framed to activate black Americans, but not necessarily non-black ones.

On the notion of black religious referents, like black liberation theology, the data while of limited generalizability given the qualitative nature of the study, may be suggestive of broader trends and of the ripeness of theological frames for research. During the Haiti debates, African American legislators were more likely to proffer religious language than non-black members with similar ADA ratings. While both sets of legislators emphasized prayers, CBC members' religious references were more specific and additionally, were steeped in language familiar to those familiar with black church culture and/or liberation theology.

Haiti Earthquake: Have Faith

During the 111th Congress, one member of the Congressional Black Caucus spoke as though she was encouraging a congregation rather than fellow members of Congress and constituents to action on Haiti relief.

> have faith. Never give up the faith, for in this time of need you will find that the human community will rally toward you and they will be your wind beneath your wings. They will be your Good Samaritan. They will be your brother. They will be your sister. (Sheila Jackson Lee, D-TX)

Congresswoman Lee's reference to fellow humans as brothers and sisters is an invocation of family common in the black church. Historically, such honorifics bestowed on fellow "family members" of the black church emphasized their creation in the image of God in an era where society where their humanity was degraded by names like "nigger" and "pickaninny," not to mention the radical notion of inclusivity of God's multi-colored family in an era where Scripture was used to justify slavery and then segregation. Beyond bestowing dignity, the honorifics also emphasized the sense of black communalism or linked fate that persists in African American culture and politics today (see for example, Dawson 1994).

Lee's reference to a Bette Midler song notwithstanding, her emphasis on keeping "the faith" is a frequent metaphor in the black church. A popular hymn in the black church penned in 1963 proclaims "We've Come This Far by Faith" (Goodson 1963) and has become symbolic of the black freedom struggle.

> We've come this far by faith, leaning on the Lord.
> Trusting in God's holy word, God never failed us yet.
> Oh . . . can't turn around, we've come this far by faith.
> God led us all the way, through each night and day.
> When the way was dark and hard, we always called on the Lord.

Oh . . . wonderful grace, we've come this far by faith.
In God's word we still believe, reaping victory,
Blessings we have always found, no need to search around.
Oh . . . sing out His praise, we've come this far by faith.

Even in the post-civil rights era, the hymn serves as a reminder to African Americans that black Christianity was a crucial component on the long road to social justice and that black faith remains central to political endurance today. In the context of the Haiti earthquake, the injunction to "keep the faith" has a particular meaning to many black constituents that may be lost on non-black constituents.[8]

Lee's reference to the Good Samaritan is also emblematic of black liberation framing. In this familiar parable of Jesus Christ, a robbery victim is bypassed by two societal elites but finally receives aid from a Samaritan. Samaritans were beleaguered minorities—half Jewish, excluded from worshipping in the temple in Jerusalem, and subject to miscegenation laws given their mixed race status. Nevertheless, the socially oppressed Samaritan becomes the hero in Jesus' parable—and the oppressed becomes the symbol of a gospel of liberation. Congresswoman Jackson Lee's inclusion of this metaphor is indicative of the solidarity of black members of Congress with the victims of the Haiti earthquake and is evidence of black liberation themes extant in some CBC members' framing of political issues.

Welfare Reform: The Least of These

During the welfare reform debates of the 104th Congress, members of the Congressional Black Caucus also emphasized what black liberation theology terms "the least of these." Pure religion is defined in Hebrew Scripture as caring for the oppressed: "seek justice, encourage the oppressed, defend the cause of the fatherless, plead the case of the widow" (Isa 1:17).[9] In the welfare reform speeches of some black members of

8. Of course, some non-black Christian religionists might understand this code and resonate with the imperative to be steadfast, but this phrase is particularly salient in black church parlance.

9. This imperative is a salient aspect of Judaism as well as of Catholicism, thus, I was attentive to these themes in the speeches of non-black members of Congress who might concur with some of the themes of black liberation. The language of *black* liberation and church culture, however, as expressed in Sheila Jackson Lee's quote, often accompanies liberation refrains.

Congress, however, there is a marked framing of specific welfare recipients who stood to be oppressed by the bill, namely children.

> Mr. Chairman, this bill is a hoax. . . . And it is mean spirited and mean to children. They did not do anything to deserve this. Why would we punish children for in the name of welfare reform? (Rep. Melvin Watt, D-NC)

Non-black members, on the other hand, framed welfare recipients as *undeserving* of public aid as opposed to *oppressed and vulnerable* due to poverty.

> Most Hoosiers want to help people in *genuine need*. They are willing to aid people who cannot work because of disability, or who face dire economic distress through no fault of their own. What they oppose is assisting people who are capable of working but unwilling to do so. (Rep. Lee Hamilton D-IN, emphasis added)

In effect, Rep. Hamilton contrasts the *deserving poor*—those whom he presumes to have genuine need (e.g., the disabled) with the *undeserving poor*—those whom he presumes to be merely lazy or unwilling to work yet able to do so (e.g., the able bodied). This member of Congress implies that the able-bodied poor are to blame for their plight while the disabled poor are blameless—poor through "no fault of their own". The implication of this framing is to cast the preponderance of welfare recipients as irresponsible individuals rather than vulnerable to, and oppressed by, structural factors beyond their control like the economy. Per this type of welfare trope, most welfare recipients are to blame for their plight and an exceptional few actually deserve aid.

What might account for black members' framing of welfare recipients in terms of the oppressed as opposed to undeserving? Some scholars liken the black church to the state church of the black community, terming it a semi-involuntary institution (Ellison and Sherkat 1995) for African Americans. In the African American community, the church plays such a central role, one need not be a member to understand and be acculturated to black church symbols, norms, and language. The black church provides cultural energy (Morris 2000) for black politics, including moral frames, music, and stories salient to the African American experience writ large. Thus, despite humanitarian language utilized by black and non-black members of Congress alike, black members of Congress framed both welfare and the Haiti earthquake as an opportunity to stand in solidarity with the black poor across the globe and as an opportunity to do justice on behalf of the economically oppressed in their backyard, consonant with themes of black liberation theology. This is also consistent with the claim of the CBC that it is the "conscience of Congress." Frames rooted in black liberation theology are used to prick the conscience of all members of Congress on policy issues. Black liberation theology is alive and kicking in black politics.

Old Time Religion or Partisan Politics?
The CBC and Policy Options

This study cannot answer the question of whether there is a direct relationship between religious motivations and policy options considered by members of Congress. Indeed, since during the two Congresses under consideration, all members of the CBC were Democrats, it is possible that religious language frames political talk, but not the solutions used to ameliorate policy problems. But this study does locate the nuance of religious language in the context of policy solutions, so we can note whether black members justify the same policies in different ways than their non-black counterparts.

Upon its founding in 1971, the Black Caucus promulgated a Black Declaration of Independence and a Black Bill of Rights (Singh 1997). This explicit racial framing of the Founding Documents of the United States reflects the sensibility of the Caucus' founders that African Americans have "permanent interests," rooted in historical and cultural experience. For example, the Congressional Black Caucus proffers a "black agenda" every congressional term, inclusive of an Alternative Budget that highlights issues of particular importance to black and brown communities across the U.S., such as poverty, environmental justice, and healthcare. What follows is the CBC's mission statement:

> Since 1971, the Members of the Congressional Black Caucus have joined together to strengthen their efforts to *empower America's neglected citizens*—including but not limited to Americans of color—by more effectively addressing our legislative concerns. The Congressional Black Caucus is committed to utilizing the full Constitutional power, statutory authority, and financial resources of the Government of the United States of America to ensure, insofar as possible, that everyone in the United States has an opportunity to live out the American Dream.

> The legislative agenda of universal empowerment that the Members of the Caucus shall *collectively* pursue shall include, but are not limited to: the creation of universal access to a world-class education from birth through post secondary level; the creation of universal access to quality, affordable health care and the elimination of racially based health disparities; the creation of universal access to modern technology, capital, and full, fairly-compensated employment; the creation and or expansion of US foreign policy initiatives that will contribute to the survival, health, education, and general welfare of all peoples of the world in a manner consistent with universal human dignity, tolerance, and respect, and such other legislative action as a majority of the entire CBC membership from time to time may support. (emphasis added, Congressional Black Caucus n.d)

The black liberation emphasis upon empowerment of the oppressed via collective action finds expression in black legislative goals. The CBC's mission statement reflects the fact that individual African Americans view their fortunes as inextricably linked to the fate of the group as a whole (Dawson 1994). But if black Americans have permanent interests, are policy options proffered by black members of Congress qualitatively different than those of their putative party, the Democrats?

Haiti Earthquake: Our President

African American members of Congress are consistently the most liberal caucus in the Congress. In the current sample, every member of the Congressional Black Caucus has an ADA score of ninety-five or higher. CBC members voted together 95 percent of the time in the 109th Congress. Other evidences of linked fate and collective consciousness emerged during coding. For example, members invoked President Obama in particular ways, calling him "our President" in the context of talking about the Black Caucus' leadership on the Haiti issue. The Congressional Black Caucus framed itself as leading the Congress on the Haiti earthquake response. Sheila Jackson Lee (D-TX) stated, "I want everyone to realize that the Congressional Black Caucus is leading on (Haiti)." Contrary to some white members framing of an "American response," members of the CBC emphasized a racialized response to an issue affecting the least of these in Haiti by the purveyors of black permanent interests. As indicated previously, black Protestants are more likely than any other group of religionists to support international aid.

In spite of this linked fate framing of the Haiti response, policy options were consonant with those of their Democratic colleagues. So while racial framing rooted in black communalism and in black liberation theology prevailed on the Haiti issue, the CBC's vision of the government's policy response, aid and development, was not markedly different from that of non-black members who are similarly liberal. However, black members of Congress were the only legislators who discussed debt forgiveness for Haiti while non-black members of Congress were the only legislators who emphasized accountability for relief funds for Haiti.

One plausible explanation for this phenomenon is that the earthquake offered a framing opportunity for all Democrats, not merely the Congressional Black Caucus. Both black and non-black Democrats framed the Obama's response to the devastation of black people in Haiti as swift in juxtaposition with the response of President Bush to black people in New Orleans after Hurricane Katrina, which they framed as slow. Of course, both CBC members and their non-black Democratic counterparts latched onto this opportunity to claim affiliation with the "fully engaged" (Bobby Rush, D-IL) Democratic president.

Welfare Reform: Option for the Poor—Work

The issue of welfare reform, however, produced some difference in terms of policy options. For example, whereas the non-black member of Congress emphasized time limits and work requirements, the black members emphasized job provision. In the final analysis, members of the Congressional Black Caucus overwhelmingly opposed welfare reform. Although reform was consonant with the agenda of the centrist, Democratic President Bill Clinton, members of the CBC maintained their preferential option for the poor. While CBC members tended to emphasize government programs consonant with a black agenda of jobs and linked fate (Dawson 1994; 2003, most come from constituencies with significant numbers of non-blacks and also emphasized American values like the American Dream (Hochschild 1996). How do black members of Congress reconcile commitment to a strong welfare state with their avowed American ideals?

Proud to be an American? American Political Values

Members of the Congressional Black Caucus' framing of politics is mediated not merely by their sense of linked fate and their commitment to the Democratic party, but also by American ideals like democracy, freedom, and equality. Of course, when a black member evokes symbolism about equality of opportunity, it is difficult to disentangle it from the persistent inequality which was a legal reality for black Americans for centuries in this country. Indeed, much of black politics is framed against the historical backdrop. But American ideals are forward looking, emphasizing radical equality of opportunity despite race or creed. American ideals are consonant with what one scholar describes as a "white racial frame" —one that validates "the inegalitarian accumulation of social, economic, and political resources" (Feagin 2010, 16) via an emphatic insistence that oppressive events and even oppressive eras were aberrations from the democratic norm and a refusal to integrate counterframes that highlight past and continued inequities and oppression in the United States. In short, the white racial frame sweeps race under the rug in favor of the American Dream.

Haiti Earthquake: U.S. Independence Predicated on Haitians

In the Haiti data, the American commitment to aid in rescue and recovery was discussed by black and non-black members of Congress as a first priority, but non-black members tended to address abstract American ideals as motivating aid. American-style democracy was proffered as the long-term solution to what ails the earthquake ravaged country. Additionally, the American response was framed in terms of realpolitik as Congresswoman Debbie Wasserman-Schultz (D-FL) linked emergency funds for Haiti to U.S. national security: "(Emergency funding) is vital to providing stability in that fragile country, and is in our own national security interest." Her framing of Haiti as a fragile country is akin to calling it a failed state and in her speech, implicates the necessity for democracy to be exported to Haitian neighbors in the name of *U.S. security*, not in the name of the security of Haitian people. Indeed, Schultz abstracted the fragility to the country itself, further emphasizing the need for the U.S. to consider its own stability against the presumed instability of the Haitian regime.

Black members, on the other hand, emphasized the role of Haitians in the political development of the United States of the U.S. as well as the contemporary political status of Haitian immigrants vis-à-vis the United States. Donald Payne (D-NJ) equated Haiti's history with U.S. history, explaining how the Haitians fight for independence against Napoleon weakened France's coffers and facilitated the Louisiana Purchase. Bobby Rush (D-IL) recounted the story of Haitian explorer Jean Baptiste Pointe du Sable, who settled the city of Chicago, Illinois, by exploiting waterways to establish a successful trading company.

Despite this rich Haitian-U.S. connection, several member of the CBC and at least one non-black member of Congress emphasized that Haitians have tended to be overlooked in immigration debates, especially as compared to other immigrants. Sheila Jackson Lee (D-TX) detects a double-standard where predominantly black Haitians and Cubans are concerned: "the deportation of Haitians have really fallen upon the backs of hardworking Haitians who came here, by and large, simply to work and to achieve opportunities. They came alongside of the Cubans, but did not have the same status." Prior to the earthquake, Haitians were seldom afforded Temporary Protected Status, a supposed benefit of the land of opportunity.

Welfare Reform: American Dream Tempered by Black History

On welfare reform, previous research has established that black members of Congress were as likely as non-black members to frame welfare recipients' behavior as antithetical to American values (Hancock 2004). In this study, one black member did emphasize the importance of work and even framed welfare as the "public dole," a primarily negative conception of welfare in this country. Non-black members like Lee Hamilton (D-IN) framed welfare recipients as outside the ambit of American values: "Welfare still too often conflicts with bedrock American values: it discourages work, promotes out-of-wedlock childbearing, breaks up families, and fails to hold parents responsible." This culture of poverty framing imbues welfare recipients' with second-class citizenship status at best and deems them un-American at worst.

American political values are certainly invoked by both black and non-black members of Congress, but the invocation of American themes was markedly different in both cases. During symbolic moments, like the singing of the National Anthem on 9/11, black members of Congress rally around the flag with the most patriotic of their legislative peers. Yet, this research indicates that black members funnel their American ideals through the prism of black culture and black religion at times. For black members of Congress who invoke the black liberation theology vision of Jesus as a political liberator who stands with the oppressed, there is a tendency to temper expressions of the American Dream with black historical reality. In this study, black members of Congress emphasized that some black welfare recipients hobble up to the starting line of equality of opportunity and begin the race for the American Dream at a disadvantage given historical inequities, structural impediments, and racism. For these American sins, the Jesus of black liberation theology stands not only in solidarity with the black poor, but he also prefers them. This bias of black liberation theology is reflected in policies like Alternative Budgets that privilege the poor and vulnerable of whatever ilk.

Conclusion and Future Research

Black politics is embedded in a cultural context where black religion abounds, providing ready language for political battle. The cultural influence of black Christianity, namely, black liberation theology, cannot be understated. This study suggests that black members of Congress commitment to liberal ideological ideals or partisan commitments alone did not solely punctuate their framing of policy issues. Unpacking the dynamics of religious framing of politics is crucial to understanding how political issues are framed more generally. This is important since the way that that policy problems are framed impacts the policy solutions brought to bear on those issues. If we believe that poor individuals are to blame for their poverty, we will provide less governmental assistance than if we believe structural factors are to blame for poverty. While controlling for both ideology and party in this study, I demonstrate that the policy options proffered by members of the Congressional Black Caucus differed from those proffered by non-black Democrats.

Despite of assertions that President Obama's election has entered in a post-racial era era, black politics is alive and well and is carried out in discursive and symbolic ways (Reed 1986; Tate 2004). The current research focused primarily upon the discursive element of black politics, asserting what largely differentiates black politics, and particularly the black agenda, is how black politicians frame political issues. The cultural imprint of the black church provides frames for black politicians as they articulate an agenda for African Americans. An additional implication of this research is that the symbolic ways in which members of the Congressional Black Caucus articulate, pursue, and implement the black agenda remain steeped not only in black Christianity a la Civil Rights era protest, but are also entrenched in post-civil rights tactics of politics.

Yet, caution is in order. The symbolic nature of black agenda politics can represent an opportunity for agenda denial whereby black members of Congress fail to pursue issues of import to the black community writ large (Hawkins 2009). Issues like the Faith-Based and Community Initiative, school vouchers, and a gay marriage ban remain on the margins of (or excluded altogether from) the black consensus agenda of the Congressional Black Caucus, despite the fact that black Americans evince high levels of support for all of the above issue positions.

While the platform and the size of the audiences certainly differs, the religious framing of black agenda issues by some members of the CBC is not entirely unlike President George W. Bush's appeals to his evangelical base during some of his State of the Union Addresses. The following excerpt is from the 2003 State of the Union address:

> Our fourth goal is to apply the compassion of America to the deepest problems of America. For so many in our country—the homeless, the fatherless, the addicted—the need is great. Yet there is power—wonder-working power—in the goodness, and idealism, and faith of the American people.

While his reference to "wonder-working power" was a nod to evangelicals as the phrase comes from a hymn, "There is Power in the Blood" (Jones 1899) President Bush's emphasis on needy and oppressed constituencies resonates with a broader swath of religionists, including adherents of black liberation theology. Indeed, President Bush's Faith-Based and Community Initiative sought to more affirmatively inculcate religious providers of social services into the nexus of government funds and contracting.

A lesson of this research for evangelicals is that there is an apparent double-standard in terms of religious language in the public square. Evangelicals are often critiqued for religious framing and called upon to exclude it from public policy debates. Perhaps evangelicals would do well to take a page from black Protestants. This study indicates that the black church may be more immune from critique to the extent that their employ of religious language in public is most often utilized 1) in reference to the historical experience of the black collective and 2) in speaking truth to power. Conversely, evangelicals often utilize religious language in the public square 1) in reference to a sense of individual rights inherent in the American story and 2) in combating other societal groups. For example, rather than speaking boldly against economic injustice broadly as the black prophetic politician does, white evangelicals engage the broader rights debate, even in the midst of their moral critique—the rights of the unborn versus the rights of the mother. Of course, many evangelicals, notably abolitionists, utilized religion during the Progressive era on behalf of the public good, but the contemporary evangelical landscape tends to invoke priestly aspects of the American civil religion over the prophetic ones which the black church tends to emphasize.

While liberation frames and religious references were generally less frequent for non-black members of Congress, future comparisons of the religious framing of CBC members and evangelical Republicans, Mainline Protestants, and Catholics, may indicate points of both convergence and divergence in religious framing of politics. While non-black members of the Republican party are unlikely to utilize liberation theology, other non-black members of Congress—namely white and Latino Catholics—might also frame issues in a manner that invokes Catholic Social Teaching, which also emphasizes liberation in a manner similar to, albeit different from, black liberation theology.

3

Reading is Not Simply Black and White: Comparisons of Health and Non-Health Literacy in African Americans and Caucasians

Dr. Rihana S. Mason, Emmanuel College

Chizara Ahuama-Jonas, University of Cincinnati

Introduction

Literacy can be defined as the ability to read and write; it is "the set of basic skills that provide individuals with entry into the realms of written language and communication" (Salkind 2008). Literacy spills over into the comprehension of everyday types of information like health information. When individuals have good health literacy, they are able to read above a fifth grade level, read and interpret charts/graphs, understand and apply information provided in medication inserts, and correctly calculate simple mathematical formulas (Glassman 2013).

Unfortunately not everyone is equipped with this important capability (Arozullah, et al. 2006). There are a growing number of individuals in the United States who have poor literacy and reading skills (Kutner, et al. 2007). Recent estimates suggest that 14 percent of adults lack basic health literacy (HL) (Kutner, et al. 2007). This lack of knowledge in certain medical settings (e.g., hospitals, medical offices, health clinics) can affect patient well-being and access to healthcare (Baker, et al. 1997). Communication gaps in individuals with poor health literacy have also been linked to various factors: 1) mismatches between the complexity of instructions and the patients' reading level; 2) use of medical rather than standard vocabulary; 3) confusing or ambiguous symbols included on labels; and/or 4) directions requiring multiple steps (Wolf, et al. 2006). With the increasing number of culturally and linguistically diverse populations as well as with the increased responsibility that youth have for their own health, it is essential that individuals understand how to protect their health (Manganello 2008).

Several groups of Americans who differ culturally and linguistically from the majority culture in America are at increased risk for poor health literacy (HL). These groups include families living in poverty, individuals from minority backgrounds, and English language learners. Shea, Beers, McDonald, Quistburg, Ravenell, and Asch (2004) found that though HL ability increased with education level, underrepresented groups such as African Americans performed lower on HL assessments across all educational backgrounds when compared to white Americans. For a period of years, particularly the 1970's–1990's, black-white gaps in non-health literacy (NHL) performance have been documented (Jencks and Phillips 1998) but have narrowed markedly in recent years (Lee 2002).

In this chapter we investigate several potential sources of the gap. The divergence may result from cultural and linguistic differences that arise from the social distinctions between Caucasians and African Americans. These differences may be apparent in the ways in which these racial groups respond to various testing formats. Performance differences may be more or less exaggerated on formats that require more facility with the English language or knowledge of the "black and white"-printed words. Because health genre has its own domain-specific "black and white," any differences that may be attributed to linguistic variation may affect the way in which information from the health domain is interpreted to a greater degree in African Americans. We explored the issue of whether racial literacy performance gaps are globally present on both HL and NHL assessments or are restricted to one genre (HL or NHL) when readability of the text and vocabulary level of the participants was controlled for. The chapter begins with a discussion of typically used NHL and HL assessments. Characteristics of examinees which translate into performance differences are also discussed prior to the description of the empirical data gathered from adolescents and adults.

Non-Health Literacy Assessments

Across the lifespan literacy is assessed in a variety of ways in order to determine who will succeed in society. A common purpose is the use of literacy assessments in school-based contexts. Common non-health literacy assessments are administered to measure reading comprehension and achievement. NHL assessments can be categorized by their format. Williams, Ari, and Santamaria (2011) reviewed the usage of popular formats such as sustained silent reading tests and cloze formats in post-secondary age adults. The sustained silent reading format can be group administered. It requires one to read extended passages and answer comprehension questions that vary in their type. These question types either require the reader to revisit information that is explicitly written in the text or requires the reader to make an inference. The *Nelson-Denny Reading Test* (Brown, Fischo, and Hanna 1993) is a timed standardized measure with seven passages and nineteen comprehension questions of both literal and inferential types. Cloze tests can be of the maze or open-ended variety. Cloze tests are constructed such that every seventh word is removed in a passage. In a maze the seventh word is replaced by three answer choices. In an open-ended format every seventh word is replaced by a blank. Williams, Ari, and Santamaria (2011) found intercorrelations among these formats in adult readers which ranged from .52 to .68 with the strongest correlations observed between the Nelson-Denny and the maze.

Health Literacy Assessments

The standard practice of HL assessment includes the administration of rapid measures of word reading and comprehension using various formats. Though there are few measures that measure the amount of HL in adults, there are currently three major literacy measures that assess HL ability: The Test of Functional Health Literacy in Adults (TOFHLA) the Rapid Estimate of Adult Literacy in Medicine (REALM) and the Newest Vital Sign (NVS) (Davis, et al. 1993; Parker, et al. 1995; Weiss, et al. 2005). The TOFHLA is probably one of the most used HL measures and was one of the first assessments of HL (Lo, Sharif, and Ozuah 2006). With the reading comprehension section of the TOFHLA, individuals use their health knowledge to complete a reading passage where they have to circle the correct word of a choice of medical words (Parker, et al. 1995). The Rapid Estimate of Adult Literacy (REALM) is considered to be one of the most widely used test of literacy ability in medical settings (Davis, et al. 2005).The REALM primarily assesses the ability to recognize and pronounce words commonly used in medical situations fluently (Davis, et al. 1993). The Newest Vital Sign (NVS) assessment consists of a nutritional facts sheet that individuals have to look at and be able to answer questions orally using the nutritional label as guide (Weiss, et al. 2005). Studies have found relations between all three measures (Al-Tayyib, et al. 2002; Bass, Wilson, and Griffith 2003; Chisolm and Buchanan 2007; Davis, et al. 1993; Hanchate et al. 2008; Parker et al. 1995; Weiss et al. 2005).

Health Literacy Assessments vs. Non-Health Literacy Assessments

Though there are many studies that have looked at HL measures in relation to other health literacy assessments, few studies, if any, have investigated the differences between the three major HL measures and NHL measures that are of the same formatting style. Some findings have shown that there are correlations between various measures of HL (e.g., REALM v. TOHFLA; NVS v. REALM) (Al-Tayyib et al. 2002; Bass, Wilson, and Griffith 2003; Chisolm and Buchanan 2007; Davis et al. 1993; Hanchate et al. 2008; Parker, et al. 1995; Weiss, et al. 2005). Few studies have looked at NHL assessments (e.g., TOWRE, Cloze, and Nelson-Denny Reading Test) in comparison to HL measures to see if there is any relation as well as to see if HL is an adequate measure of NHL. Some studies have compared the TOFHLA and the REALM to non-health related literacy assessments such as the Wide Range Achievement Test (WRAT) and the correlations were determined to be significant (TOFHLA: r=0.72; REALM: r=0.88) (Baker et al. 1999; Davis et al. 2005). In order to understand the differences between HL and NHL measures it is necessary to examine whether there are any relations between standardized health related assessments (NVS, TOFHLA, REALM) and their NHL related counterpart assessments.

Examinee Differences in Literacy Assessment

Across several HL studies characteristics of examinees like age, gender, parental background and race have been demonstrated to affect literacy performance. Younger examinees, females, those with college educated parents, and Caucasians score better than other examinees. Younger (ages forty-five to sixty-four) adults perform better on the REALM than older adults (ages 65 and older) (Shea et al. 2004) and on the National Assessment of Adult Literacy (NAAL) (Kutner et. al. 2007) when level of education is not included as a variable. Rudd (2007) demonstrated performance differences between younger and older adults on the Health Activities Literacy Study (HALS). Females perform better than males on the REALM (Barber et al. 2009) and on the NAAL (Kutner et. al. 2007). Non-minority adults perform better on the REALM (Shea et al. 2004) on the TOFHLA (Ickes and Cottrell 2010) the NAAL (Kutner et. al. 2007) and on the HALS (Rudd 2007).

Adolescents

Are comprehension difficulties the result of the type of genre used in assessments or are comprehension difficulties the result of the format that is used to assess comprehension? Forty-five African American high school students and their parents in a large southeastern urban city were recruited from a summer college preparatory program to participate in the research study. All adolescents and their parents signed informed consent documents to participate in the study in accordance with the IRB regulations at the time the study was conducted. Parents of adolescents completed a short demographic survey with questions pertaining to family background characteristics. The average age of adolescents was 14.98 years. Ages ranged from fourteen to seventeen years of age. The mean rising grade level was the tenth grade. Grades represented ranged from rising ninth grade to rising twelfth grade. The average vocabulary level for adolescents was equivalent to that of a 9th grader as assessed by the Nelson-Denny (Brown, et al. 1993). The majority (75 percent) of adolescents was female and from low-income (60 percent) non-college educated (92 percent) households.

Students were randomly assigned to read both HL and NHL passage in varying formats. HL passages had themes related to cancer, asthma, and schizophrenia. NHL passages had themes related to narcotics usage and crime outcomes, albinism, and violent crime. Literacy test passages within each genre were formatted as follows: a) *mazes*—three answer choices (one correct and two incorrect) for every seventh word in a passage, b) *open-ended cloze*—every seventh word in the passage was deleted and replaced with a blank, c) *sustained silent reading*—intact passages followed by multiple-choice comprehension questions. The *maze* format was similar to TOFHLA (Parker et al. 1995) and the *sustained silent reading* format was similar to the health literacy item on the *National Assessment of Adult Literacy*. Passage length and readability were controlled across passage topics and genre. All reading passages that were used to develop the Maze-Cloze procedures were taken from the *Timed Reading Passage* book series (Spargo and Williston 1973).

We hypothesized that adolescents would comprehend NHL related topics more than HL passages and this would be reflected in differences in literacy test scores. Table 1 shows the descriptive statistics for all literacy formats. A series of paired-samples t-tests were conducted to test the effects of genre on literacy scores. Results indicated that there was no difference in performance across HL and NHL assessments on any literacy test format. Literacy test scores were transformed into z-scores in order to compare the distributions across literacy test formats. There were also no significant differences between literacy test formats. There were significant correlations between the three formats which provide insight into the validity of using particular formats within this population. Table 2 displays all correlations between all formats across genre types. The strongest correlations were between maze and open-ended cloze formats, HL maze and NHL maze: $r=.69$, $p<.05$ and HL open cloze and NHL open cloze: $r=.69$, $p<.01$ respectively. Other notable significant correlations were between NHL open cloze and HL maze: $r=.50$, $p<.05$ and between HL sustained silent reading and NHL maze: $r=.41$, $p<.05$.

Table 1. Overall Performance on Literacy Measures in Adolescents.

Measure	Mean Average	Standard Deviation
ND-RC	36.27	15.26
NHL Maze	32.34	10.08
HL Maze.	34.22	10.12
NHL Open Ended Cloze	7.77	3.70
HL Open-Ended Cloze	7.62	4.15

NHL Sustained	3.56	1.49
HL Sustained	4.07	1.35

Table 2. Intercorrelations Among HL
and Non-HL Measures in Adolescents

	NHL Maze	NHL Open Cloze	NHL Sustained Silent Reading
HL Maze	69***	.50**	.45*
HL Open Cloze	.19	.69**	.39*
HL Sustained Silent Reading	.41*	.33	.30

An additional analysis was conducted to determine if adolescents' facility with the English language (e.g., their knowledge of the "black and white"-printed words) was related to their performance on NHL and HL measures. Adolescents were separated into moderate (40 percent to 73 percent) and low (14–38 percent) vocabulary groups using a median split of their accuracy scores on the *NDRT* vocabulary subtest (Brown et al 1993). Adolescents with moderate vocabulary accuracy performed better than participants with low vocabulary accuracy on all measures. All one-way Anovas comparing the mean scores across vocabulary groups on the NHL and HL measures were significant at the .01 level with effect sizes ($\eta2$) ranging between .07–.40. The greatest performance gap was observed on the mazes. Adolescents with moderate vocabulary completed ten (HL) and twelve (NHL) more completions than the adolescents with low vocabulary.

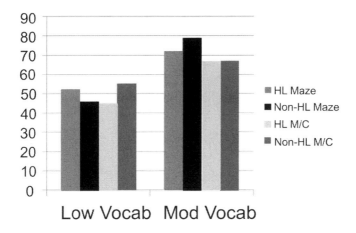

Figure 1. Comparison of adolescents' performance (percentage correct) on NHL and HL measures by low and moderate vocabulary ability

Adults

Adult participants were recruited from the student population enrolled in undergraduate Psychology classes an urban research university in the Southeast of the United States. Participants received course credit for their participation. All adults signed informed consent documents to participate in the study in accordance with the IRB regulations at the time the study was conducted. A total of fifty-nine adults volunteered in the study. We excluded the fourteen (25 percent) who self-identified as other than African American or Caucasian (0 percent American Indian, 15.5 percent Asian, 1.7 percent Hispanic, and 6.9 percent "other"). Forty-four students met the race characteristics for the study. Out of the remaining participants twenty were Caucasian and twenty-four were African American. The average age of the sample was 21.60 (SD= 4.69) with a range from sixteen to thirty-nine years. The majority (75 percent) of adults was female and from college educated (76 percent) households. Both groups performed above 75 percent correct on the Vocabulary subtest of the Nelson-Denny (Brown, Fischo, and Hanna 1993).

Adults were randomly assigned to read the same HL and non-HL literacy mazes as the adolescents. In addition, several other experimenter-designed and normed tests on HL and Non-HL literacy were administered. The HL tests included the REALM, a passage modeled after the NAAL, and the NVS. The REALM contains sixty-six words which participants must recognize and pronounce out loud. The words are common words used in medical settings. The raw scores collected were adapted to range from one to three reading levels: Score 0–46 (sixth grade and below); Score 45–60 (seventh to eighth grade); and score 61–66 (9th grade and above).

A sustained silent reading passage was created to model the format of the NAAL survey. The topic was related to blood pressure (Spargo and Williston 1973). The passage had a Lexile level of 1080L and consisted of 410 words. The Flesch-Kincaid readability measured at the 8th grade level. Participants read the passage and were required to answer a question the answer of which was described in the passage. The NHL reading passage was a reading article taken from the Times Reading Passages series (Spargo and Williston 1973). The passage was related to getting lost in the woods and how to get out if one should become lost. The passage had a Lexile of 1080L and a Flesch-Kincaid readability level to be measured at the 4th grade reading level. Compared to the Blood Pressure passage, the reading grade level was significantly lower. The created question based on the passage was, "According to the article, what ways can you get out of the woods if you become lost?" Participants had to be able to understand and interpret the question and the information in the passage in order to correctly provide an answer in one sentence.

The NVS (Weiss et al. 2005) consisted of a nutritional facts sheet which had information that was taken from the label of a pint of ice cream. Participants were asked six questions about the ice cream label and needed to use their health knowledge in order to interpret and answer the questions correctly. Most of the questions were related to quantitative literacy, which is where students have to compute the answer to questions using numbers (e.g., "How many calories is in the container?").

There was no analogous NHL test that was similar to the NVS. However the Nelson-Denny Reading Test (Brown et al. 1993) was used as a normed measure NHL in participants. Participants had 20 minutes to complete the reading comprehension subtest of the Nelson-Denny Reading Test on the same answer sheet. The first minute of the Nelson-Denny was recorded as Reading Rate and used as an additional measure of NHL word recognition skill. The Nelson-Denny Reading Test has been correlated with various literacy measures and has been found to be an accurate measure of reading comprehension and vocabulary knowledge (Petersen, Glover, and Ronning 1980).

Among the HL measures administered in the present study, complimentary formats of NHL measure were also administered. The complimentary format to the REALM was the Test of Word Reading Efficiency (TOWRE; Torgesen, Wagner, and Rashotte 1997). Most commonly used to assess the skills of children, the TOWRE is a word recognition test similar to the REALM in that participants must orally recognize and pronounce familiar and nonsensical words (Torgesen, Wagner, and Rashotte 1997). The entire assessment was timed for ninety seconds with each section timed at forty-five seconds. Participants were asked to pronounce each word correctly and to recite the words as fast as they could in order to receive a higher score. The TOWRE consisted of two parts: the Sight-Word Efficiency section and the Phonemic Decoding Efficiency section. The Sight-Word Efficiency section contained 104 familiar words that became more difficult as the list continued. The Phonemic Decoding Efficiency contained sixty phonetically nonsensical words which participants had to pronounce as fast as they could in forty-five seconds (Torgesen, Wagner, and Rashotte 1997). The raw scores of both sections were measured, combined, and converted into Standard scores which were used in analysis.

The difference between the REALM and the TOWRE was that a time limit was used for the *TOWRE* but not for the REALM. Instead of timing the REALM similarly to the TOWRE during initial data collection, the data that was recorded from the REALM was rescored for 45 seconds after the assessment took place. The original scores of the REALM will be identified as REALMorig and the rescored REALM will be identified as REALM(:45).

Participants were given the measures described above in two sessions, Part 1 and Part 2. The order of the measures was randomly assigned with individuals receiving either HL or NHL measures in both sessions. Depending on random assignment participants either received mostly HL assessments or NHL assessments first, making sure that assessments with the same format were completed in different sessions (e.g., TOWRE, REALM, Reading Passages etc.). The sessions ranged from one hour to one and a half hours depending on the assessments administered as well as how long participants took to complete untimed assessments (e.g., NVS, Reading Passages). Participants completed the experiment in a secluded room with the researcher there to administer the tests.

In order to accurately measure the differences between scores on similar assessments with different genres, it was necessary to see if the HL measures were significantly correlated to the NHL measures with the same formatting before analyzing the detailed data. Using SPSS data analysis software (SPSS, 2009) a Spearman's rho non-parametric correlation test was conducted to identify if there was a relationship between the measures that were HL or NHL related. The Maze-Cloze procedures were all significantly correlated to each other. This finding may have been due to the fact that all passages were created from the same reading series. Also, there were no significant correlations between the reading passages (Blood Pressure, Lost in the Woods) which shows that these assessments were not similar enough to be measured against each other.

Table 3 shows that overall adult performance was similar for HL and their analogous NHL counterparts. For the HL maze (M= 39.54; SD= 9.37) and the NHL maze (M= 39.18; SD= 8.41) in the entire sample, there was virtually no difference between the two measures. The two sustained reading passages also showed little difference between formats, HL passage (M= 1.08; SD=.27) and NHL passage (M= 1.13; SD= .34). The simplest format (single word reading) elicited differences between HL and NHL assessments. REALM(:45) scores were compared with TOWRE scores. Adults read 14 more words on the TOWRE compared to the words read on the REALM(:45) [(MTOWRE= 88.33;SD=8.79); (MREALM= 64.06; SD=3.05)]. These results show that participants found NHL words to be easier to identify than the common health words that were given on the REALM.

Table 3. Overall Performance on Literacy Measures in Adults.

Measure	Mean Average	Standard Deviation
ND-RC	58.87	10.39
ND Reading Rate	234.23	57.27
TOWRE composite	88.33	8.799
REALM(:45)	74.67	17.66
REALM(orig.)	64.00	3.37
HL Blood Pressure Passage	1.08	0.27

Measure	Mean Average	Standard Deviation
NHL Lost in the Woods Passage	1.13	0.34
NHL Maze.	39.54	9.37
HL Maze.	39.18	8.40
NVS	4.80	1.36

Data related to performance differences between African American and Caucasian American adults was examined. Table 4 shows that we observed achievement gaps on several assessments both HL and NHL. Caucasians pronounced 5.53 more words on the TOWRE than African Americans, $F(1,26)=4.34$, p=.05. The reading rate of Caucasians was 63 words per minute faster than African Americans, $F(1, 41)=9.04$, $p=.005$. Caucasians answered 7.94 more completions on the HL mazes than African Americans, $F(1, 26)=9.14$, $p=.006$. Caucasians answered the NVS more accurately than African Americans, $F(1, 41)=7.44$, $p=.009$. There was not a performance gap between African Americans and Caucasians on NHL mazes, $F(1, 27)=1.14$, $p=.295$.

Table 4. Performance on HL and Non-HL Measures by Race

Measure	African American	Caucasian
ND-RC	60.00 (SD=8.67)	59.57 (SD=9.76)
ND Reading Rate	199.13 (SD=64.03)	261.68 (SD=70.70)
TOWRE composite	87.56 (SD=9.22)	93.09 (SD=4.27)
REALM(:45)	49.85 (SD= 10.69)	51.16 (SD=10.04)
REALM(orig.)	64.56 (SD= 1.78)	65.20 (SD=1.06)
HL Blood Pressure Passage		
NHL Lost in the Woods Passage		
NHL Maze.	40.31 (SD=7.86)	43.69 (SD=8.94)

HL Maze	36.82 (SD=8.20)	44.75 (SD=5.61)
NVS	4.39 (SD=1.79)	5.50 (SD=.69)

Within African American adult participants alone, we found no significant differences between the mean averages of between the HL assessments and their NHL counterparts of the same format. This replicates the finding we described above with adolescents.

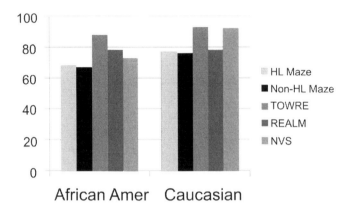

Figure 2. Comparison of adults' performance (percentage correct) on NHL and HL measures by racial groups

Correlations between literacy assessments were analyzed using Spearman correlations. Table 5 below highlights the significant correlations below the diagonal for the African American adults and above the diagonal for the Caucasian adults. Overall there were no significant correlations between HL measures in either racial group. The pattern of relations among measures was similar among racial groups. The strongest relations were between the TOWRE and mazes. We observed a positive correlation between the TOWRE and non-HL mazes for African Americans and Caucasians, $r=.65$ and $r=.51$, respectively. We also observed a positive correlation between the TOWRE and HL mazes for African Americans and Caucasians, $r=.52$ and $r=.53$, respectively. We observed a pattern that is qualitatively relevant. The pattern of correlations between the NVS and REALM were different across racial groups. We observed little to no correlation in African Americans ($r=.02$) and a moderate correlation in Caucasians ($r=.25$). The magnitude of correlation for Caucasian participants is consistent with the pattern observed by Barber et al. (2009) in a much larger sample of adults ($N=310$).

Table 5. Inter-correlations between Literacy Measures in Adults[1]

	REALM	TOWRE	HL Maze	Non-HL Maze	NVS
REALM	1	.40	.06	*.51*	.25
TOWRE	.18	1	*.53*	*.59*	.34
HL Maze	-.15	*.52*	1	*.71*	-.04
Non-HL Maze	.22	*.65*	*.72*	1	.15
NVS	.02	*.45*	.04	.15	1

Discussion

We examined the performance of African American adolescents and adults on two types of literacy measures, HL and NHL. We attempted to test the hypothesis that HL assessments were more difficult than NHL assessments by comparing scores on these measures to their NHL counterparts. In addition, we investigated whether there would be the presence of racial (black-white) performance gaps on HL and NHL measures when vocabulary level in both African Americans and Caucasians was controlled for. We observed a pattern of results that indicates both a difficulty with particular HL assessments and racial gaps on both HL and NHL assessments.

Our adolescent data did not shed much light on answering the question of what makes performance on HL assessments more difficult in African Americans. We did not observe any significant differences in performance on any of the formats we tested as HL and NHL. This finding may have resulted from the fact that our adolescents were restricted in their individual characteristics. Even though we had a range of ages, it is possible that because the majority of adolescents came from non-college educated households, performance ranges may have been suppressed (see Williams, Ari, and Dortch 2011 for a similar finding). Our data did provide a source of concurrent validity between the HL and

1. African American adult correlations are below the diagonal and Caucasian adults are above the diagonal. Spearman correlation coefficients in bold are significant at p=.05 level.

NHL in the adolescent age group. This is notable since there are special measures being designed to assess HL in adolescents (Manganello 2008).

Our adult data began to show promise in indicating a source of difference between performance on HL and NHL assessments and between racial groups. There was not a significant of race on NHL mazes. Adults in the current study did have a more difficult time with particular HL assessments. This was evident when the TOWRE was compared to the REALM(:45). These assessments only required adults to either read health related words or non-health related words aloud. Both races read fewer health related words compared to non-health related words. The REALM(:45) proved to be equally as difficult for African Americans and Caucasians compared to their performance on the TOWRE. Both groups achieved scores on the REALM(:45) that can be characterized as having a literacy level that would allow them to read most patient materials and scores on the TOWRE that are average for their age.

Several comparisons in adults demonstrated performance gaps that favored Caucasian adults. African Americans completed fewer HL mazes, completed the NVS less accurately, and read fewer words on the TOWRE, and read fewer words per minute than Caucasians. We observed significant quantitative differences on HL mazes between African Americans and Caucasians that were consistent with gaps previously reported on the NAAL (Kutner et. al. 2007) and on the HALS (Rudd 2007). The combined gaps on the HL maze, TOWRE, and ND reading rate is consistent with the suggestion of Williams, Ari, and Santamaria (2011) that the maze format was particularly sensitive to differences in word recognition skills. The reading rate difference we observed in African Americans is potentially a contributor to reading difficulty across both HL and NHL formats and should be explored in future studies.

The gaps observed on the NVS and TOWRE were not substantial enough to classify African Americans at a different level of literacy compared to Caucasians. This suggests that at least on some formats, even though there are significant quantitative differences, they do not have clinical significance. We observed a different pattern of intercorrelations between the NVS and REALM between racial groups. We do not have enough data to conclude whether this pattern challenges the concurrent validity of these measures in the African American population.

We explored the pattern of intercorrelations among assessment formats in each participant group in order to provide sources of validity among assessment formats. Even with the inclusion of some experimenter adapted assessments, our data is consistent with previous studies have found that there are significant correlations between HL assessments (Baker et al. 1997; Cutilli and Bennett 2009; Osborn et al. 2007). Additionally, the HL mazes were correlated with the NHL mazes. Our open-ended cloze were also correlated with other formats in both HL and NHL genres. When looking at comparisons among standardized assessments, the TOWRE was significantly correlated with the REALM(:45) assessment. These findings are similar to previous literature that express that various HL assessments are correlated with standardized assessments (Davis et al. 2005; Friedman et al., 2009; Osborn et al. 2007; Weiss et al. 2005). Baker et al. (1999) found that the TOFHLA and the REALM were correlated with the WRAT which also shows that various HL assessments are related to standardized tests.

There is an assumption that health disparities can be eliminated by increasing literacy. Our investigation points towards increasing basic word recognition skills. Improving facility with pronunciation and decoding may free up resources for the inferential processes needed to process the domain specific information related to health related materials. Despite the observed racial performance gap on the NVS, African Americans were still with the range of adequate literacy. Better or faster word recognition skills may also translate to better performance on measures like the NVS. We do not have data which can pinpoint the cause or source of weaker word recognition skills in the adults in the current study. Other researchers who have studied the influence of individual characteristics on reading performance have attributed home environment and exposure to print to differences in word recognition skills (Snow, Burns, and Griffin 1998).

Reading performance differences as we have described in this chapter are not simply black and white racial differences in health literacy performance. Our chapter does highlight the importance of familiarity with the "black and white," or printed words on the page. Both of our populations presented with vocabulary levels that were comparable to that of a ninth grader. A vocabulary level of 9th grade is beyond the level which is needed for good health literacy (www.nnlm.gov) and the target readability level for patient educational materials (Sabharwal, Badarudeen and Kunju 2008).

African American adolescents and adults did not have greater difficulty with HL assessments when the readability of the passages was comparable to the NHL passages.

Readability of any printed material is a combination of semantic difficulty and sentence complexity. Semantic difficulty is generally determined by the frequency with which words appear in printed materials. This seems to suggest that when it gets down to the same general "black and white" or familiar pool of printed words, the task of comprehending health related materials is similar to that of comprehending non-health related materials. You can essentially eliminate black-white racial performance gaps on assessments like NHL mazes and Nelson-Denny reading test where the domain for the passages is more common than that of the specialized domains (i.e., asthma, cancer, etc. assessed by the HL mazes).

Current health literacy assessment practices may be aided by including measures of one's facility with the "black and white" vocabulary by pairing the REALM with other NHL word recognition tests like the ones we used in our investigation (e.g., TOWRE and Nelson-Denny Reading Rate). Rapid screening for vocabulary in healthcare settings may also improve patient and consumer health knowledge, utilization of health services, and health outcomes.

Author Notes

Research for this chapter was conducted while first author was at Georgia State University. Research was supported for the second author through the Ronald E. McNair Baccalaureate Program while she was also at Georgia State University. Parts of the research study were conducted to complete the requirements to fulfill an undergraduate Honors thesis for the second author. Data included in this chapter was presented at the Division 45 meeting of the American Psychological Association.

4

African American Women Scholars in Christian Higher Education: A Perspective on Sistah-hood

Dr. Yvonne RB-Banks,
University of Northwestern–St. Paul

Introduction

A Critical Reflection: Framing History and Shared Experiences

In spite of the career gains women have made and their obvious appearance in many traditionally male dominated fields, women in general still face new challenges. The cultural narrative of African American women brings to light various patterns of experiences related to the field of higher education. Upon study it appears that currently African American women scholars are experiencing barriers similar to those faced by their historical contemporaries. Understanding why this is occurring requires a critical look at the data. Looking at the experiences of African American women on a specific pathway of scholarship should offer even more detail as to their real experiences in Christian Higher Education (CHE). It is important to see how this group of women scholars' experiences line up with the expectations they entered with as they stepped through the doors of CHE.

One view addressing this question about the experiences of African American women scholars is discussed by Dr. Linda E. Thomas, Assistant Professor of Theology and Anthropology at Garrett-Evangelical Seminar. Thomas speaks of "critical reflection upon black women's place in the world that God has created and takes seriously" and states that "categories of life which black women deal with daily (that is race, womanhood, and policy economy) are intricately woven into the religious space that African American women occupy" (1998). Dr. Thomas continues to outline the positive and negative outcomes for black women within "the institutional church, culture, and society [which] impact the social construction of black womanhood" as well as within their church communities. If change is to occur in a larger context it will mean that data that reflects the voices, the experiences, and the successes of African American women scholars will need to come forth.

Collecting data related to African American women scholars' experiences in higher education is relevant due to the lack of research covering their experiences. Literature talks about absent narratives in the data for this population of women and states that "there is a lack of data prior to 1990" (Townsend-Johnson 2006, 1). The lack of research on this group makes it noteworthy and underscores which groups have been included or excluded in the databases. The African American women scholars sharing their stories for this writing live with the impact of this truth. Accessing their narratives can allow higher education to understand their experiences and prepare for change.

African American women scholars are worthy of the efforts needed to collect the data to ensure continued and specific progress in CHE. Their shared experiences can open a new chapter for the data needed. The need for a specific field of research that highlights data on black women in the academy was warranted almost thirty years ago (*see* Bonner and Thomas 2001). Critical reflection on women in the workforce indicates gains, as previously stated; however, sufficient data tied to black women's experiences in higher education is lacking. It follows, therefore, that in order for CHE to appropriately set the tone for this population's entry, a look at what has historically been a closed door to this population's entry into CHE is relevant. Learning directly from their experiences will be an asset. So to that end, fourteen African American women scholars currently working in the field of higher Christian education were asked to lend voice to the topic.

Reviewing at an expanded level, not only what is found in the literature on this topic, but what is offered through the voices of women scholars in the field about what influences and barriers in the workforce, may reveal socialized messages about gender role. Accepting that such messages for women scholars are not left at the door upon entering CHE would allow leaders to create the right support for this population. As leaders in CHE institutions gain a broader understanding of the inherent and often unseen barriers faced by women scholars it would be hoped that they would address the matter systemically from the perspective of how gender roles impact scholarship in the academy. The societal messages are no less impactful for women who identify with the African American culture. Barriers faced by African American women scholars are often due in part to perspectives held by others in the academy about their collective personhood, contributions or even worth, which are tied to gender, race and culture (Henderson, Hunter, and Hildreth 2010). Sistah scholars, entering higher education with all the benefits bestowed upon them from their framework of faith and culture, feel eager and well-prepared to make a significant difference. However, many discover quickly that in spite of their cultural fortitude and deep faith they face unexpected complexities, even from other women scholars.

It is important to note the similarities among women's experiences in the workforce due to gender, but the commonality in experiences ends at the point of gender for African American women. What does this mean for African American women scholars? It means bringing with them Gutierrez and Rogoff's definition of culture: a dynamic, situational and historic construct influenced by a number of additional variables, including group membership (Gutierrez and Rogoff 2003). This means that African American women scholars in the CHE community experience mixed messages. Within the shared experiences of this population, many hazards exist that men and women scholars from other cultural backgrounds may never experience. In some cases, additional messages leave this group outside the walls of access without the support of their Christian sisters from other social cultural experiences. This group of alienated sistahs is a category of women who bring to CHE specific cultural embodiments related to the African American experience. For the purpose of this discussion, the 14 scholars conceptualized their sistah-hood in three main components; gender, faith and the African American experience.

Sistahs of Faith: Who Are They?

As already mentioned, this group of women comes from a common heritage, but according to Thomas, women of faith from the African American experience bring a binding anthropological paradigm to academe (Thomas 1998). The concept of being sistahs of faith in the academy is created by a common belief system. Their faith creates a deeper bond within the walls of CHE. The messages from a collective cultural understanding guide these women to engage fully for the betterment of the whole community. This population comes to higher education to engage in ways that support, guide, share, sacrifice, mother-others, and stand in the face of overwhelming odds. The CHE community benefits from this group of women scholars' presence. What would help CHE understand how to prepare for the best experience possible for everyone?

First, CHE should understand that African American women scholars traditionally come from a *collective* culture experience. Also, it is relevant that they adhere to messages existing in deep caverns of their faith practices that may not be found in the context of higher education, which is traditionally an individualistic culture. When put under the microscope by others from non-African American experiences about these issues, this population can be mistakenly viewed by others as playing the gender or race card. Data and stories provided by this population, however, show that when they enter academe with a history of demonstrated scholarship and terminal degrees in hand, they are often not accepted as equals, even in their fields of study. The fact that they face this unspoken denial of the affirmation of colleagues comes at a cost to their continued and successful progress in higher education. How many leave without seeing the end of the road to promotion or tenure? How many fail to return due to feelings of isolation or vulnerability during the evaluation process? How many from this population exit higher education because of cultural conflicts associated with gender and faith?

When asked to describe their experiences in CHE, the African American women scholars for this writing were often surprised by the need to face events alone within CHE. Social constructs exist that this population did not expect to find in the walls of a Christian institution. Surprisingly, some of the issues are related to encounters with their peer groups. When asked to talk about the support received from other women upon entry, the scholars questioned why, as sisters in Christ, they had not been fully accepted within the context of CHE. In fact, some shared that during times of professional reviews for tenure or promotion, some of the other non-African American women colleagues appeared to avoid engaging in the usual sisterhood support on their behalf. Upon critical reflection, it appears that barriers from the past still exist and are the primary reasons for this population's lack of progress in higher education. Such barriers frame the experiences of African American women scholars in ways that should ask why this population is still facing what Anthony Bradley calls the "credibility obstacle within white universities" (Bradley 2011).

Women and Barriers

As stated earlier, research reveals that compared to other institutions, CHE has been progressive in acknowledging barriers faced by some groups. Yet, there appears to be an oversight as to what it means to enter academe as both an African American and a woman. This population of scholars faces the unsophisticated concept of the "double whammy." This term references the barriers tied to gender and racial discrimination (Bonner and Thomas 2006, 121–23). The number of women has grown over the past twenty-five years for women in many professional fields, including higher education. Yet in spite of their education, experiences, and training, women continue to face obstacles. They still do not receive the professional accolades at the level of their male colleagues; in several cases they are simply denied. For women, increase in numbers does not equal increase in access (López 2011). The matter is not about increase, but access to designated points of fulfillment in a related field of study.

The advancement scholars need in higher education is tied to access to mentoring and other key facts. Limiting the focus of research to the growth of women's numbers in any field misses the fact that women often lack the social power or connection to advancement. They have unequal access to covenant partnerships, scholarships, and administrative opportunities that their male counterparts receive. Why is this happening in CHE? A quote made in the 1980s by "Bailey Smith, former president of the SBC, [who] stated that marriage, propagation and submission were the highest possible callings for women" highlights strongly how at different points in its history the church has had various perspectives on the role of women (*see* Leonard 1990, 153). Those changing perspectives have influenced the treatment of women throughout society, as well as within CHE. For example, a review of this population's experiences compared to their counterparts' reveals that what is true for most new faculty members—such as having multiple options of individuals who are willing to mentor, guide committee work choices, direct research choices, inspire and support—is not true in the case of most junior African American women scholars. The fourteen voices shared in this writing indicate that African American women are likely to receive less support in CHE settings.

Historically, barriers associated with the social construct of race create invisible barriers for women of color, especially this population of scholars. Creating awareness for better understanding is one place to start (*see* PBS 2003). African Americans have been locked out of the road that leads to upward-mobility positions. Women in general have also struggled with the hidden agenda related to advancement. A key piece to understanding advancement in higher education in general is tied to the evaluation process. For many, not only African American scholars, the process of evaluation has appeared hidden. In spite of the overarching themes of service and sacrifice in CHE this group of scholars is dismayed at the lack of balance in the evaluation process. Some of the 14 scholars in this writing, when reporting on the process leading to the submission of the promotion dossier, found the lack of available coaching or mentoring during this intensive process astounding. It is unfortunate that the point of evaluation or review for promotion/tenure is often the point at which knowledge of what *should have* happened to advance is unveiled. This lack of understanding in general adds to the barriers and becomes a gap in the bridge between their experiences and their success.

It can be seen as critical that CHE drill deeper to explore how the evaluation process impacts scholars in general, and then apply that knowledge to understand further what African American faculty face daily and how such experiences influence the evaluation process (Bradley 2011, 1). Bridging the gaps by gaining understanding of their experiences should show a positive impact on productivity and longevity in CHE. It is expected that this increased understanding of the barriers and hidden pitfalls faced on the road to promotion will help to prepare for a better experience for scholars who come from the African American context.

CHE: Themes and Hidden Rules

Part of the ethos of CHE suggests that as a Christian community, help will be given along the way. Some scholars expressed that before entering CHE they believed that the *family* of Christians would be different than mainstream higher education. They believed that having a spiritual mentor as a part of their professional experience would fit with the ethos of Christian belief, and they thought one would be provided, offered, or recommended. However, for this group of scholars that wasn't the case. In fact, many stumbled upon strong barriers without a mentor or coach, which did not allow for smooth access or inclusion. This experience, it is believed, goes back to the church's influence over the role of women. In fact, research reveals that women in general received less mentoring in faith communities because of set notions tied to women's role in the church, the workplace, and in the halls of CHE (Henderson, Hunter, and Hildreth 2010).

Some scholars lending voice to this writing felt that having a discussion prior to entry about the culture of the *actual* Christian environment and expectations would have been helpful. Many from the African American group approached entry in CHE based on their black church experience. Needless to say, CHE operates very differently than the black church family. In most black Christian church experiences, African American women find reciprocity and gain benefits from giving and serving. The benefits often come in the form of support, words of affirmation, recognition for who they are, what they have achieved, and what they contribute to their faith communities. However, the CHE experience seems to lack reciprocity for African American women scholars. It appears that neither support nor reciprocity is available to them for the giving they do, the wealth of knowledge they bring to the academy, and rarely do they experience words of affirmation within CHE from either the leadership or other scholars.

The new skills and insight this population brings to the field of scholarship are often overlooked or minimized in the review/promotion process. There is documented gender and race bias in faculty evaluations (Huston 2005). There appears to be no current exploration on ways to assess the professional resources that come with this group's personhood or to assess the value they add to the institution. The evaluation and promotion process was a common point of concern for the fourteen contributors.

The concern here is related to time lost in establishing the right steps leading to an appropriate dossier that supports advancement. What is actually required in each is often revealed only once one starts the process, which comes years after entering the academy. Some scholars discovered that they had pursued the wrong focus in relation to the institution's strategic plan for faculty or some other preferred direction of the institution. Some learned too late that some outside community services applied to the calculations tied to promotion. The demands of the required work in the areas of committees, publication, office hours, on- and off-campus event attendance, advising, and other non-documented services done within the community left this group of women facing a lack of confidence in how to succeed. It appears at times that the women must explore and realize CHE life simultaneously.

The topic of evaluation opens up many hidden needs that require resolution in order for women to be on equal ground in CHE. On this topic, Mary Ann Mason lays out the hidden rules and what women face in male-dominated fields of leadership. Mason goes further and offers tips that can help women in general navigate and improve their experiences in higher education (2009). African American women can benefit from the directions offered for women in higher education, overall, but will have to probe even deeper into the literature to find answers to how they will as a group need to approach and resolve the world of CHE as the "outsider within" (Henderson, Hunter, and Hildreth 2010). Continued research appears to be the answer for women scholars who need to discover how to make choices within CHE in a manageable cultural context. The underlying and unspoken barriers arising from social biases exist on many levels for this population. To address the long-term goal of scholarship investigating such experiences should lead to the discovery of successful strategies that apply to this group. Of course it will need to be in a vernacular identifiable with both the female and the African American experiences (Henderson, Hunter, and Hildreth 2010).

Sistah-hood in the Vernacular: A Common Contextual Heritage

African American women as scholars face a cultural conundrum that requires them to examine their experiences in reference to a common vernacular. The concept of a common heritage and how it manifests for African Americans is explained well in the foreword of the book *This Far by Faith* (*This Far by Faith* 1999, 8–12). The experience of being African American and female brings about a dialect of experiences that can be *described* to others outside the culture, but is rarely comprehended. The similarities in the experiences, celebrations, and challenges faced by many African American women scholars can be considered a cultural vernacular.

Behaviors that express a way of being or a depth of identity come out of deep cultural and family roots tied to the African American experience. The behaviors are expressed in the way they engage in community, the way they offer to serve others, the way they embrace their faith, their style of worship, their care giving, their choice of career paths, and their strategies for overcoming conflicts. For this population these experiences appear to be linked and tied as one (2011, 1). If CHE leaders sought to view how this group of scholars identity is shaped and guided, through seeking to understand their behaviors then a lot about this population could be explained. Therefore, looking deeply into how and why African Americans women carry their souls, voices, views of life, and even their music with them into CHE could offer a useful context for support and change. When speaking and describing their experiences, some related it as speaking in the black vernacular of life. Some of the scholars described their experiences as being naturally mosaic: intertwined and rich, in spite of historical challenges. To gain a sense of their vernacular it is important to understand the formation of a common contextual heritage, as well as how their culture is tied to a faith developed over three hundred plus years of history as African Americans. For this population of scholars, life experiences are not left at the threshold of higher education upon entry. Therefore, having an awareness of how this population's behaviors, thoughts, and choices are linked to their heritage is significant in creating a foundation that is inclusive and supportive.

The exploration for this writing created a platform for the fourteen scholars to drill deeper into the shifting landscape of higher education. This approach of collecting their voices as a shared common experience is a much needed gathering of data, as echoed by Stacey Patton. In her article, she focuses on how "Black studies continue . . . to address silences and to look at how race is constructed" and impacts the lives of blacks (Patton 2012). The research offered by this population of scholars lending their voices to this writing aligns with the common context of what black women face as scholars. From their shared reality, themes evolve and fit well into what is seen as a common vernacular associated with the context of heritage. A variety of factors under this concept stress the need for more formal data that speaks to this population's place in the CHE.

The Power of Place

One question directed at the scholars revealed an expression related to not having a place to belong. Several mentioned feeling out of place and lacking power, hence the power of place of knowing you belong. Some felt like they were under a microscope while in CHE. An echo started to surface from discussions related to this population of scholars not having a place of power in the academy. This created for many what they termed a lack of placement for self. This reference to place warrants more in-depth research at a later date. However, for now it can be explained as a strong link between one's faith community and how a sense of place (acceptance) is established and one's academic community and how a sense of place is established. For this group of women scholars a grounded sense of place in their faith community and academic community appear to be the foundation for them having power in place to grow.

At one point in the discussion it was explained that tensions can be carried over from one place of community to the next, with no buffer, and this can impact a scholar's growth. A point that directly highlights when a sense of place can be disturbed relates to the lines between service and promotion. These lines can become indistinguishable when there are unspoken church relations with the academy. Some women scholars have found it difficult to experience the power of place when they needed to negotiate salary with their CHE institution because of an affiliation between the CHE and their faith community in some way. If discussions were held prior about the relationship between their church community and their CHE institution then women scholars would experience more power of place along their journey in the academy. When crossover occurs between faith communities and CHE institutions some African American women scholars are left feeling a sense of lost for their power of place. This lost stemmed from their concerns which could not be expressed or legitimized in either place due to the crossover between the church and the academy. The best that can be expected is that women scholars learn to put the discussion on the table with their CHE institution and their faith community, if there is a pre-existing relationship. Delineating the boundaries clearly will support women scholars in having a clear power of place in both their CHE community and their faith community.

One strategy that would empower, support and legitimize this discussion regarding power of place is found in the work of Linda Sechrist. In a short piece on the power of place, she writes about "the qualities that make a place special" (Sechrist 2012). This relates to the place being highly personal and helping us to define who we are. Understanding how to find one's place in any new social group could be a step in the right direction for avoiding additional complexities regarding retention. The church world and the world of higher education are complex institutions, and trying to navigate both in a seamless manner may leave no room to breathe. The power of place is an important theme to understand when looking at the matrix of complexities for the population of scholars (Sechrist 2012). Using this concept in relation to sistah-hood for African American scholars is a good way to understand how the concept of place is created within the context of CHE.

For this population, all components are linked in the African American experience, as stated earlier, like a mosaic or a woven tapestry. Their history has produced a style of existence that weaves together each part of their lives from childhood, through womanhood, and even into motherhood. Finding a place of acceptance within the walls of CHE appears to be essential to the success of this group of women scholars. Finding a sense of place within CHE equates to finding a place of belonging, security, safety and ultimately the freedom to contribute. The concept of having a place within CHE for this group relates to having all the benefits that come with the power of place or home or family tied to scholarship in the academy. When African American women scholars are unable to establish a sense of place, belonging, or acceptance (meaning security within CHE) complexities arise. Their tapestry of self may start to feel disjointed due to categories related to the whole-self such as self-esteem, self-expression, self-acceptance, or self-actualization (*see* Sechrist 2012, 25). Further exploration is beyond the scope of this writing at this time, but is surely a topic that warrants further development. The need to feel the power of place, the power of acceptance for the formation of personhood as a scholar within CHE should not be understated for women as a group, and especially for African American women scholars. Since this population often chooses to express their faith as full-body experiences it is important for the academy to be prepared as they make transitions into CHE (*This Far by Faith* 1999, 8–12).

What does being comfortable in one's professional place look like for this group? Some examples may be how one interacts with students or the level of freedom expressed in class settings. It could encompass singing in class to make a point about scripture, embracing the phrase "amen" as an affirmation of personhood or in reply to an on- or off-point comment, wearing clothing that combines African and mainstream expression, and engaging in code-switching to make a point and to bring *the flavor* of their cultural heritage to the experience. Some scholars even shared how they have cooked samples of their ethnic dishes to share. Such experiences create a consciousness of place and empower them to share the creation of this personhood.

This ability to breathe is important as they daily experience the complexities of being an African American woman scholar in a faith-based institution. Understanding the power of place adds to their feeling of connectedness, and creates a sense of putting down roots. It is a feeling of being a part of the village as it relates to "it takes a village" (African Proverb). As African American women scholars develop this concept of place, it lends to what may have been missing in their narrative in the past.

Womanhood, Workloads, and Seeking Balance

Galvanizing themes have surfaced and are centered on the multiple facets of the various experiences women face in higher education. Seeking balance in the midst of these experiences creates a stanza of rich voices from this group of fourteen scholars. The two primary notes that came up repeatedly were how faith for many was tied to their view of womanhood and the duplicity of purpose found in CHE. This section will touch lightly upon the two hindrances that received multiple nods during this project's writing.

One facet of the data gathered that seems to affect retention for women in higher education is how stopping to care for others impacts their workload. The voices of the fourteen gave examples of students sitting or standing outside their offices seeking help. Some expressed feeling a strong need to have an open door to students of colors, even for those who were not their departmental advisees. This group of scholars is aware of the need to be available for certain populations of students in college. Research discusses how it is common for this population of scholars to have a self-defined commitment to help mentor other marginalized groups (Henderson, Hunter, and Hildreth 2010). They concur that they often feel pulled to meet their personal professional goals, yet also be there for this often fragile group of students. Looking for balance and seeking direction in this area is critical enough in their development and success in higher education to warrant attention.

Going back to the phrase "it takes a village," it was seen by some of the group that this concept was missing when it comes to helping certain students within CHE. The question of balance is a real theme for this group, especially when it is expected that only women scholars of color will provide guidance to students of color. Not all of the scholars felt that they should have this responsibility alone, and some felt unspoken expectations to be available without witnessing similar expectations directed toward other scholars. Strong comments surfaced that the institution overall should be responsible for all faculty members being accessible to students.

The traditional church community is still struggling and debating internally about women and their role as leaders. As cited before, the church has influenced the worldview systemically on the role women play in society. The struggles over women's roles appear to have carried over into CHE and are reflected in the complexities found in the role of women as they pursue their scholarship in a balanced manner. One point relates to the challenges that come from trying to balance the Martha/Mary complex (Luke 10:38–42). Are women to be in the role of servant or the role of learner/scholar? Which rules to obey and how to gain recognition for the choices they make as scholars are real areas of concern which impact balance for women scholars.

In their various narratives, the group of fourteen revealed surprisingly similar experiences along the journey. African American women scholars have already faced steep climbs just to be at the threshold of higher education. Even when the door opens they still face a steep climb once inside the walls of academe; this awareness can leave them feeling even more disenfranchised when facing unbalanced and unrealistic expectations. A common key point that may send a wrong message to this group of women was received by many of them as they entered CHE. Comments such as, "I am so glad you are here," sound welcoming, but when they are followed by "Can you help. . . ," or "I always wanted to know. . . ," or "I hope it is safe for me to ask. . . ," scholars are knocked off-balance. This type of early engagement upon entry signals additional burdens that could impede their scholarship. The struggle for balance is very pressing for this group, and learning how to address or even avoid unspoken misinterpretation of stereotyping can't be underemphasized as this group enters CHE.

Hazards and the Imposter Phenomenon

Helping scholars new to CHE create space for dialogue about such matters is an important step in preventing events that can become hazards. As outlined earlier, there are many risks along the journey from entry to review and promotion, to securing tenure in higher education. One such risk for this group as they seek balance is what Trotman terms the "Imposter Phenomenon" among African American women in higher education. She lays out the challenges these scholars face being women and black. Being "doubly invisible" is the state of experience for this population (Trotman 2009). The work of R. D. Cade adds to the concept by talking about how such experiences could be thought about as a form of taking on temporary embodiment that allows one to cope (Cade 2007, 230). How are African American women as scholars coping with experiences in CHE?

Entering with the passion to give their all, as they were culturally raised to do, may cause many African American women scholars to overextend while striving to achieve the needed markers of scholarship (Trotman 2009). Are they unknowingly creating the hazards for themselves by expecting reciprocity? A review of the overlapping experiences of marginalized groups could offer a framework for the issues specifically confronting African American women scholars. The issues that confront high risk populations and the hazards that place them at risk are worth reviewing. The literature is laden with a broad range of data that covers the topic and offers strategies that outline success. In an interesting twist, some research offers that marginalization does not always equate with failure. Work by Robertson, Larose, Roy, and Legault on non-intellectual learning factors on college students offers insight on the topic. When the factors that cause risks are understood, harnessed and resourced, the risks offers an opportunity to be turned into success (Robertson, Larose, Roy, and Legault 1998). It seems the message from the research is that with perseverance, this population can thrive. Since sistah-hood is often described as an ardent and collective experience, harnessing their experience could be the right step for a new entry plan.

The intertwining sisterhood of faith and culture tells these scholars to rise and help, rise and support, rise and guide, rise and share, rise and sacrifice, and rise and stand no matter what the need. However, for women pursuing scholarship and achievement this approach incurs risks for scholarship, risks for time management, and risks of over-extending.

Christian women as sisters in Christ receive powerful messages about Christian womanhood, and when they enter CHE no reciprocal for such commitment is found. Since faith and culture are so interwoven for this group of African American women scholars, some have no separation in their thinking upon entering the doors of CHE.

Let's assume that most scholars feel the first entry into the academy and stepping on the track of scholarship as full emotional commitments. It seems that the difference for this group of scholars can be summed up in a reference made by one contributor to this writing, who said that entering the academy and facing the unexpected challenges felt like the song "On the Battle Field for My Lord." The risks for this population are tied to missing key opportunities to guide their achievements. They may feel like imposters in their own skin as they strive to reach profession-al milestones that demonstrate scholarship, through research, secured publications, and awarded grants.

As CHE embraces understanding of the hazards for this group of scholars, it is important to listen in a way that embraces and legitimizes their voices. Understanding is the vehicle through which change will come. For the leaders of CHE institutions it appears that willfully and boldly engaging in steps to raise awareness is a good place for CHE to start addressing the unique social construct of this group. By following in the footsteps of Judith Weisenfeld's history, those coming after them into CHE can benefit greatly from their work, activism and hopefully, with guidance, avoid similar hazards (Weisenfeld 1997).

Moving Forward: Learning from Experienced Voices

"All I really needed to know I learned from Black women" (Randolph 1997). The quote by L. B. Randolph speaks volumes for how CHE can start to move forward. The lack of rich literature can actually be taken as a form of documentation that shouts out for the need to increase the voices of ex-perienced African American women scholars. The silence can be removed by listening to and learning from their experiences. The fourteen voices in this writing align with what the research recommends to help higher education move forward. Their commentary supports the need for a set place at the table for understanding black women's experiences in CHE. The halls of CHE are slippery to navigate for all scholars, and coping effec-tively with the daily experience can be described as tediously emotional. It can't be overstated how their experiences clarify the overall need for more research on the various experiences and women in higher education.

Dr. Thomas' writings highlight how the use of theology and other social constructs that show up in higher education, reminds black women as scholars of their assigned role, which is often a carryover from unspoken societal mandates. Dr. Thomas provides a useful foundation of information that should not be minimized for this group of scholars during times of review and promotion. Her work focuses in on the resources African American women scholars bring to CHE. The data from Dr. Thomas' work and the combined voices of this group can be used by administrators to establish clearer institutional intentions. More direct focus on affirming what comes with this group can help avoid "deleterious forces seeking to keep black women in 'their place'" (Thomas 1998). Such actions would create a context of inclusion and remove the appearance of neglect of this group of scholars' personhood.

It was revealed that choosing to change the way one works after making a series of unexpected discoveries can be the beginning or the ending of one's academic career. How to handle such discoveries safely is a key to success. All who enter higher education will at some point face the dilemmas that come with making changes in communication styles, performing services, advising, and even adapting within their non-academic life. As African American women within higher education stumbled upon these discoveries, they found no simple way to proceed. They were often left alone to handle the silence that may come from the experiences with others (Ladson-Billings 1996, 79). Again, this is a key point that supports the need for establishing early mentoring relationships.

What a benefit it would be to learn early from the voices of others who have traveled the same path. Without mentoring or coaching, this group enters danger zones. The dangers can be revealed in the loss of time or resources, both of which are needed for securing retention in higher education. All of the time commitments tied to gender roles can slow a scholar down when seeking a position of tenure. They have to put in the right amount of standardized availability, which is better known as face time with students and work on committees. The "publish or perish" barrier is real for all seeking to advance in higher education, and early effective mentoring could guide the way. Many of the experiences shared by the women are supported by the findings in the literature, which highlight that mentoring works.

Some scholars for this writing expressed an interest to know what other people groups experienced upon entry as scholars. How much mentoring was offered and how quickly was it *offered* upon entry? This theme, if termed *offering*, is one that requires further research in the future. It appears to have an emotional component that was not explored further in this writing, but carried a message of acceptance. Several scholars pointed out that in their educational training to prepare for their areas of scholarship, matters of gender and ethnicity were not discussed as potential barriers. Many only discovered the impact of their personhood on the institution after encountering a situation that brought forth the unspoken expectations. There appear to be no learning modules to help this population prepare for such dilemmas, leaving many to be stunned by the barriers they encountered. If the academy of CHE wants to move forward more strategically, this awareness gives a deep nod for the importance of mentoring early on for retention to occur.

"What's Wrong? I'm Just Saying": Engaging in Meaningful Cultural Exchanges

In order to engage in meaningful cultural exchanges, research encourages us to get past the use of negative stereotypes. The overview on "Women and Negative Stereotypes" by Divya Bhargava (2009) combined with the work of David Bensman (1999) gives a good starting point for what it will take to engage in meaningful cultural exchanges. Bensman states that it is the process by which members of groups with different traditions, values, beliefs, and experiences gained a greater degree of mutual understanding (Bensman 1999, iii). Also, work by David Myers outlines how stereotypes toward African American women as scholars show up in conversation (Myers 2005). Again here is a tie back to how the church has viewed and still views women's roles. Some of the fourteen scholars offer examples for what happens when African American women within the academy engage in professionally appropriate assertive behaviors that align with the behaviors of male colleagues, and even model the behaviors of direct females with other cultural roots. The experience, as explained, usually results in black women's behaviors being labeled as disagreeable, or viewed as negative or even aggressive (Dace 2012a).

Research confirms that African American women receive the least support in group settings and at times the harshest judgment from colleagues on topics about group dynamics (Dace 2012b). Even evaluations from female students bring forth that *gender matters*, as well as race. Interestingly, it was expressed that even in their field of expertise this coarse view of their personhood existed. Institutions should note that such negative perceptions of African American women scholars exist and can occur with department teams, committees, and other group arenas, all of which impact the review process. Due to such exposure, they are likely to be the most stressed, receive the least amount of support, and be the most overworked, locked out, and disillusioned. Knowing this information can move CHE to appropriate actions regarding the underlying reasons impeding the road to scholarship.

Addressing Change: Starting Points for Preparation

Data shows that over the past twenty years the numbers of this population in higher education have grown steadily, as stated earlier (*see* "10 Surprising Statistics" 2010; Buying Influence n.d.). Therefore, as the numbers will continue to grow, higher education can assume that African American women are coming to stay. The most common theme that can be pulled from the data offered from the fourteen voices is that CHE needs to be prepared to receive African American women scholars. To prepare and connect, CHE can start by embracing opportunities with the increasing numbers of this population. This requires changes in the general attitudes about workload, the clarity of the roles within CHE and the events that impact personhood as it relates to gender and race. Preparedness, especially for the entry of those twice marginalized, is an essential ingredient for positive change.

CHE might start by considering the way people often think about the issues that confront populations deemed marginal or at-risk. Putting the focus on preparing and connecting is the key. Research supports that early connections and "innovative practices" tied to mentoring help all scholars better understand the nature of higher education (Pye 2012). As higher education prepares for the next chapter of scholars who come from diverse life experiences, the following spectrum offers opportunity for a structuring focus:

The above spectrum offers realistic and intentional input based on the experiences of this group in CHE institutions. Issues of preparedness are key starting points and areas of immediate need. Higher education needs to ask bold questions, probing to what degree is CHE ready to welcome African American women scholars and what involvement is needed by the community to reduce challenges.

The work of Henderson, Hunter, and Hildreth offers key strategies for addressing the current resistance for African American women scholars to receive early mentoring (Henderson, Hunter, and Hildreth 2010). Incoming female faculty members, in general, need mentors in place upon arrival. Mentors should be individuals who can relate across disciplines, who have demonstrated cultural competency and are able to offer ways to balance the new discoveries in CHE. An effective mentor should understand the matters facing incoming scholars and be able to engage in cross-pollination, sowing seeds of expectations across blended individualistic and collective cultures.

It is also important to seek understanding of how an imbalance in perspective can occur when cultural norms clash without interventions (Chamblee 2012). Preparation means having a starting point and a focus on change. Preparation means being upfront about the adjustments that will need to occur overall in order to change the direction of this group's experiences in higher education. There are several avenues for structuring higher education environments to constructively incorporate the talents and experiences of African American women scholars. Differences can be beneficial, and African American women as scholars bring a heritage that has always pioneered and paved the way for improvement. The short list for improving the success rate in general for women in higher education falls under a few key themes.

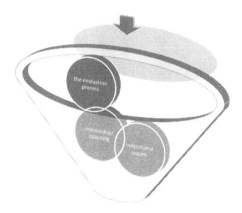

Improving issues of equity related to the evaluation process is one of the key themes for ensuring this population's longevity within the institution. Reviewing the evaluation system will give women faculty members' contributions equal weight. This is an understandable need given the impact of gender bias in association with the review process. When administrators start to address the topic of service and use measures that validate the contributions that women scholars make to the academy then change will come. Women scholars have skills that nurture the student population and validating the importance of those skills to the mission of the institution will bring about a positive shift in how women scholars' contributions are measured. As institutions improve in their general understanding of women scholar's contributions, they will need to look even deeper into the interconnectedness of the contributions African American women scholar make to the academy. African American women scholars through their service, scholarship and support to students bring an abundance of gifts to CHE. Administrators will be prepared better to evaluation through the validation of the total contributions this group makes by taking steps to improve what is measured and how. The evaluation process for women, specifically African American women should be based on crediting areas often associated with mothering or nurturing skills, doing this will allow for balance during the evaluation process. Within CHE especially, this improvement in the evaluation process would be a good starting point for preparation that will help to encourage change and promote service to students with women faculty without them needing to fear sacrificing their scholarship which lead to promotion.

Administrators who design evaluations can analyze different narratives and set ways for integrating diverse skills into the evaluation process. There are few models that successfully address the equal and fair discussion for promotion that have the traits of women as the foundation for measurement. Finding different ways to address more descriptive measures of a scholar's work, thereby honoring varied talents brought to the academy by women, seems a fair step to take in improving the evaluation process. A suggestion that resonated from several of the women in this body of work was to look more in the affective domain and have skills tied to qualitative measurements instead of the traditional quantitative measures (Roberts 1998–2012). Higher education should include the benefits of gender and race, and add those traits as standardized scoring components that lead to retention and tenure. All data is not measurable in the same way, and some data is not measured with the current tools of evaluation used in the academy. Some data are observed but not measured or counted in the promotion process. For example, literature is starting to surface about the barriers that are seen within the academy related to how faculty and/or staff at times feel like mothers to many of the students entering.

Students appear to need more hands on guidance, or even face time, to move through successfully. It appears that when it comes to measuring this concept of *mothering* or contributions that come from such acts, the academy is at a lost for how to measure or give credit for such service to faculty during the promotion process. For women faculty, this is a serious matter with serious implications that impact their scholarship and promotion. Therefore, it appears relevant for CHE officials seek answers to the mothering question and how to measure the impact on faculty in order to address the matter of equity. Seeking answers to the following questions will benefit the evaluation process for women: What is the impact of being the unofficial surrogate mother to students on a college campus? What is the toll on female faculty, especially African Americans when they find themselves in this unexpected role *mothering*? How does one document for promotion the services of nurturer, listener, problem-solver, etc.? How does one navigate being placed in a role that should have been left behind upon entering the doors of CHE as a scholar? For administrators, learning how to give weight to this often unspoken or unacknowledged role termed "mothering" or "other mother" regarding women faculty is essential to changing institutional evaluation norms. Improvement in the assessment process for all scholars is important, but this matter is especially relevant to the experiences of African American women scholars who enter the academy facing deeply anchored challenges that are a part of the historical construct of CHE institutions.

Conclusion

The data is rich, and now more is available through the fourteen experiences shared. These voices offer a perspective that been lacking in the research and reveal the experiences of a diverse population. The tone for future research has been set by the offered recommendations, noting that clearly there is "diversity among diversity," and it will be key for CHE to include this knowledge of how there is diversity between race, and diversity within race itself (Austin 2012). This perspective is meaningful as further data is gathered on women scholars in order to avoid the one-size-fits-all approach when studying the impact of women experiences in CHE.

One would expect a more favorable account on the entry and retention of African American scholars in CHE over experiences in their secular counterpart, but little has been distinguishable in the stories shared. The fourteen voices reveal how faith shapes their perspectives, and there is still work to be done in this arena. There appear to be strong bonds and a commitment to continue adding to the changing ethos of CHE. Their collective voices resonate with deep faith and culture. Borrowing research from another field of study, Jane Goodall gave the insight that "most people are not evil" and that "people mostly do bad things because they haven't understood or haven't bothered to think through what they are doing. It's when people begin to understand in their own hearts that they will do something [different]" (Irwin 1995). These scholars have a willingness to share their stories and add to the body of knowledge needed for change, in spite of the complexities faced.

Understanding what it takes to successfully navigate as African American women scholars within the walls of academe may continue to need attention, but a rich foundation will be laid when CHE starts to think about the presence of Christian African American women scholars and the complexities within the community. Acknowledging that change takes time, patience, skills, tolerance, and collaboration, this population of fourteen has shared their perspective to help CHE begin changing the agenda for African American women scholars. They have offered tangible, current, and clear opportunities to look at how their embodiment of both gender and race impacts their daily experiences. So as the new ethos of CHE institutions takes its first steps, this group is listening for how their voices and experiences will be used to pave the way for the next generation of women scholars.

5

Becoming an African American Academic Leader on a Predominately White Christian Campus: The Use of Autoethnography as a Method for Exploring Mentoring Processes

Dr. Michelle R. Loyd-Paige, Calvin College

Introduction

Self-Reflective Writing Entry, June 20, 2011.

> Pre-ME-LDI Question #1: What short term (next five years) career aspirations do you have? Answer: *Strengthen my position (office) at the college and prepare for my replacement.*

> Pre-ME-LDI Question #2: What long-term career aspirations do you have?

> Answer: *None. I just want to get through the next years without becoming bitter, broken, and burned out.* (Loyd-Paige June 20, 2011)

In June 2011, the Council for Christian Colleges and Universities (CCCU) held its first Multi-Ethnic Leadership Development Institute (ME-LDI) as a part of its regularly offered Leadership Institutes. The CCCU Leadership Institutes provide professional development resources to member CCCU institutions and affiliates. From 1998 to 2010 238 people had participated in either the *Women's Advanced Leadership Institute,* the *Leadership Institute,* or the *Advanced Leadership Institute*; however, only forty of the 238 had been persons of color. The ME-LDI program was developed to more intentionally identify people of color within the CCCU as having senior-level administrative potential (Council for Christian Colleges 2011). I was one of twenty-one people in the first ME-LDI class. The year-long ME-LDI program began with a five-day intensive leadership institute held at the Cedar Springs Christian Retreat Center, located in Washington State near the Canadian border, June 20–24, 2011. The intensive leadership institute involved leadership lessons, one-on-one meetings with Resource Team members (CCCU member institutions administrators of color) daily prayer and mediation, team-building activities, and self-reflective exercises. My purpose for applying for ME-LDI, and participating if selected, was to connect with leaders-of-color who were associated with CCCU schools. I had not anticipated having a life-altering experience. However, two early writing assignments that proved to be both revealing and troubling and an invitation to participate in a research collaborative about mentors dramatically changed my understanding of whom I was and my research agenda for the year to follow.

The very first ME-LDI writing assignment was a short pre-intensive questionnaire about career aspirations. The questions were: "What short term (next five years) career aspirations do you have?" and "What long-term career aspirations do you have?" Everyone in the group wrote out their answers understanding that we would share our responses with the group and turn in our responses to the Resource Team for review. Most of the participants were either not in administrative positions or were very new (fewer than two years) in their administrative roles, and all were in higher education and on campuses that were predominantly white. Of the participants, I was one of two that had had more than two decades experience in Christian higher education and over five years experience as an administrator. While I knew that my role as the Dean for Multicultural Affairs was exhausting and, at times, disillusioning, I was nevertheless surprised by my own pessimistic outlook. As I answered the questions—What short term (next five years) career aspirations do you have? Answer: *Strengthen my position (office) at the college and prepare for my replacement.* What long-term career aspirations do you have? Answer: *None. I just want to get through the next years without becoming bitter, broken, and burned out.* —I realized that I neither had positive academic aspirations nor had ever been asked *How* or *What* I saw as my academic future.

The second reflective writing assignment asked ME-LDI members to create and analyze a list of mentors. The mentoring relationships were to be reviewed in terms of types of relationships, demographics of mentors, and present and past status of mentoring relationships. I generated a list of nineteen past and present mentors. My list contained four relational mentors, nine academic mentors, and eight spiritual mentors. Additionally, only five of the nineteen were current mentors; of those five, four were spiritual mentors, one was relational, and three were female. The exercise brought to the forefront a truth of which I had not been conscious: I did not have a current academic mentor. Most of the people in the group had current academic mentors, many had more than one. I was beginning to see a connection between not having an academic mentor and my answers to the pre-ME-LDI reflective questions. Having to list mentors and then reflect on what the list was telling me about my life was a "reality check" that came to me after five years as an academic leader on a predominantly white private liberal arts Christian campus in the Midwest, twenty-five years as a faculty member within the same context, and a total of thirty-five years as either student, faculty, or administrator within the same context and school. I was also beginning to ask myself in what ways mentors mattered and why I did not have a current set of academic mentors. Dr. Heewon Chang of Eastern University led the list-your-mentor writing exercise. In her debriefing of the activity she invited people to participate in an optional collaborative research project exploring mentoring. I was one of seven who volunteered for the year-long project which used autoethnography as a tool for exploration. I had believed that participating in the project would help me to answer my own questions about mentoring and help me to better understand my pre-ME-LDI reflective writing answers. I was correct in those assumptions.

This introduction is followed by five sections. Within the first section I present a concise literature review which includes theoretical contexts used for examining the mentoring relationships of People-of-Color on predominately white college campuses. Within the second I present an overview of the methodology supporting this project. Within the third I share autoethnographic observations about my own mentoring experiences from my time as an undergraduate student through my early years as a college dean. The fourth section provides a framework for interpreting the data presented within the third section and the fifth section offers concluding remarks.

Literature Review and Context

> Academic women of color face excessive demands for service, to
> create token diversity, or support minority students, cutting into
> the scholarship they need to advance. As they rise in leadership,
> they find speaking out on racial and ethnic issues can backfire.
> *There's a shortage of mentors* who've been there to help them sort
> it out.—S. G. C. (2010, emphasis added)

In the fall of 2009, some 7 percent of college and university faculty were
black (based on a faculty count that excludes persons whose race/ethnic-
ity was unknown) 6 percent were Asian/Pacific Islander, 4 percent were
Hispanic, and 1 percent were American Indian/Alaska Native. About 79
percent of all faculty were white; 42 percent were white males and 37
percent were white females. Staff who were black, Hispanic, Asian/ Pacific Islander, or American Indian/Alaska Native made up 19 percent of
executive, administrative, and managerial staff in 2009 and about 33 percent of nonprofessional staff (Snyder and Dillow 2011). Higher education
within the United States of America is a predominantly white and male
profession (Fong 2007). Women of color, according to a 2009 AAC&U
report, while growing in their presence in academe, make up a small
percentage of females in the most senior of academic positions. "28%
of Chief Academic Officers are women (35% are white women and 3%
are women of color). Among all senior administrators, white women are
38% and women of color are 7%. 23% of college presidents are women,
with 19% of all female presidents being women of color" (Touchton, Musil, and Campbell 2009). The small number of women of color in the
academy is directly related to "American history, legal restrictions, and
traditional customs" (Wilson 1989).

> The recruitment and retention of faculty of color remains one
> of the most difficult challenges facing American Higher Edu-
> cation. Research findings—whether qualitative or quantitative,
> whether numerical or narrative—demonstrate that American
> Indian, African American, Latino, and Asian Pacific American
> faculty comprise, at most, 10% of the faculty, and many describe
> experiences of racial and ethnic bias in the workplace. – *Caro-
> line Sotello Viernes Turner* (1998)

JoAnn Moody in her book *Faculty Diversity: Problems and Solutions* asserts that all new faculty can expect to experience some sorts of

stressors. But she further contends that white women, U.S. minority, and international under-represented faculty on predominately white campuses are likely to experience additional stressors. "These have been termed cultural, racial, gender, or class taxes that are exacted from non-traditional faculty fulfilling the role of pioneer, outsider, and token" (Moody 2004, 12). These additional stressors include: internalizing feelings of inadequacy, being seen as an "affirmative action" hire, being given too little attention, having scholarship undervalued, experiencing negative racial incidents, overcoming isolation, and managing excessive committee assignments and student demands (Moody 2004, 235). Charmaine Clowney in *Best Practices in Recruiting and Retaining Diverse Faculty* corroborates Moody's list of stressors with a list of common complaints from diverse faculty and professionals impacting retention. Clowney's list includes: isolation from departments and marginalized research, perceptions of being incompetent or an "affirmative action hire," left out of informal networks, and lack of critical mass of other diverse faculty for support (Clowney 2012). Moreover, Chavella Pittman in *Racial Microaggressions: The Narratives of African American Faculty at a Predominantly White University* found that "racial microaggressions were a common and negative facet" (2012) of the lives of African American faculty on predominantly white campuses. And in *Racial Microaggressions Against Black Counseling and Counseling Psychology Faculty*, Constantine and associates found that African American faculty felt that they had received inadequate mentoring (2008).

A fundamental definition of mentoring is provided in *The Mentor Handbook*: "Mentoring is a relational process in which someone who knows something (mentor) transfers that something (resources) to someone else (mentoree) at a sensitive time so that it impacts development" (Clinton and Clinton 1991). Traditionally, mentoring is "a single dyadic relationship designed to provide developmental assistance by a more senior individual with a protégés organization" (Higgins and Kram 2001). Traditional mentoring programs focus on a single or primary mentoring relationship. This primary relationship generally provides high amounts of both career and psychological assistance. "This tends to be the predominant method of mentoring faculty of color due to an emphasis on the transfer of career, marketable, or discipline-specific skills, behaviors or attitudes. Social and emotional interactions make the transfer of knowledge and skills possible" (O'Quinn 2010). Broadening the insights of traditional mentoring is a body of research which examines the extent to which peer relationships inside and outside the mentoree's organization and from a wide range of social systems provide both career and psychosocial support (i.e., non-work related organizations, family members, friendships, etc.). These peer mentoring relationships are called Developmental networks or relationship constellations (Higgins and Kram 2001; Davis 2008). Developmental networks or relationship constellations are composed of multiple individuals. The configurations of these networks and constellations often change over time in response to the developmental and psychosocial needs and the environment of the mentoree.

Whether mentoring occurs in a traditional method or within the context of a relational network, there are three basic expressions of the mentoring process: formal, informal, and non-formal (O'Quinn 2010). Formal mentoring is intentional, strategic, and structured (e.g., an employer-initiated mentoring program for first-year faculty, professional leadership development programs). Informal mentoring is generally occasional, periodic, and is often unstructured (e.g., conversations with co-workers, periodic advice from a former colleague). Non-formal mentoring is passive mentoring. There is generally no direct contact and tends to be more inspirational or aspirational (e.g., the life and work of a historic figure, the work of a well-known scholar in one's field, discernment perceived as divine inspiration). Relying too much on an informal mentoring system can mean that women and faculty of color are inadvertently overlooked (Moody 2004). Faculty of color, and especially women of color, on a predominantly white campus may struggle to find "someone like them," someone with whom they share a natural affinity or feel comfortable approaching (Lois 1997; Bower 2002; Alex-Assenoh et al. 2005; Moses 1989).

> The few women of color who manage to enter the halls of academe as students, faculty, or administrators quickly discover an entrenched and finely tuned system of gendered and raced privilege, power, and exclusionary practices. Learning to navigate the multi-tiered academic systems of oppression and pass survival strategies along to other women of color is both a rite of passage and a badge of honor.—*Pat Washington* (2006)

The experiences of African American women in the academy have been documented in several studies from a variety of perspectives and a number of the studies use a qualitative method of investigation. A brief survey of the literature reveals the breadth and scope of the research to date. Vargas in *Women Faculty of Color in the White Classroom: Narratives on the Pedagogical Implications of Teacher Diversity* (2002) and Hendrix in "*She Must be Trippin': The Secret of Disrespect from Students of Color* (2007) examine the classroom experience of African American faculty. Hamlet in *Giving the Sistuhs Their Due: The Lived Experiences of African American Women in Academia* (1999) Marbley in *Finding My Voice: An African American Female Professor at a Predominantly White University* (2007) Gregory in *Black Women in the Academy: The Secrets to Success and Achievement* (1995) Astin and Astin in *Meaning and Spirituality in the Lives of College Faculty: A Study of Values and Authenticity and Stress* (1999) and Butner, Burley, and Marbley in *Coping With the Unexpected: Black Faculty at Predominantly White Institutions* (2000) look at coping strategies. Gregory in *Black Faculty Women in the Academy: History, Status, and Future* (2001) Johnson and Pichon in *The Status of African American Faculty in the Academy: Where Do We Go From Here?* (2007) and Sotello Viernes Turner, Gonzalez, and Wood in *Faculty of Color in Academe: What 20 Years of Literature Tells Us* (2008) provide a survey of the presence of black women in the academy and in literature about the academy. And in *The We and the Us: Mentoring African American Women* Crawford and Smith (2005) more specifically examine how mentoring affects the career choices of African American women who become administrators in higher education and how their sociocultural and gender experiences define their career choices and development as does Jackson and Branscome in *African American Women's Mentoring Experiences* (1996).

> [We need theories] that will rewrite history using race, class, gender, and ethnicity as categories or analysis, theories that cross borders, that blur boundaries—new kinds of theories with new theorizing methods. . . . We are articulating new positions in the "in-between," Borderland worlds of ethnic communities and academies . . . social issues such as race, class, and sexual differences are intertwined with narrative and poetic elements of a text, elements in which theory is embedded. In our mestizaje theories we create new categories for those of us left out or pushed out of existing ones.—*Anzaldua* (quoted in Solorazano and Yasso 2002)

Many who research the lives of African American female faculty would concur with Anzaldua that it is important to bring social issues such as race and gender to the forefront of inquiry. Research confirms the marginalization that many African American women in the academy experience. Understanding the marginalization requires sensitivity to what Solorzano and Yosso call "the intercentricity of race and racism with other forms of oppression [and] the centrality of experiential knowledge" (Solorazano and Yasso 2002). Similar to intercentricity is intersectionality. The term intersectionality was coined by legal scholar Kimberlé Crenshaw in order to reveal the "multidimensionality" of marginalized subjects' lived experiences (Crenshaw 1989). "Intersectionality emerged in the late 1980's and early 1990's from critical race studies . . . from its inception, intersectionality has had . . . a particular [interest in] the intersection of race and gender . . . the various ways in which race and gender interact to shape the multiple dimensions of black women's . . . experiences" (Nash 2008). This project follows in the intersectionality and intercentricity conventions.

Methodology

"Autoethnography is a qualitative research method that enables researchers to use their autobiographical and contextual data to gain a hermeneutical understanding of the social context, and in turn, a socialcultural meaning of self" (Duncan 2004). More specifically, autoethnographies are case studies that follow in the tradition of ethnographic research. Though following in the tradition of ethnographies, there is a key difference between the ethnography and autoethnography. Ethnographies explore the experiences of a people within a cultural context. Autoethnographies explore the self as a cultural being in relation with others within a particular cultural context. Autoethnographies use personal experiences as the primary data. Data is in the form of personal memory, personal inventory, self-observation, self-reflection, and external data (Chang and Boyd 2011; Bird 2012). Autoethnographies are about method, process, and product. They produce a type of literature which captures personal experience. The telling of personal experiences within a cultural context allows for an examination of how we make sense of the world and for the exploration of the intersectionality of the self and the intersection between self and community. Autoethnographies, like ethnographies, use an investigative process of data collection, data analysis, and data interpretation. As with other forms of research this project begins with a question. The question here is, "What has the mentoring looked like in my life and why?"

This project grew out of the ME-LDI collaborative project—multiple contributors writing about their experiences for one study. This project, however, has only one investigator and contributing author. The type of data collected for autoethnographies is dependent upon the type of project. Chang describes four different styles of autoethnographic projects: "confessional-evocative" (2008, 145) "imaginative-creative" (2008, 148) "descriptive-realistic" (2008, 143) and "analytic-interpretive" (2008, 146). Confession-evocative and imaginative-creative tend to incorporate more artistic writing than scientific inquiry while descriptive-realistic and analytic-interpretive tend to include less self-narrative and more contextual analysis. This project is a descriptive-realistic autoethnography.

Active data collection, in the form of reflective writing on mentoring, began June 2011 and continued through June 2012. The data collection involved self-reflective writing in a personal journal, participation in a series of WIMBA[1] discussion groups with a subset of the ME-LDI group members, and the retrieval of artifacts written prior to 2011 by or about the author. The data collected for this essay was in the form of personal memory, personal inventory, self-reflective data, and autobiographical artifacts (Bird 2012). Following the data collection, the data was reviewed to determine possible themes and research questions. A writing retreat for ME-LDI group members who were writing autoethnographies was held in March 2012. The writing retreat afforded a time to reconnect with ME-LDI members, sharpen themes, write independently, collectively discuss writing progress, and receive feedback. It was during the writing retreat that I choose a descriptive-realistic style of autoethnography for a self-narrative about my mentoring experiences throughout my academic career.

Autoethnographic Observations on Mentoring

The observations which follow are separated according to the three states of being and identity within my academic career: student, faculty, and

---

1. WIMBA, a brand of web-conferencing technology, included discussion boards and chat rooms. Meetings were in electronic chat rooms with the option of video connections. Meetings were held one monthly from July 2011 to February 2012. Each session had a particular topic based on prompt questions supplied by the collaborative project principle investigators and posted on the discussion boards. Sessions were recorded and transcribed.

dean. Each state of being is briefly introduced. After the introduction representative reflective writings reveal the contours of that particular state pertaining to mentoring. The majority of the writings from the earlier stages of my career are excerpts from an unpublished intellectual autobiography (Loyd-Paige 2007). The majority of the writings from the middle and later stages of my career are excerpts from the reflective writing exercises[2] associated with my ME-LDI participation.

Student

I graduated from a high school that was predominantly white and twenty miles from the college I would attend to work on my undergraduate degree. The college, Calvin College, was a small private liberal arts institution with a strong ethnic and religious heritage and identity. I attended the college knowing that both my ethnic and religious identity would cast me as double-minority. I would eventually major in sociology and graduate in four years. In the fall following my graduation from Calvin, I was enrolled in a terminal PhD program at Purdue University. I would, again, major in sociology.

> My parents valued education. Growing up I was not asked the question of "if" I was going to go to college; I was always asked "where" I was going to go to college when I graduated from high school. I graduated from Wyoming Park High School in 1977. I was one of two Black students in the National Honor Society while I was there. I was ranked eighth in my graduating class, the only African American student in the top ten. (Loyd-Paige 2007, 10)
>
> "Defining Moments"
>
> The first thing that comes to mind is a conversation with a female faculty member who asked me if I was planning on attending graduate school. When I told her "no", she encouraged me to think about it. Because of her and that brief conversation after a class meeting, I applied for graduate school. She also wrote a letter of recommendation on my behalf. I pursued my

---

2. Michelle R. Loyd-Paige, ME-LDI transcripts. The transcripts only contained the comments made by Loyd-Paige and were complied in a single document for the purposes of research. The comments include the transcribed verbal comments made on conference calls, the contents of postings to the ME-LDI discussion board, and the comments—both verbal and written—made during WIMBA sessions with ME-LDI members committed to the collaborative project.

PhD at Purdue University. As a TA I had to take a "teaching sociology" seminar. Once I took on teaching responsibilities, I knew I wanted to be a college professor (Loyd-Paige 2011, 13).

When I completed and defended my dissertation; I was scared that someone would discover I was not bright enough to have a PhD. . . . I was full of fear. I was fearful that no one really wanted to hear what I had to say; fearful that people would not think my work was very important; fearful that maybe I was only in graduate school because of some affirmative action quota or mandate. . . . Part of this insecurity about my intellectual abilities stem from my lack of connections to an intellectual Black community. I didn't see any Black scholars and so it was hard to see myself as a Black scholar. I never had a Black professor—as an undergraduate or as a graduate student. Very few of my courses included readings with Black authors and I read even fewer studies, essays, and social commentators authored by African American females. I didn't know that there were Black sociological theorists until I started teaching an introductory sociology class at Calvin and the textbook I was using mentioned WEB DuBois. I felt cheated out of my intellectual heritage.[A] combination of low self-esteem and lack of a Black intellectual role model left me doubting my own abilities . . . My childhood fears of not being good enough were being carried over into my adult life. (Loyd-Paige 2007, 15)

Perhaps also noteworthy would be the counsel I received from the professor [a White older male] I worked for as a TA. . . . I had a good working relationship with the professor I was assigned to. We would spend time talking about how he approached teaching and about the introductory sociology textbook he was working on. One afternoon I told him that I was planning to pursue a career as a college professor. He told me that I should do fine, but cautioned me not to teach a course on race relations. When I asked him why he told me that as a Black woman, people would already assume that they knew what I was going to say and proceed to not listen. He continued to say that people would write me off as an angry Black woman before I even opened my mouth. He said that I would have more influence in the academy if I choose to write and teach in an area other than race relations. Something about his counsel didn't sit right within me. But his counsel would influence the direction—or better yet, lack of direction—of my early scholarly life. (Loyd-Paige 2007, 13)

Faculty

I began teaching sociology classes at Calvin College in 1985. This proved to be my first and only teaching assignment after graduate school. For several of my twenty-some years as full-time faculty member I was the only African American faculty member out of 300 faculty members. Currently, less than 4 percent of the faculty is African American.

> I can remember starting out in my career teaching at Calvin and because I was a student there, people just assumed that I knew who were the people to talk to or that I was very familiar with the campus and even the Christian Reformed Church. But it wasn't true, people just assumed it was true because I was a student there. They were used to students [who would come back to work for the college, students who had had a family tradition of attending Calvin] so they didn't treat me like a new person. They treated me like someone who was not new— someone who was very familiar [with how the campus worked] but I wasn't very familiar (Loyd-Paige 2011, 2).
>
> One day [early in my teaching career and I was talking with another department member] we were talking about what my teaching load would look like the following semester. I asked him where he thought I would be in ten years. I was expecting him to say something about improved teaching or published author, instead he said, "not here." I was dumbfounded. He went on to say that he did not see me as a part of the department that far out. I am not sure how he meant it, but I interpreted as I was either not good enough to stay or that I was not welcome to stay. I continued working at Calvin College not really thinking that I would last longer than a few years. (Loyd-Paige 2007, 15)
>
> I wanted to bring my cultural context into the classroom. My context was that of an African American female. I was living in a predominantly Black community, but felt academically and intellectually isolated. I did not know of any other Black female sociologists. I didn't think I was the only one, I knew my kindred sisters existed somewhere, but I was not very good at finding them. (Loyd-Paige 2007, 16)
>
> With the help of my colleagues from the Consultation of Afro-Christian Scholars in Higher Education I have begun to see myself as a social scientist, not just a student and teacher of sociology. I have begun to see that some of my fears about not being "good enough" were unfounded. And that perhaps what I was really afraid of was that I really was as good as some people had said that I was—people like my professor from summer

school who urged me to go to graduate school, people like my major professor who had champagne chilling in his office on the day of my defense, or people like myself when I would read over my dissertation and think, "this is good." (Loyd-Paige 2007, 15)

Dean

I had been teaching for about twenty years as a full-time member of the department of Sociology when my provost asked me to serve as the interim Dean for Multicultural Affairs. I had been asked to fill the position because a national search had failed. As a faculty member I had been the department chair and had served on several all-campus committees—including the anti-racism training team. The combination of longevity, leadership experience, and passion for diversity led to my being considered for the open position. Since that initial year, the qualifier "interim" has been removed from my title.

> In the beginning his [an African American male from another college] guidance was focused of the intersectionality of a spiritual and academic life AND about surviving as an Afro-Christian scholar on a predominately white campus. When I was asked to consider taking on the role as dean, he was one of the few people I called. He provided great insight and encouragement. He affirmed my gifts and challenged me to make this position my own. He shared his mistakes [as a dean] and encouraged me not to repeat them. He gave me "permission" to redesign my job description, to set my own boundaries, and to use my voice strategically. He also provided a listening ear in the first two years of my administration (Loyd-Paige 2010 12).
>
> I do not have a [current] mentor for my role as an academic dean . . . and have not had one for six years (Loyd-Paige 2010, 17).
>
> For myself, I think I lacked a mentor because I really didn't have ambitions of doing anything more than what I am doing. Yes, I think that is part of the reason. The other part is because I really didn't see anyone around me that was doing what I was doing or someone that was someone that I aspired to be because even though I admired some of the things that people were doing, the way that they did things were not some of the things that were inspiring me to want to follow after them. (Loyd-Paige 2010, 4).

An Analysis of My Mentoring Processes

> In comparison to majority faculty, the numbers of faculty of color in higher education remain disproportionately low. Mentoring is an important strategy for retaining these faculty members. There is nothing more isolating and alienating than to be the first or only person of one's race and/or ethnicity to be hired in a department, and a mentoring relationship is one way to escape from that isolation. (Stanley and Lincoln 2007)

Rarely during my academic career have I been mentored by an African American within the academy—male or female. During my graduate school years I had two traditional mentors. The first of these traditional mentors was the person I worked for as a teaching assistant. The second traditional mentor was my dissertation advisor —both of these mentors were middle-aged white males. After graduate school, however, both of these mentoring relationships ceased and no one filled the role of a mentor in a formal manner. At the time I joined the faculty (in 1985) there were no mandated formal mentoring programs for new faculty as there are now at the college. I was not treated like a new faculty member when I joined the sociology department because I had graduated from the college just three-and-a-half years prior to my first day of teaching. The lack of formal mentors within the academy was mediated by formal and informal mentors associated with other aspects of my life; these mentors provided the socio-psychological support needed to sustain an academic career. Space has not permitted an exploration of these socio-psychological supports found outside of the academy in my life within this essay; however, the research substantiates the presence and importance of such socio-psychological relationships in the lives of academics of color.

Although traditional formal mentoring has been a part of my academic journey, it becomes clear when looking at the breadth of my academic profession that my experiences best support the notion of mentoring as developmental networks and as constellations of relationships. Through the process of writing an autoethnography I have realized that what I had thought was an absence of mentors in my life was, in fact, an absence of traditional mentors. Being able to identify a collective of people who have moved in and out of my life as mentors has helped me to better understand my academic experience. Being able to juxtapose my feelings of isolation and inadequacies with the remembrance of people who have positively influenced and supported my academic journey has helped me to better understand my self within my context as a student, faculty member, and college dean. Engaging the self-narrative processes of the autoethnography came easy to me and challenged me to view my individual experiences as part of a larger story of all African American female professionals on predominantly white campuses.

Additionally, my journey highlights the impact of formal, informal, and non-formal mentoring. These different forms of mentoring lend themselves well to developmental networks and constellations of relationships. The external-data-gathering portion of the autoethnographic process provided an avenue for identifying others—both white allies with the academy and people of color outside of the academy—as informal and non-formal mentors who were instrumental to my thriving within the academy. At every stage of my academic life there was a dynamic assemblage of formal, informal, and non-formal mentors. The make-up of the assemblage changed, not only from stage to stage, but often from year to year. For example, during my early faculty years, I lacked a formal (traditional) mentor; a white female staff member and a white female colleague were informal mentors (periodic conversations over lunch); when a black male joined my department he became an informal mentor (he was one informal male mentor during my early faculty years and the only other black faculty member on campus at the time); and my non-formal mentors were, and continue to be, Ida B. Wells, W.E.B. DuBois, and E. Franklin Frazier (all historic black sociologists). Whether formal, informal, or non-formal, mentoring has been an integral part of my academic journey.

While reviewing my personal memories and self-reflective writing about my mentoring experiences, a pattern of relationships became evident. All but one of my formal professional mentors were white and male and were associated with whatever institution I was affiliated with at the time (the only one that was not white was an African American male); almost all of my informal professional mentors were female, white, and peer co-workers (of my same faculty rank); and all my non-formal professional mentors were black historic figures (both male and female, but predominantly female). Moreover, I noticed that I relied upon my non-formal mentors to negotiate the *intrapersonal* aspects of my academic life (countering the feelings of inadequacies). I relied upon the informal mentors to negotiate the *interpersonal* aspects of my academic life (learning to negotiate a specific academic culture). And, I relied upon my formal mentors to negotiate the *institutional* aspects of my academic life (advancing through graduate school and achieving tenure).

Conclusion

ME-LDI Self-Reflective Writing Entry, June 24, 2011

Post-ME-LDI Question #1: How has your participation in ME-LDI affected your previous career aspirations? Answer: *Greatly, I am now thinking about my development as a leader. I see that I have more to do.*

Post-ME-LDI Question #2: What has contributed to the shift, if any? Answer: *Hearing from leaders of color who work in predominately White Christian colleges; seeing the possibilities modeled in front of me; conversations with people in similar situations; being open to the Spirit.* (Loyd-Paige June 24, 2011)

My expedition towards understanding the presence and place of mentors in my life started with the ME-LDI retreat exercise of generating a list of past and present mentors. That exercise was an eye-opening experience and a reality check of my professional academic life. Recalling the critical moments in my life as I researched the experiences of other African Americans within the academy helped me to focus my thoughts on what it meant for me to be in my own cultural context. It helped me to focus my thoughts about being an African American student, faculty member, and administrator on a predominately white private liberal arts Christian college in the Midwest. The autoethnographic process moved me away from venting and self-silencing towards analysis and elucidation.

My academic journey, in many ways, is a reflection of the literature on African American women in the academy. My journey through the academy, from student to dean, is one that has been impacted by the presence and absence of professional academic mentors. The absence of mentors in my life is not surprising given the relatively low numbers of African American females in the academy. While it is not necessary for one to have a mentor who shares the same racial-ethnic and gender identity as oneself, my story would indicate that where there is such an absence, one becomes more vulnerable to feelings of isolation, feelings of not being good enough, and the challenges associated with "otherness."

The term autoethnography literally means "one story." However, in the telling of my "one story" it becomes clear that my "one story" is impacted that the stories of many others—the stories of those who have been allies, the stories of those who have discounted me, the stories of those who guided me, and the stories of those who inspired me. But my story is not about aloneness. My story is one of a constellation of relationships who have helped me become an empowered "I" in my own story. I am because of those who have gone before me. I am because of those who have walked beside me. I am because of those who have tried to silence me. I am because of those who have helped me to survive long enough to become an academic leader. I am because of the formal, informal, and non-formal mentors in my life who have facilitated my becoming an African American leader on a predominantly white campus.

6

Ain't I a Student?
Thinking through Spaces
for Black Female College Students

Dr. Deshonna Collier-Goubil, Biola University

IN THE YEAR 1850, Sojourner Truth, a well-known abolitionist and women's rights advocate, sat in a meeting of a coalition of women's rights activists. For a full day of sessions, Truth sat and listened while different pleas about the woman's cause were made. Finally, Sojourner Truth spoke through the jeering of racial comments by women who were afraid that her comments would comingle the women's rights cause with the cause of equal rights for blacks in the country (Painter 1996). Despite calls to forbid her from speaking to the forum, Sojourner Truth opened her mouth and recited a now well-known challenge to the issues of gender and race in the U.S.: "Ain't I a Woman?" In this prolific speech, Truth put forth a challenge to those in her hearing to look at her also as a woman. In this moment, the challenging intersections of race, class, gender, and status come together beautifully in the mind and body of a woman who had a strong sense of her own identity, self-efficacy and spirituality. Sojourner Truth spoke boldly as an African American woman with a strong sense of God.

Isn't this what Christian colleges seek to produce, students who are able and willing to serve the world, speaking boldly into matters that necessitate a Christian ethic, while never losing sight of their spiritual core? However, the question for Christian colleges remains: how exactly are we providing this for students of color? This particular chapter seeks to understand the need for spaces, particularly for black female students at Christian colleges, that will allow the growth potential to produce students who are confident in their identities, spiritually grounded, and skilled in leadership in order to speak boldly into places where their voice is needed.

In 2011, Christian colleges and universities boasted a grand total of 48,052 students. Of this number, 11.4 percent of the student population were black students (5.3 percent black women). These statistics are a slight increase from 2010 percentages, which were 10.4 percent and 5.1 percent respectively[1] and a large increase from 2006. The trend of increasing enrollment of black students at evangelical Christian colleges was well noted in a study by Cross and Slater (2004). A continued increase of black students in Christian colleges is a welcome notion. The question remains, however, what happens to these students once they arrive? How many of these students are evangelical Christian colleges able to retain? Of those retained, what is the quality of their experience while in college? Research literature indicates that black students at Traditionally White Institutions (TWIs) often face additional stressors which make matriculation through to degree difficult. Black students attending Christian universities experience many of the same stressors as black students attending non-Christian universities, with the added stressor of a religious experience that may be very different than what they are used to encountering. The multiple stressors compressed together, with the added issue of systems of difference, white privilege oppression (showing up in formal or informal ways) often leave a bad taste in these students' mouths and lead them to transfer out of the Christian college setting. This chapter explores the unique challenges of black female students attending Christian colleges and proposes some programmatic ideas to aid in supporting these students throughout their college enrollment.

This Generation of Student

In an age when an African American female is First Lady of the United States, heralded for her credentials and her commitment to a healthy lifestyle, adored for her fashion sense, and loved by many (representing all races and nationalities) how do we confront the issue of feeling so alone on a college campus? What is it like to experience racism, sexism, and classism on a college campus? How does it feel to be invisible, asexual, an afterthought, or completely ignored in university planning

1 Data drawn from the Integrated Postsecondary Education Data System (IPEDS).

and student activity groups? What is the experience of being a student in a supposed post-racial society? These are questions that I imagine confront many students of color on college campuses. The Christian college student might add: where is God in all this and what is God saying to me in this experience?

The Next Great Generation

Millennial students are heralded as being the next great generation (Howe, Strauss, and Matson 2000). They have been told by their mostly Baby Boomer generation parents that they will accomplish great things. This "on the brink of greatness" mantra leads millennials to feel that they are very special. De Bard (2004) discusses other characteristics of millennials: they have been sheltered; they are confident, conventional, and team oriented; they have a need to achieve; and they are under pressure to do so. This optimistic view of millennials would lead most to agree with the notion that this generation can accomplish great things.

As it relates to diversity, millennials boast of being the largest and most diverse generation that this country has seen (Howe, Strauss, and Matson 2000). With their aptitude for teamwork, the problem of the "color line" discussed by DuBois at the turn of the twentieth century (DuBois 1903) seems an issue of the past. Millennials appear to be champions of diversity. They are the first generation to grow up with celebrities who readily identify as LGBTQ (lesbian, gay, bisexual, transgender, and/or questioning) and they have had the opportunity to hear and participate in discussions of immigration reform during their generation. Hearing that they are able to accomplish what this country has not been able to accomplish in over two hundred years—that is, creating an actual society that is inclusive of diverse groups—would leave any person buying into the idea. As the old adage goes however, if it seems too good to be true, then it probably *is* too good to be true.

The Other Side of Greatness—Being Not So Great

Research on millennials has often focused on the group as a whole. Few researchers aggregate their data by race when speaking of millennials. This has led to some misconceptions about how millennials feel about and experience race relations in the United States, beginning with the issue of segregation. While millennials are proclaimed as being the most diverse generation and a generation that is the most accepting of diversity, they have grown up and attended primary education in very segregated neighborhoods and classrooms (Broido 2004). Lacking the benefit of actual cross-cultural contact limits the understanding of acceptance of other races and cultures. In short, it is very easy for one to say that they accept other races and cultures: it is a totally different thing to interact in a meaningful fashion with another culture. Millennials must move past eating cultural food, attending cultural festivals, wearing cultural fashions, and interpreting "being culturally accepting" as looking for fun (Broido 2004). Millennials' interpretation of accepting racial diversity lacks depth of reasoning regarding power, privilege, and oppression and how these forces affect race, gender, and cultural relations in the U.S.

The reality is that millennials are entering college with about the same amount of cross-race contact as their predecessors' generations, the difference being that they mask their lack of cultural humility in the garments of colorblindness and post-racial language. Students of color on campuses committed to a colorblind ideology suffer in silence. Lewis, Chesler, and Forman (2000) note that the effects of colorblindness lead to racial stereotyping, marginality, expectations to assimilate, interpersonal awkwardness during cross-race contact with white students, and white students' resentment of and hostility towards diversity programs.[2]

Further, when data is parceled out, it appears that the myth of a post-racial society is blown out of the water. Cohen's 2011 study uncovered that when millennials' survey responses regarding race are disaggregated by race the results are very different. Whites, blacks, and Latino millennials have divergent views on the impact of race on young blacks in society, and the treatment of blacks by the healthcare system and the government. In most cases, black millennials felt that black people are treated more poorly than whites in society, with most white millennials having the opposite response and Latino millennials falling somewhere in the middle of black and white respondents. The one area in which Cohen found agreement between the races was on the question of the treatment of blacks by the police in society. In this all groups agreed that law enforcement discriminates against black youth more than any other

---

2. It should be noted that white millennials also experience interpersonal awkwardness, often making inappropriate racial comments when interacting with millennial students of color.

group. Lastly, when asked if racism will be eliminated within their life-time, most were pessimistic.

With this vast difference in the ways in which millennials perceive race relations in the U.S., how might these millennials of different racial and cultural groups interact once thrown together on a Christian college campus? Students of all races, ethnicities, and cultural backgrounds have similar reasons for choosing to attend Christian colleges. These include proximity to the student's family/home, the student having a positive experience during a campus visit, and financial assistance provided to the student to name a few (Confer and Mamiseishvili 2012). Spiritual development, meeting spiritual needs, wanting to attend a university where their faith will be integrated into their course materials are of course primal reasons for students to choose to agree to doctrinal statements, university contracts, and statements of faith most Christian colleges require their students to sign.

In looking toward the future of our next generation of leaders, the greatness of this generation only extends to the point at which an authority figure has laid out a roadmap for millennials. Millennials were reared in very structured, planned, and organized environments. This trend towards organization and structure has caused millennials to trust that authority figures around them will set them on an action plan. This action plan should be described in detail and should also encompass points of celebrating their achievement along the way. The problem as it relates to race and race relations is that no other generation in the U.S. has been successful in eliminating any structural matrix of domination. In no other time in history have we been able to successfully eliminate racism as an ideology or as a structural practice. Rather, we have adjusted to it, added to it, and/or attempted to ignore it. For millennials to conquer this social ill and become a truly diverse and multicultural society calls for some independent creative thinking on their own. The paradox is that while millennials are awaiting a grand plan from some authority figure, this may be the area in which millennials are able to live up to their distinction of being truly great and lead us into a world that we have never known. A true diverse and multicultural nation, however, will require humility, recognition, and action. It will necessitate learning true intercultural humility, recognizing the structural forces of racism and how it impedes society's growth, and practicing including new groups into large-scale political, economic, and social dialogue.

On Being a Black Female in This Generation

Not all millennials are created equally. In looking at African American millennials, Strayhorn (2010) found that while this group of millennials fits into the mold of the average millennial in some areas, the group faces challenges in other areas. African American millennials, like their generational counterparts, are more numerous, more affluent, and better-educated than African Americans of previous generations. The gender gap for those entering college however has widened for African American millennials, a fact not true of their counterparts.[3] African American women in college now outnumber African American men two to one. In addition, while data reflects a widening of the black middle class in the U.S., one may wonder how millennials will fare in continuing to grow the number of college entrants, as the recession, workforce reductions, and flailing economy have hit the black community harder than other communities.

For black female students to matriculate, they must shoulder not just general education requirements, but also the weight of discerning how to be a black woman in a complex generation. Images of Michelle Obama on magazine covers and television interviews are shattering some of the controlling images of black women in popular culture.[4] Mrs. Obama represents intelligence, health, and fashion, in addition to strength for these young women. Simultaneously, the treatment of Mrs. Obama in some media venues also reflects the very present reality that racist ideologies continue to abound in our society.[5] Black female students live in this dichotomous relationship every day on predominantly white college campuses. On the one hand their colleagues (other millennials) celebrate their acceptance of everyone no matter their race, country of origin, or sexual preference. On the other hand this acceptance rarely moves beyond a person choosing to practice cultural idioms as a fashion statement

3. Gender gap for African American women entering college has increased from 54.5 percent in 1971 to 59.3 percent by 2004.

4. Patricia Hill Collins in her landmark work *Black Feminist Thought* discusses the imagery of the mammie, the matriarch, jezebel, and the welfare queen as being controlling images of black women that have lasted throughout time and through which black women are judged, whether or not they actually exhibit any behavior suggestive of the images.

5. Mrs. Obama's every move in the public's eye is scrutinized as being "un-American," there have been cartoon images of her drawn in a derogatory fashion, and her husband has been publicly heckled.

or holding an unspoken expectation of compliance and assimilation with the dominant culture.[6] This generation embraces the message, "You have an equal opportunity to compete in the workforce," yet the fact remains that African American (and Latina) women continue to be underrepresented in professional workforces (Miller, Kerr, and Reid 2010). A glass ceiling continues to exist for women of color (compared to both white women and white men) at the administrative professional level in both public and private sectors (Campbell 2009).

Black women on predominantly white college campuses find themselves in the midst of an identity crisis not experienced by previous generations. Many have never experienced the more overt forms of racial discrimination that their predecessors likely encountered (Henry 2008). Similar to their white millennial counterparts, they have been sheltered from these types of experiences and many will encounter their first experience of difference on their college campuses. Having been sheltered from these experiences, these young ladies have not been armed with the social prowess to respond to these incidents in a healthy fashion. Unfortunately, these women end up internalizing experiences of microaggressive behaviors, or bottling up their feelings until one day the stress from holding things in gets the better of them, or withdrawing completely and eventually leaving the institution. All possible results have a direct effect on the students' academic progress and pursuits.

One of the most blatant forms of this generation's oxymoronic relationship with race relations as it pertains to black women on college campuses can be found in these women's dating relationships. While the multiethnic student demographic has grown with this generation, and sentiments regarding interracial dating appear to have changed, black female millennials continue to find displeasure in seeking dating relationships. While black men are often sought after on predominantly white college campuses, black women do not always receive the same attention. Although this may seem to be an insignificant portion of college life, being viewed as asexual in an environment that prides itself on marriage

6. In her book *Generation Me* author Jean Twenge saves a conversation about minority groups for last. In the discussion of race in the chapter, Twenge points to African Americans and Latinos being able to integrate professional jobs and all persons enjoying ethnic cuisine. She admits that racism and discrimination still remain; however, one can walk away from her work thinking that the strides made in Equal Employment Opportunities overshadow the reality of a more covert form of racism with which people of color must contend in U.S. society.

preparation and pre-marital relationships[7] adds to the frustration, stress, and sense of not belonging that many black women on Christian college campuses experience. This calls for the creation of a space for black women to have these conversations to remain psychologically healthy.

Other Issues with Which to Contend

Images of Black Women in Society

With hip hop being a prevalent cultural expression engaged by a diverse and international audience, the culture continues to predominantly espouse an image of black women that upholds previous stereotypical ideologies (of black women as sexual objects). Research is inconclusive as to whether hip hop has a positive or negative influence on young people (Henry, West, and Jackson 2010). Black women have successfully used hip hop to garner civic engagement and to redefine images of beauty (Henry, West, and Jackson 2010). However, the world around black women is using the stereotypical images espoused in the culture to define, interpret, and then interact with black women. Black female college students are faced with the added obstacle of attempting to navigate these troubling waters while working through their own developmentally-appropriate definition of womanhood.

First-Generation College Students
and Low SES College Students

Roughly 48 percent of the black incoming freshmen are first generation college students, this down 2 percent from previous generations (Bonner, Marbley, and Howard-Hamilton 2011). Although the numbers of first generation college students (FGCS) are gradually decreasing in this demographic, there are still a good number of black FCGS entering college who present a range of additional need. FGCS are often older, live off-campus, and are less involved in campus athletics and activities (Pascarella, Pierson, Wolniak, and Ternzini 2004). These students typically

---

7. Many students on Christian college campuses experience increased stress in attempting to locate a dating relationship that will lead to marriage while in college. It is often thought, "Where else might a young Christian college student find other suitable mates than on the campus of a Christian university?"

work a greater number of hours on outside jobs and take fewer academic units.

FCGS often face challenges that other college students enter college prepared to handle. These can include contending with differences in family and university culture, which can create multiple identities within the student. Students who are the first in their family to attend college often come from family environments which do not exactly understand the culture of a university and college life. These students often face a psychological pull between both environments. Ecklund (2013) theorizes that the families of origin for many FGCS of color tend to have a collective perspective while the university culture leans more toward an individualistic perspective. The student then has to learn how to operate and thrive in both environments. Another challenge faced by FGCS is needing additional assistance navigating university culture (Dennis, Phinney, and Chauteco 2005). FGCS may require assistance determining what is needed to matriculate in a timely fashion, how to take notes and study effectively, how to seek out faculty and staff, and how to handle stress of the unknown—not knowing what to expect from the multitude of experiences that occur during college. In addition to these things, students of color who also happen to be FGCS have another layer of burden in dealing with racism and micro-aggressions they may experience on predominantly white college campuses.

Although we'd like to hope that students at Christian colleges are not having these types of experiences, the fact remains (and data confirms, as previously stated) that millennials have had very little cross-race contact prior to attending college. Thus it is actually a foreign task to most students to live, interact, and learn in environments with people who are different than their own race. This issue spans across college experience. Even students of color who are not the first in their families to attend college, still need additional support and assistance while attending traditionally white institutions (TWIs).

Where Is My Faith/Religion in All This?

While several studies have uncovered that the presence of spirituality and faith have aided students of color in their transition into a TWI, the unique opportunity for Christian colleges is that they are communities of faith where people purposefully live out their faith in community with others living out the same or similar faith. A problem however arises for students of color when the faith communities they enter in college are starkly different from the churches they were attending as youth. In this way their expression of faith can be questioned, in either direct or subtle ways. Sometimes the absence of diverse worship styles or prayer styles can send subtle messages to young freshmen that their style of worship is not the "correct" way to worship.

In my own experience, my spiritual roots were shaken when I began to realize that the style of teaching and preaching that I had grown accustomed to was called "Black Liberation Theology" and that that form of theology was supposedly wrong, according to the TWI I was attending at the time. I received subtle messages in classes that it was not a "biblical" theology, rather a socio-political one. This sent me on a quest to prove wrong all that questioned my form of theology. I read several books, wrote many papers, and even had the opportunity to lecture in a few classes (imagine that). This, given my demeanor, was an opportunity for me to find my own voice. But for a younger student (in my experience, I was in a graduate program when my theology was challenged) during a time in their life when they are much more susceptible to ideas from outside of themselves, this can lead to a questioning of many things. As a professor on the campus of a Christian University I have too often heard students of color professing that they are not searching for a black theology or a liberation theology or a (you enter the name) theology, rather they are searching for a biblical theology, as if everyone else isn't. The question remains, however: can a person separate their social experience, their location in society, and the experiences that they have had in life from their reading of the Scripture? Some argue that the ideas and concepts that come to each of us from our unique experiences should help us to realize the importance of diversity within the community of believers. I wonder how much of this fight for a so-called biblical theology is more an outward expression of students who are fighting to fit in with their colleagues. In a sense they do not want to be labeled one thing or another; they want their expression to be considered the norm. Unfortunately, as a sociologist I have a full understanding that this is an uphill battle in a world where you are not part of the majority culture.

I do feel however that there are some things that Christian colleges can do to assist students in this manner. As a good friend told me once, all things are tied to identity. When a student feels secure in their identity, challenges to their identity will not have such a grand effect on them. They may even receive such a challenge as an opportunity to grow and learn more about themselves and the person whom they have chosen to be.

Toward a Leadership Development Program Model

Developing Our Next Leaders

The needs of black female college students at predominantly white Christian college campuses appear to be vast but are addressable. A leadership development model would aptly address the ills facing this community. Confer and Mamiseishvili (2012) advocate for integrative approaches that allow for faculty, staff and peer support to students of color to ensure they are receiving the social support they need to matriculate through graduation. A program that utilizes a networking mentoring approach while focusing on the pillars of identity development, leadership development and spiritual development, may aid in retention efforts, matriculation through to graduation, and ultimately recruitment of new students of color to Christian college campuses.

The discussion of leadership here focuses both on capacity and efficacy issues. Leadership capacity encompasses those skills, knowledge, and abilities that most characterize a leader, while efficacy refers to the degree to which a student believes (internally) they have leadership capabilities and/or resources. I chose this definitional model as oftentimes on predominantly white college campuses students of color are not afforded a plethora of leadership roles. Thus to measure leadership development by obtaining a position of leadership in, say, a student organization, would eliminate several students from any pool. This is relevant to note since a student's self-efficacy towards leadership is just as important as that student's actual leadership competencies.

As discussed previously, many black students attending college are first generation college students. For these students there is a need to ensure that they first have a grasp on college life. Any leadership program which includes first generation college students would do well to cover topics such as navigating college courses, locating internships, understanding how internships can aid you, basic and advanced study skills, etc. While these topics may not be as useful for other students, the first generation college students in the group cannot possibly begin to delve into the more advanced training of leadership competency development if they are in jeopardy of failing classes. Even those African American students who come to college with higher GPAs will sometimes lack basic and advanced study skills needed to compete and do well at the collegiate level.

In addition to ensuring that black students are able to compete at the collegiate level in classes, additional leadership knowledge, skills and abilities would serve them well. Kodama and Dugan, in their 2013 study, found that once leadership data is disaggregated by race, different items were found to be statistically significant for different groups. For African American students, community service, leadership positions in student organizations, student affairs mentoring, socio-cultural conversations with their peers, and personal beliefs about how well they function as a member of a racial group all led to a greater sense of the student's self-efficacy towards leadership abilities (Kodama and Dugan 2013). Thus for black female students there appears to be a correlation between identity formation and leadership self-efficacy. One could seek to determine whether a positive identity formation should lead to a positive outlook on the student's own abilities to lead and capacity for leadership. Additionally, in order to build and develop leadership skills, seminars or workshops should be provided that discuss communication skills, navigating potentially difficult conversations,[8] public speaking, working in teams, networking, etc. In addition to this, Kodama and Dugan found that community service correlates as a positive predictor for African American students' leadership self-efficacy. Thus, one should also strongly consider having any black female group to participate in some form of community service. Lastly, an integral part of any leadership development plan for young black female college students is to ensure that an array of background experiences are represented in selecting and recommending students to campus leadership positions. Group leaders should be careful to not overload one student, but rather should provide leadership opportunities to several different black female students in an effort to present the vast array and beautiful diversity captured within the black community.

A Search for Identity: Identity Development

Studies reveal that African American students enrolled at traditionally white institutions of higher learning encounter numerous instances of

---

8. Cross-race contact can also aid with the practicing of the skill, learning how to respond to difficult conversations.

racial micro-aggressions and overt racism. A student who encounters numerous smaller events on a daily, weekly, monthly, and extended basis can begin to show outward signs of stress (fatigue even) on the physical, emotional, and psychological health of a student resulting in what the literature refers to as Racial Battle Fatigue. "Racial Battle Fatigue addresses the physiological and psychological strain exacted on racially marginalized groups and the amount of energy lost dedicated to coping with racial micro-aggressions and racism" (Smith, Allen, and Danley 2007). Black students need a place where they are able to process negative interactions among others who share similar experiences. Students need a space where they are able to dialogue about coping strategies, discuss possible solutions with university administrators, and receive aid in refocusing their time and energy back to their own matriculation, growth, and development.

Sorting out one's identity is a journey that may very well last a lifetime. I do not advocate that a person have their identity entirely configured and worked out by the time they graduate from college, nor even that developing one's identity should be the main focus of their college experience. The argument being made here is that providing a space, place, and educational materials to encourage black female college students in formulating their identity can create a buffer for the student in the other experiences they may have in a predominantly white environment. Jones and McEwen's 2000 study found that many students are working through multiple identities often involving multiple oppressions. They conclude that educators and student development personnel should encourage students to consider different aspects of their self-identity. Students in their study wanted to be accepted and treated according to their own self-identified identity. The problem for many black female college students attending predominantly white Christian colleges is at what point will they work on developing this strong sense of self?

The popular discussion at many Christian colleges is to turn your focus to developing your "Christian identity." That Christian identity is then discussed and described as being much more important than a racial, ethnic, or gendered identity. This rhetoric is reminiscent of a colorblind ideology, which allows those who feel uncomfortable discussing issues of race to try their best to ignore race while continuing to perpetuate the race-related issues that those in subordinate positions of power continue to face. Similarly, to completely ignore a person's race, socio-economic class standing, gender, etc. as having a great impact on their identity is like attempting to ignore "color," which is one of the harshest forms of racism in our supposed post-racial society. A person's race, class, gender, etc. impacts their identity in one of two ways: 1) It affects how they see themselves, their internal identification, and 2) It affects how they are received, perceived, and responded to in society, or their external identification.

One major issue with the idea of being colorblind is that we actually do see color. When one says they are being colorblind they are attempting to ignore the color that they see. This fails to address aggressive behavior that some members of society experience based on their race (or color) at the micro level of interaction. It also ignores and invalidates the systemic layers of oppression that are felt by groups of historically marginalized people at the macro level of analysis. Many liken colorblindness to the most threatening form of racism (see Bonnilla-Silva 2007 for a full discussion of the tenants of colorblind racism). In this same regard, taking a position that one's religious/spiritual identity trumps all other facets of a person's identity formation is problematic for several reasons.

As discussed regarding one's race or ethnicity, this stance presumes that a Eurocentric expression of Christianity is the appropriate one. It fails to address the idea that there are many different facets of Christian expression that are not unbiblical or heretical. What's often stated with this stance is that one is attempting to locate and follow the "biblical" way of doing things as if it is ever possible to completely remove one's social location (socio-economic status, racial and cultural idioms, etc.) from a reading of the text. By the mere fact that a human being is reading and interpreting the text, the experiences and circumstances of that human being are brought into the reading and interpretation. Additionally, the colorblind stance fails to deal with 1) The aggressive behaviors that a person experiences in society based on the multiple oppressions they might face and 2) The ways in which differences and inequality based on race, class status, gender, etc. are woven into the structure of our society.

For black women in society there are multiple oppressions, what Patricia Hill Collins refers to as a matrix of domination,[9] with which one must learn to contend. Providing a space for these college students to explore the intricacies of not only a racial, cultural, and ethnic identity, but also a gender identity, religious identity, socio-economic class identity,

---

9. In her landmark work *Black Feminist Thought*, Collins refers to the intersection of the different ways in which black women experience inequality in society (oppression, omission, suppression and exclusion) as the matrix of domination.

sexual identity, etc. is needed. These students need a space to explore how these different identities intersect, interact, and interplay with one another in society. Lastly, being able to connect with other women who are also attempting to figure their way through these issues will provide a sense of community, belonging, and acceptance for these students which will have short term (remaining at the Christian college and completing their degree) and long term (learning how to have positive relationships with other women who share similar life traits) positive effects on their overall outcome. In seeking to develop a model for black female students to begin a conversation about their identity, one should have workshops/seminars that discuss and describe the different racial and ethnic identity models, being keenly aware to present models that include girls with a multiracial identity and that address micro-aggressions, gender discourse and identity, sex-role stereotypes, etc. Discussions should be sure to provide a multitude of examples of women from differing walks of life and should also take care to discuss how these identities intersect and operate together.

Spiritual Development

African American female students attending Christian TWIs are often expending additional energy dealing with constant racial and gendered micro-aggressions. They are focused on disproving stereotypical controlling images of black women. They work hard to be the best in their class, they are constantly fielding questions about their hair, their speech, their clothing, the other black people they happen to know on campus, etc., and they are battling to feel "normal." In the midst of this battling, coping, and attempts at assimilation their own spiritual development can be neglected.

Just as most other students at Christian colleges, an assumption can be made that these women have decided to attend a college that will not only challenge them intellectually but will also engage them spiritually. Looking to sort out how one's faith connects with their everyday life is uniformly an important topic at Christian colleges. A problem can emerge for the student, however, when subtle experiences of racism and/or difference are not explained, confronted, or even discussed in their theology courses. It is the practice of some theologians to discuss additional forms of theology (ethnic theologies) only to point out how they are wrong. But if described properly, attempts at making theological sense of a racialized world can be healing to a person of color, explaining some of the anguish they feel deep inside. Further, the notion that one form of theology is the "biblical" form asserts that other forms of theology are not biblical. This places the discussion into a dichotomy of right vs. wrong rather than as multiple experiences which are all right (so to speak) but reflect the life experiences of different people in the world.

Love and Talbot (1999) argue for five interrelated propositions to spiritual development in the collegiate student. They focus on the internal process of seeking personal authenticity, recognizing concerns beyond oneself, developing a greater connectedness to self and others, deriving meaning and purpose in one's life, and gaining an increased openness to exploring one's relationship with God. Speck and Hoppe (2007) focus their discussion of spiritual development on three main areas. These are the student's inner quest for purpose and meaning, spiritual activities that a student may use during their quest (meditation, reflection, and contemplation) and lastly, the student's development of a meaningful philosophy. This third area is accomplished through considering profound questions. A combination of these two definitions can be used to ground a plan for student spiritual development. The thoughtful process in which a student engages in a search to discover meaning, connect more fully with God, struggle with profound questions, gain a greater sense of personal authenticity, and cultivate a concern for others beyond oneself is what should be sought after for black female students on predominantly white college campuses.

The idea of spiritual development is especially important for students who may find the spiritual culture of their predominantly white Christian college foreign. While their white counterparts will locate comfort in being able to join in with worship songs during their first chapel at the university, for example, students who come from a different church background may find this experience their first hint at being different, not fitting in, and not belonging in the setting. Additionally, an African American spirituality encompasses not only intellectual spiritual practices (e.g., contemplation, meditation) but also includes cultural practices (ethnic identity, church and family) life adversities, faith in God, and a belief in divine intervention (see Newlin, Knafl, and Melkus 2002). This particularly includes a surrendering prayer, or prayer in which problems are surrendered or turned over to God. In seeking to ensure that black female students fully develop spiritually during their matriculation in a

Christian college, one should make it a point to address topics of spiritual practices (contemplation, mediation, prayer) spiritual maturity (hearing from and growing in relationship with God) struggling with profound questions, being authentic with Christ, facing adversities in life, and building a concern for others. One should never shy away from confronting issues of inequality in society, or the historical treatment of people of African descent around the world, or other social issues. Lastly, one should be sure to include, incorporate, and infuse the essence of African American spirituality (musical traditions, surrendering prayer, and cultural practices). Ultimately, a student's spiritual development can aid the student in combining all facets of their selves into a single identity.

Creating Safe Spaces for Black Female College Students

As outlined in this chapter, safe spaces for black female students are not only helpful but necessary in an effort to aid the growth and development of the students attending traditionally white Christian colleges. Just as Sojourner Truth was unafraid of stepping out onto her own path and shining light onto the realities of the intersections of multiple oppressions that women of color often face, these students need a safe place to cultivate their own voice in these institutions of higher learning so that they too can gain the confidence, opportunity, and self-efficacy needed to make their voices heard in society. While the notion of a "safe space" has been discussed as problematic in educational literature (*see* Barrett 2010) what's called for in this writing is an co-curricular space in which black female college students are able to work towards developing their multi-layered identities, free to express themselves (thoughts, beliefs, opinions, creativity, and experiences) and challenged to take risks.

Black female students encounter a campus climate wrought with multiple oppressions, fighting against controlling images of black women that their administrators, professors and peers subconsciously hold in tandem during student interactions. They strive to achieve academic excellence, sometimes being the first in their families to make such strides, while having to navigate micro-aggressions. They seek spiritual development in environments where a Eurocentric model of Christianity is exalted as the only and/or best cultural representation of their faith. But as Sojourner Truth charged a room full of women's rights activists in 1850, aren't they also our students? While we tend to have a focus on multiculturalism, cling to notions of colorblindness, seek to travel across the ocean for missionary purposes, and challenge our students to diversity, we sometimes miss the necessity of producing ethnically diverse students who are comfortable in their own skin. This includes students being able to critically examine and develop their identities (racial, ethnic, cultural, gender, etc.) in a space where critical analysis, risk taking, and acceptance of their experience is not a battle but is celebrated. This is not a call for complete separatism and a lack of cross-racial contact: for the student of color on a predominately white campus this notion would be impossible. Rather, this is a call for the creation of spaces and places where a person can work towards determining who they are and become confident in that, while also developing necessary skills that will aid them in broader society, both on the academic campus and beyond.

7

Erasing Race: Racial Identity and Theological Anthropology

Dr. Vincent Bacote, Wheaton College

Introduction

"YOU DON'T SEE ME," he said. With these words a close group of Christian college graduates (and their wives) found themselves plunged into the depths of a complex and difficult conversation about "race." Seated around a campfire, this was not an easy conversation, nor was it readily apparent what this African American male meant when he told his good friends that he believed they did not *really* see him. What did this statement mean? From the speaker's perspective, it meant that although he had been in this circle of friends for nearly twenty years, he had arrived at the perception that his friends only knew him in a partial way because they were unable to see him as a black man. His main point was that there was an effort required to acknowledge some very important and central aspects of his identity, and that these old friends were essentially blinded by the glare of normative whiteness. It was very difficult for him to say this, and even more of a challenge for his friends whose initial response was characterized by hurt, rage, and rejection.

This anecdote is not an isolated incident, but one example of the difficulties that remain for evangelicals as a result of the ongoing effects of the modern concept of race. As Ed Gilbreath observes,

> What really troubles some black evangelicals . . . is that their white counterparts don't even realize how much their "whiteness" affects their faith. After confessing that she was "sick and tired of racial reconciliation," my young friend who wrote me . . . added "The white Christians I encounter often display a

shocking provincialism—a real naiveté about the world around
them. Frankly it is as if they are stunned to find out that their
cultural, political, and religious frame of reference is not the
only one." (Gilbreath 2008, 18)

Gilbreath then explains the title of his book, *Reconciliation Blues*: it is
about "the loneliness of being 'the only black,' the frustration of being
expected to represent your race but being stifled when you try, the hidden pain of being invited to the table but shut out from meaningful decisions about that table's future. These 'reconciliation blues' are about the
despair of knowing that it's still business as usual, even in the friendly
context of Christian fellowship and ministry" (Gilbreath 2008, 19). As
the initial anecdote reveals, these frustrating episodes often occur in
a manner where the problematic dimensions are barely apparent, if at
all, to those in the majority. The white members in the circle of friends
were unaware that they needed to "see" anything beyond what they
already knew of their friend, and once the topic was broached around
the campfire, it was clearly a struggle for all involved. More broadly,
the repeated efforts to facilitate constructive conversations and create
welcoming environments in evangelical settings (whether institutional
or simply interpersonal) often become exhausting, at times leading
minorities of various backgrounds to migrate to other communities
beyond evangelical shores.

Minority inhabitants of the evangelical world often find themselves
traversing a difficult path in a context that emphasizes "biblical" Christianity. In settings where the Bible is received as God's word and there
are various statements of fidelity to divine revelation, the expectation is
that such environments could be contexts of fellowship where Christians
live together in mutual love and understanding across differences of race,
culture and ethnicity. In spite of this hope and expectation, frustrating
events like the anecdote above occur and the dissonance is often so great
that frustration and exhaustion often ensue. What should we do? I propose the following: in order for evangelicals to make significant progress
in negotiating the relationships between different persons (often categorized by "race") it will be necessary to erase "race." The modern concept
of race is fiction that operates as a social and cultural reality, and as a
result "whiteness" is the normative standard for humanity. This "normal"
view of humans makes "race" a category that obscures and blinds many
of us from truly "seeing" those who are non-white; we could even say
that the modern conception of race itself "erases" vital dimensions of the

humanity of those not identified as white. Such persons are perceived as deficient in some way by virtue of their "otherness," while at the same time a respectful recognition of this otherness is often absent. Moreover, race facilitates the construction of false idols that correspond to a "color" scheme. Evangelicals can take the lead in one of the greatest efforts of Christian faithfulness and social transformation if they participate in the difficult but necessary work of erasing race with the help of the core doctrines of creation and redemption with a particular emphasis on the implications for our theological anthropology. Before we get to the vital biblical and theological work that may propel us forward, we must first spend some time understanding our context.

The Myth of Race

It is valid to ask, why this proposal about "Erasing Race"? It can certainly seem I am proposing that we reject something we all recognize as a legitimate part of our identity. Yet, it is this assumption which needs to be challenged. We are born into a world where "race" occupies a prominent place in the mythology of the modern West, and it has a unique expression in the United States where we have the idea of an "American." Myths are grand stories people tell in order to frame and understand their world and which may contain true and or false elements. Most of us perceive "race" as a simple matter of fact. In many cases where one is asked to identify themselves, race is one characteristic that we use as a definitive category. Yet, the manner in which we use the term "race" has not always existed.

One of the chief reasons for erasing race is because it is a fabrication. It is a public fiction that seems to have a scientific basis, but this is a falsehood. Steve Fenton helpfully explains:

> The error base of the concept of race lies in the fact that for much of the 19th and 20th centuries the term race was taken to mean discrete divisions of humankind with visible characteristics marking those divisions. This classification was combined with the idea that races had characteristics of temperament, ability and moral nature, which constituted a racial inheritance. Race was seen to be a "natural"—in scientific terms "biological" —grouping of human populations and the primary determinant of civilization. (Fenton 1999, 66)

A good early example of this can be seen in the classification scheme of eighteenth century scientist Carl Linnaeus: "Each race had certain characteristics that he considered endemic to individuals belonging to it. Native Americans were choleric, red, straightforward, eager and combative. Africans were phlegmatic, black, slow, relaxed and negligent. Asians were melancholic, yellow, inflexible, severe and avaricious. Europeans were sanguine and pale, muscular, swift, clever and inventive" (Datatorch. com 2009).[1] Such classifications can lead us to almost regard the various "races" as different species given the level of distinctions. These classifications are not as objective as they might have seemed to Linnaeus, however. Eloise Hiebert Meneses explains: "Of course, the problem with Linnaeus's taxonomy of people was that it was based thoroughly in what is now called ethnocentrism, that is, interpreting and evaluating other people and their cultures with the worldview and values given to you by your own culture. Linnaeus was Swedish, and 'naturally' assumed that his own people and their ways were the most advanced" (Meneses 2007, 40). Meneses further notes that while ethnocentrism was not unique to Europeans like Linnaeus (in fact it has been common across time and people groups) the significant difference for European ethnocentrism was that it was bolstered by the world dominance of Europe under colonialism and also coincided with the emergence of modern science as a respected discipline that justified such classification schemes (Meneses 2007, 40). These kinds of theories of the inheritance of character and moral stature as connected to racial traits were based entirely on a form of speculation, yet the concept of race as linked to biology came to be regarded as simply the way things are. Today many of us take it for granted as if it has "always been this way," even though "race" was invented.

1. "People were part of Linnaeus's natural order, under the order 'anthropomorpha' in the genus 'homo.' All people were members of the same species for Linnaeus, which meant God created them to be distinct from other forms of life. There were, however, four basic 'varieties,' which meant that they had acquired some superficial differences from differing climates:
    Americanus: Reddish skin, black hair, scanty beard, obstinate, merry, regulated by custom.
    Asiaticus: Sallow skin, black hair, dark eyes, severe, greedy, covered with loose garments, ruled by opinions.
    Africanus: Black skin, black, frizzled hair, indolent, women without shame, governed by caprice.
    Europaeus: White, long, flowing hair, blue eyes, gentle, inventive, covers himself with close-fitting clothing, governed by laws." In Jackson and Weidman, *Race, Racism and Science*, 16.

If "race" is an invention, then how has this purportedly scientific classification scheme been discredited? Among the reasons are 1) the impossibility of sustaining this system of classification because the variance within the "races" was actually greater in degree than the variance between them, 2) the realization that historical factors and cultural differences better account for differences among groups of humans, and 3) that "by the middle of the twentieth century it was cruelly evident that the science of racial difference had been allied to the denial of dignity and the very right to life of 'races' perceived as lower and dispensable" (Fenton 1999, 5). Meneses points out one particular example of how this happened:

> In the United States, the anthropologist Franz Boas did much to reverse the scientific opinion on race. Boas demonstrated immigrant children were significantly taller than their own parents, indicating a strong influence on stature from nutrition. In 1940, he published *Race, Language, and Culture*, arguing that biology does not determine culture, and that the various cultures of the world are to be equally valued. In addition, over time, the hard facts from studies of anatomy, brain size, intelligence, and genetics just kept contradicting the idea of race. So, in the end, the attempt to classify the races failed, not only due to lack of evidence but also due to the example of ample counterevidence. (Meneses 2007, 43)

While it has been discredited among some in the academy, most of us in the West still await the messenger to arrive with the official declaration that race as we know it is a grand falsehood. From the standpoint of simple observation, the deficiency of race as a classification scheme should actually be apparent. For example, I recall being a small child and wondering why people were called "black" and "white" when none of the people with those labels matched the description. Yet the classification lingers in spite of the fact that it has been discredited for over half a century. Perhaps the answer can be found in answering this question: Why would someone want to be regarded as "white" in the United States? What does "white" actually mean? Why would someone find the label desirable and worth keeping instead of something that is more true to what science tells us about the rich complexity of the human race? Obviously Linneaus's scheme gave prominence to those of European descent, to those of the Caucasian or "white" race. Why does this linger and how is it central to the crisis in this chapter's opening anecdote?

J. Kameron Carter's *Race: A Theological Account* makes an argument based on a reading of Immanuel Kant which explains how "whiteness" is established as normative and rational humanity (*see* Carter 2008, 79–121). The following quotes are illustrative:

> Functioning also as teleologically structured philosophy of history, Kant's theory of race articulates an account of the destiny the species as coinciding with the global perfection and spread of whiteness. (Carter 2008, 81)
>
> In contrast to his lengthy account of the origins of Negroes, Huns, and Hindustanis in which he is clear that they are races, Kant refers to whites with terms ranging from *Gestalt* (form) to *Abartung* (deviation) to *Schlag* (kind). As he sees it, whites are a group apart. They are a "race" that is not quite a race, the race that transcends race precisely because of its "developmental progress" (*Fortgang*) toward perfection. . . Thus, whiteness is both "now and not yet." It is a present reality, and yet it is also still moving toward and awaiting its perfection. The teleological end, which is the consummation of all things within the economic, political, and aesthetic—in short, within the structural—reality called "whiteness," is on the one hand made present and available now in white people and in white "culture." And on the other hand, it is through these white people and culture that the full reality of whiteness will globally expand to "eschatologically" encompass all things and so bring the world to perfection. (Carter 2008, 88–89)

Carter argues that Kant articulates a theological vision (ultimately a Gnostic one) that establishes "whiteness" as superior and distinct, a unique characteristic linked to advancing and achieving the goals of civilization. One interesting dimension of how this occurs is by cleaving the Jewish ethnic particularity from Jesus and reconceiving him as the ultimate rational and moral autonomous figure. This creation and, if you will, "baptism" of whiteness as the pinnacle of humanity is then woven into the fabric of the modern world.[2]

2. Carter has recently summarized this in an online magazine: "The white, western god-man is an idol that seeks to determine what is normal. It is a norm by which society governs the body politic or regulates, measures, evaluates, and indeed judges what is proper or improper, what is acceptable or suspicious citizenship. . . . Whiteness is that story that one must aspire toward if one is to be deemed a proper citizen, a proper American. Rather than being biological, then, whiteness is better understood as a kind of discipline, something one must be disciplined into and thus something one must achieve and continually accomplish within oneself.

It is important to note that Kant was not alone in conceiving whiteness as superior, as figures such as Hume, Rousseau, and Voltaire all regarded darker races as inferior.[3] Jews and blacks fare less well. The importance of the argument to this point is that it suggests that the frame for viewing other human beings became what we might call a lens of whiteness. If Kant and others were only theorizing about race but had no influence on the modern world, then this discussion of race would only be of historical interest, but this is not the case. The concept of race with "whiteness" regarded as superior has been a profound element of the modern world.[4]

George Yancy's work helps illustrate the effect of the gaze of whiteness and the effects on others (particularly those defined as "black"):

> Felt invisibility is a form of ontological and epistemic violence, a form of violence initiated through white spectatorship, a generative gazing that violates the integrity of the Black body. The white gaze defines me, skewing my own way of seeing myself. But the gaze does not "see" me, it "sees" itself (Yancy 2005, 230).
>
> Substituting the historical constructivity of whiteness for "manifest destiny," whites remain imprisoned within a space of white ethical solipsism (only whites possess needs and desires

---

"Understood in this way whiteness is a story of assimilation, a story that hails or calls out to us—especially to immigrant families. It awaits our answer to its call and through our answers (which can take the form of everyday practices like neighborhood watching, for example) we establish ourselves inside of or relate ourselves to the narrative of the proper citizen, to proper Americanness. Indeed, immigrant history in this country is the (very often violent) history of the achievement for some (and the failed achievement for others) of assimilation into the national narrative of the proper citizen." In J. Kameron Carter, "Christian Atheism: The Only Response Worth its Salt to the Zimmerman Verdict," *Religion Dispatches*, July 23, 2013, http://www.religiondispatches.org/archive/atheologies/7204/christian_atheism__the_only_response_worth_its_salt_to_the_zimmerman_verdict/.

3. For example, David Hume stated "I am apt to suspect the negroes to be naturally inferior to the whites. There scarcely ever was a civilized nation of that complexion, nor even any individual, eminent in either action or speculation. . . . Such a uniform and constant difference could not happen, in so many countries and ages, if nature had not made an original distinction between these breeds of men." David Hume, "Of National Characters" in *David Hume Selected Essays*, ed. S. Copley & A. Edgar (Oxford: Oxford University Press, 1993) 360.

4. Luke Harlow provocatively suggests that "White Supremacy was an article of faith in the United States in the era leading up to the Civil War." Luke Harlow, "Religion, Race, and the Significance of Civil War-Era Kentucky," (paper presented at the Symposium on the Civil War and Sacred Ground, Raven Foundation and Wheaton College, Wheaton, Illinois, March 17, 2012).

that are truly worthy of being respected [Sullivan 2001, 100]). It would seem that many whites would rather remain imprisoned within the ontology of *sameness*, refusing to reject the ideological structure of their identities as "superior." The call of the Other qua Other remains unheard within the space of whiteness's sameness. Locked within their self-enthralled structure of whiteness, whites occlude the possibility of developing new forms of ethical relationality to themselves and to non-whites. (Yancy 2005, 238).

Yancy[5] helps provide one possible reason for the confusion that ensued in the opening anecdote. The latent privilege of whiteness in the modern West as well as the unconscious yet functional dimension of the lens of whiteness often leads to circumstances of interpersonal engagement in which the ability to "see" others is difficult apart from discovering that the lens is at work. So it makes sense, in a way, that some of the friends could not understand what was meant by the statement "you don't see me."

More than perception (and as stated by Carter above) the modern approach to race is linked to formation of society. For example, Fenton states "white supremacist America and apartheid South Africa were both societies which were politically and legally structured by ethnic differentiation (Fenton 1999, 14). While few would deny this claim as a matter of historical record, what is more difficult for many to see is that the legacy of white supremacy remains. Some might counter that the United States is a country which has some bad racist history but now allows all to become part of the great melting pot: "Understand that America is God's Crucible, the great Melting-Pot where all the races of Europe are melting and reforming! A fig for your feuds and vendettas! Germans and Frenchmen, Irishmen and Englishmen, Jews and Russians—into the Crucible with you all! God is making the American" (Zangwill 1914).

While Zangwill only referred to Europeans, the argument today (and for decades prior) is that this metaphor refers to anyone who comes and takes advantage of the American experiment. In response, the question is who decides and defines a "normal" American? What makes us all one? What is it that erodes prior ethnic identities and produces this thing called an American? It is here where the persistence of "race" comes into play. A century ago it was very important to be regarded as "white" or "Caucasian," because that made it possible to have better access to the best

5. For more of Yancy's work, see George Yancy, *Look, A White!: Philosophical Essays on Whiteness* (Philadelphia: Temple University Press, 2012).

opportunities in the United States. While it has been a few decades since the end of Jim Crow laws and while racial discrimination is illegal, the privilege associated with whiteness lingers. If we do the thought experiment of imagining a person that is a reasonable and successful American beyond the world of sports and entertainment, there is a good chance that most of us will envision someone we label as "white." The reasons for this are more complex than stated here, but a significant factor lies in the fact that the United States is a society we could label as "racialized."

In *Divided by Faith* by Michael Emerson and Christian Smith, they define a "racialized society as *a society wherein race matters profoundly for differences in life experiences, life opportunities, and social relationships*" (Emerson and Smith 2000, 7). They indicate that one of the difficulties is that

> We tend to understand race, racism, and the form of racialization as constants rather than variables. . . . But things look different when we see that the form of racialization changes. . . . By 1955, the problems of race and the racial hierarchy had not disappeared at all. The forms had changed to be sure, but so ever-present were the problems that major social movements and upheavals resulted. These upheavals ushered in a new era of race relations in the United States—the post-Civil Rights era. Our understandings of race relations, however, remain stuck in the Jim Crow era, leading us to mistaken conclusions—racism is on the wane, and racial division and the racial hierarchy are but historical artifacts. Rather than incorrectly examine race in the United States using and old standard, we must adapt our understanding and analysis to the new, post-Civil Rights era. (Emerson and Smith 2000, 8–9)

This newer understanding helps reveal why "race" remains a dominant influence in our perception, but in newer ways. Racial practices today in the United States "(1) are increasingly covert, (2) are embedded in normal operations of institutions, (3) avoid direct racial terminology, and (4) are invisible to most Whites" (Emerson and Smith 2000, 9). It is important to note that Emerson and Smith recognize that "race" is a fiction, but they use the term because it operates as a "true" fiction as long as societies continue to function in a racialized way. Because contemporary expressions of a racialized society are often invisible, the idea that white supremacy remains as part of the fabric of society is difficult to see. Yet, our use of racial categories is itself a vestige of a frame of reference that makes "white" the standard by which others are judged, even if it is not readily apparent to us given our historical distance from the construction of race and the subterranean, lingering effects of the lens of whiteness.

Our continued use of racial categories makes it difficult for us to see others truly and makes "white" into an idol (though many are unaware of worshipping at the altar). Because of its embeddedness in our context and different forms today, it takes considerable effort to understand how "whiteness" can blind us from truly seeing each other. Yet, it is important for us to recognize how using "race" to categorize each other is misleading. When we describe each other according to race, we can mistakenly think it enables us to understand people on the basis of their skin color, suggesting a correlation between melanin and culture, with a latent core assumption that "white" is the standard by which others are judged. The result of viewing each other through the lens of race is that we have a myopic perspective. Our vision is skewed and we fail to recognize the blind spots that come with such a lens. In relationships like the one referred to at the beginning, the white friends thought that they knew their African American friend intimately, but they had never considered how race was a factor in what they could or could not see in their friend. To the extent that those of us who identity as evangelicals fail to question how race handicaps our vision, we will continue to struggle mightily to make notable and lasting changes in this area.

Erasing Race, Seeing More Clearly

It was important to spend some time on our context because we will not be able to do our theological work properly if we do not have some idea about the challenge that is before us. I propose that we erase "race" because it is unhelpful for truly understanding other human beings. By "erase" I do not mean that we should completely abandon everything in the modern concept race. Just as when one erases pencil, we should keep the "shadow" of race because understanding biological variation among humans can be helpful in areas like medicine. How do we proceed?

First, we must recognize that the modern concept of race is insufficient theologically; it fails to do justice to a proper theology of creation, particularly in our theological anthropology. One irony here is that theological anthropology provides us with an important theological basis for erasing race, yet this doctrine can also be used in a way that leaves us in our current circumstance. For some, the fact that humans are made in the image and likeness of God means that all they need to see is another human like themselves. Here we discover an irony where sometimes willful and sometime latent self-deception leads Christians to deny that a distorted dimension of their theology is being used to keep in place the distorting dimension of the modern concept of race.[6] The challenge lies in how our understanding of humans as created in the image of God facilitates *truly* seeing others rather than providing a reason for leaving the modern gaze through the lens of whiteness in place. To move forward, we need to understand what it means for humans to be bearers of the divine image.

Scripture reveals to us that human beings are God's handiwork, created in his image. Genesis 1:26–27 presents humans as the pinnacle of God's creation and tells us that we are made "in the image and likeness of God." A survey of systematic theology texts along with biblical commentaries will reveal that "image and likeness" (or the theological term *imago Dei*) have been interpreted to mean "mind" (or reason) "soul," "original righteousness," "relationality" and the function of "dominion."[7] Though debates may continue about arriving at an exhaustive definition of the meaning of the *imago Dei*, it is fair to conclude that perhaps all of these labels help us arrive at an understanding of the richness of this essential human characteristic. Nonna Verna Harrison highlights an important dimension of the image tied to the language of dominion in her explanation of the image:

> The word "dominion" speaks of royalty, which is a facet of the divine image in every human person. Royalty involves (1) dignity and splendor, and (2) a legitimate sovereignty rooted in one's very being. . . . Because everyone is made in the image of God, and because this image defines what it means to be human, people are fundamentally equal, regardless the differences in wealth, education, and social status. The church preached this

6. As Cornelius Plantinga notes, "Corrupt and self-serving uses of religion naturally follow false ideas of religion and of religion's God, but, alarmingly, they may also follow true ones." The truth that humans are all made in the divine image is often readily used to keep us from contending with the difficulties posed by race. See Cornelius Plantinga, *Not the Way It's Supposed to Be: A Breviary of Sin* (Grand Rapids: Eerdmans, 1995) 109.

7. A helpful overview can be found in J. Richard Middleton's *The Liberating Image: The Imago Dei in Genesis 1* (Grand Rapids: Brazos, 2005) 15–42.

countercultural message in the ancient world and still preaches
it now. (Harrison 2010, 90–91)

Harrison goes on to highlight the fact that one emphasis in early
church theological anthropology highlighted human dignity stemming
from the understanding the *imago Dei* as royalty granted to all humans,
which extended to women, slaves and lepers. She notes that fourth century church father Gregory of Nyssa stated that the true price of a slave
is beyond any price because the slaves were also humans that bore the
image of God and are thus worth more than the whole physical world
(Harrison 2010, 103). The *imago Dei*, shared by all human beings, is truly
something we all have in common. This commonality is a basis for human dignity, the opposite of the distortions of an anthropology where the
modern idea of race reigns supreme.

Human beings have commonality, but there is also particularity.
Acts 17:26 states that we all have a common ancestor and that we are all
part of one race, humankind: "From one man he made every nation of
men, that they should inhabit the whole earth; and he determined the
times set for them and the exact places where they should live" (NIV).
This verse acknowledges that differentiation occurs, certainly, yet the
category of race is not at work.[8] Undoubtedly, from Genesis 3 onward
humans have found ways to distinguish themselves from each other and
some groups have sought to dominate and oppress others (or perhaps all
groups have, with some having greater success as oppressors). It is a normal state of affairs post-Fall. What is clear from this text and any other
that differentiates humans, however, is that the language of race that we
commonly use is absent from Scripture. The differentiation expressed in
texts such as Acts 17:26 is based on geography and what we would today
call ethnic/cultural identity. If this is true, then what categories should we
use instead of race? I suggest that we turn to Scripture and use categories
rooted in creation and redemption in order to have an anthropology that
better promotes human flourishing and enables us to "see" better.

From the standpoint of creation, the fact that humans are themselves the pinnacle of God's very good creation should be our baseline.
As stated above, humans are created in the divine image with a royal

8. Darrell Bock argues that the larger point is God's sovereignty over all nations
and that we all have in common the same creator God, a significantly different emphasis than attempts to use the emphasis on distinct nations as a means for keeping the
races separate. Darrell Bock, *Acts,* Baker Exegetical Commentary on the New Testament (Grand Rapids: Baker Academic, 2007) 566.

dimension, which provides a basis for human dignity. In Genesis 9:6, the reason for the high cost of murder is that humans are made in God's image. If the cost of murder is this high, it should further indicate to us that there is a tremendous value and worth given to all of us simply as a result of being created in the divine image, apart from associations with pigmentation, talent, culture, geography or intellect. By virtue of being divine image bearers, an image that remains in a fundamental manner post-Fall,[9] an ethical imperative emerges: all humans should be regarded in a way that indicates a regard for both the creature and the Creator. The modern conception of race yields significant inertia against this imperative; submitting to and practicing this imperative is more difficult when definitions of humans along racial categories comes (or "came with") with the stamp of approval of another authority, modern science, even though we have seen that this is actually discredited science. The modern concept of race, operating in a racialized society, produces a perspective based on a story that is different from the one given to us in Scripture. It tells us that nature has given us humans in different races, with some clearly inferior. This is a different narrative than one which compels us to begin with the belief and conviction of the tremendous value of all persons. In the process of erasing race, it is necessary that we properly identify and evaluate our modern approach, which most likely is at least partly influenced by the legacy of race, against the standard set by Scripture.

Redemption must also play a role in erasing race and grinding a new set of lenses for us. Christ, the second Adam, has come to make it possible for us to move toward the fullness of God's intent for humans to live in a way that reflects divine image-bearers. While we retain some aspect of the divine image after the Fall, texts such as Colossians 3:10 reveal that through redemption we are experiencing a renewal which includes a restoration of the fullness of the divine image.[10] In part, redemption

9. Theologians and biblical scholars debate the effects of the fall on the *imago Dei*, with some arguing that the entry of sin into the world removes the image at one extreme and at the opposite with some arguing for minimal distortion of the image. My view is similar to that of Anthony Hoekema in *Created in God's Image* where he states that the "structural" dimension of the image remains while the "functional" image is distorted though not lost. See Hoekema, *Created in God's Image* (Grand Rapids: Eerdmans, 1986) 33–65, 83–85.

10. The growth into a new humanity is a process of moving into the reality that is already part of our identity as a result of Christ's work, and God provides the power behind this change, but this does not imply passivity. See David Pao, *Colossians and*

includes the gift of our full humanity (not immediate perfection, but the participation in a transformative process). If this gift is given to us in redemption, we have to embrace this truth in a way that begins to inform our perception of each other. Then we must ask: does the renewal of the divine image in redemption inform our perception of each other or does our sight remain tinted by the lens of race?

Another aspect of redemption is that God is making one people for himself. As God's people, the church, we are together citizens of God's kingdom, members of God's household, priests, and children of God. This is common to all who are redeemed. We are part of the same family. Is this aspect of doctrine an element that shapes our lens? Given the weaknesses in evangelical ecclesiology, it is not surprising if this has not had significant impact on our view of each other. This is one area where the familiar Romans 12:2 text provides light: our minds and thus our vision must be transformed if we are to resist ongoing conformity of our vision to the lens given to us by the categories of race. The redeemed, transformed mind ought to be one with a new, transformed and transforming vision of humanity, certainly beginning in the church and radiating outward.

In our articulation of a redeemed humanity, it is important for us to keep creation and redemption together if we are to erase race and begin to see each other with increasing clarity. The common identity in Christ that we have in redemption does not mean that we "only see each other in Christ" and ignore our cultural particularities. Instead, the centrality of our identity in Christ relativizes but does not obliterate our cultural identities. The best aspects of our cultural identities are expressions of the beauty and complexity of humanity created in the divine image, expressions that we should appreciate and learn about as a means of giving God glory. In this regard, Abraham Kuyper argues the following regarding the complexity of the divine image:

> For good reason, therefore, we pose the question whether the creation of man in God's image does not have significance vastly greater than what has been acknowledged up until now in individual terms. The answer lies in the simple observation that the image of God is certainly much too rich a concept to be realized

Philemon, Zondervan Exegetical Commentary on the New Testament (Grand Rapids: Zondervan, 2012) 226–27. Also see Douglas Moo, *The Letters to Colossians and Philemon*, The Pillar New Testament Commentary (Grand Rapids: Eerdmans, 2008) 268–73.

in one single person. In looking at parents and children we can sometimes see facial features and character traits of the parents to be spread out over the several children in varying proportions but always in such a way that none displays them in their fullness. How much more do we not have to confess that the image of the Eternal Being, if we may so put it, is much too full and rich to be reproduced *in one individual.* Do we not come closer to the truth by saying that the bearer of the full multifaceted image of God is not the individual person but *our entire human race?* Christ is *the* image of the invisible God since in him all the treasures of wisdom have been hidden, but can that be said in the same sense of any one of us? It can be said that the whole image of God was germinally concentrated in Adam as head of our entire race, but only in the sense that he carried the whole human race in his loins. Is it not true then that, not individually but socially, the image of God can be understood in all its dimensions only if we look at what the immensely rich development of our entire race permits us to see of it? (Kuyper 1998)[11]

Humans as divine image bearers *together* reveal the fullness of God's image. By implication, we impoverish ourselves if we elevate one group over another as if that group is comprised of better or more complete image bearers than others.

From the standpoint of the culmination of redemption, if we consider the picture we are given in Revelation 7:9, we see a diverse multitude that makes up the people of God. Though they are all wearing white robes, the text does not suggest that their ethnic particularity is eliminated by virtue of being redeemed (*see* Matthews and Park 2011, 192–195). If we also consider the glory of the nations that comes into the kingdom in Revelation 21:24, it speaks to the wealth of goodness that is produced by the many cultures in the world. Thus, when we look at each other, our aim is not a Gnostic denial of our particularity, but an

11. This idea is not unique to Kuyper, as his contemporary Herman Bavinck held the same view. Hoekema also states "Whatever great artists, scientists, philosophers, and the like have added to our store of knowledge, art, and technological achievements reflects the greatness of the God who has endowed humankind with all these gifts. We could even put it this way: whatever is in God—his virtues, his wisdom, his perfections—finds its analogy and likeness in man, thought in a finite and limited form" (Hoekema, 100). Bavinck: "The image of God is much too rich for it to be fully realized in a single human being, however richly gifted that human being may be. It can only be somewhat unfolded in its depth and riches in a humanity counting billions of members." Herman Bavinck, *In the Beginning: Foundations of Creation Theology*, edited by John Bolt, translated by John Vriend (Grand Rapids: Eerdmans, 1999) 212–13.

appreciation of the richness of our diversity centered in Christ that enables us to better regard all of us who are created in the divine image. The lens of redemption does not make us colorblind, but properly sensitive to the kaleidoscopic reality before us.

Conclusion

What is the end result? If we erase race, we remove a major impediment to addressing one of the greatest scandals of the church: the inability of Christians to live up to their identity as one people of God rather than as cousins who have an agreement to see each other on special occasions but to otherwise ignore each other. Erasing the distorted perspective of race and putting on lenses ground by the deep realities of theological anthropology rooted in creation and redemption will help us to begin to truly see each other and have a commitment to each other that models full obedience to the first and second greatest commandments. This process of erasure is not to be mistaken for the notion of ignoring our particularity, but is instead altering our vision so that incidents like the opening anecdote are reduced (ideally rendered impossible for Christians). Clearly, what I propose here expresses a conviction and confidence that Biblical and theological truths have the capacity to counter and overcome deep cultural and social realities. The change I envision relies on both theological truths and divine power that lead to actual concrete realities in the lives of individuals and further, in the society that is the church, and hopefully outside the church as well. One significant result of erasing race is that it will help us seek the flourishing of all humans. For this to become reality, evangelicals must be committed to a long, difficult process of transformation. To use two metaphors, erasing race is almost like an exorcism, and we must cast out this demon that has possessed us; we must let the scales fall from our eyes so we can see each other, and truly love each other as God has commanded. Then we might imagine that in situations like those in the opening anecdote, each person around the campfire will be an intrigued participant who wants to know more and more about the beautiful human complexity they see all around.

8

"An Open Door and a Welcome Hand": Lewis Garnet Jordan's Ethiopian Vision

Dr. Eric Michael Washington, Calvin College

ON NOVEMBER 24, 1921, Lewis Garnet Jordan, corresponding secretary of the Foreign Mission Board of the National Baptist Convention, USA, Inc. (NBC) resigned his post after serving for a little more than twenty-five years. Jordan assumed the office of corresponding secretary in February 1896 a mere four months prior to the official and legal sanctioning of racial segregation in the American South owing to the Supreme Court's decision in the landmark case of *Plessy v. Ferguson*. This period is known as "the nadir of the Negro's status in American society" as described by African American historian Rayford Logan (1997, 52). Though Jordan worked and thought during a bleak period in African American history, he spearheaded the effort of the NBC in expanding its missionary presence in West, Central, and southern Africa as it sent eighty-seven men and women into those African mission fields.

Though historically overshadowed by his contemporary Bishop Henry McNeal Turner, Lewis Garnet Jordan was an influential proponent of African missions, Ethiopianism, and emigrationism. This chapter argues that Lewis Garnet Jordan's vision for African American missions in Africa centered on his strong desire to obey Jesus Christ's commission to preach the gospel to all nations, and his belief that the late nineteenth century and early-twentieth century was God's chosen time for African redemption. Jordan clung to the belief that God had prepared African Americans especially to be agents of African redemption. Prior to Jordan's career as leader of the Foreign Mission Board of the NBC, other African American Protestants had been proponents of a theology called

Ethiopianism. By the middle of the nineteenth century, African American missionaries and colonizationists such as Alexander Crummell and West Indian-born Edward Blyden were the major proponents of this theology. Their thought influenced African American Baptists, Jordan included. Jordan's thought, captured in his historical, autobiographical, and editorial writings, represents a continuation of this 19th century theology containing a strong evangelical orthodoxy. Jordan believed that there was no disconnect between a solid and unapologetic Ethiopianism and Protestantism.

Since the Revolutionary Era in America and in the Atlantic World, literate Christians of African descent pondered the question of their enslavement and Christianization. Ethiopianism developed as a result of their question. Historian Wilson J. Moses defines Ethiopianism as

> the effort of the English-speaking black or African person to view his past enslavement and present cultural dependency in terms of the broader history of civilization. It serves to remind him that this present scientific technological civilization, dominated by Western Europe for a scant four hundred years, will go under certainly—like all the empires of the past. It expresses the belief that the tragic racial experience has profound historical value, that it has endowed the African with moral superiority and made him a seer. (1978, 160–61)

Taking Moses' definition further, English-speaking Christians of African descent in the New World had to situate themselves within not only the "broader history of civilization," but also the larger narrative of redemptive history. Just as Israel was God's chosen people in the Old Testament, people of African descent comprised the elect under the New Testament. One chief characteristic of Ethiopianism is the nexus between the history of world civilizations and a biblical understanding of God's dealings with the nations. For Raboteau, African American Christians peered back at Ethiopia and Egypt as representative of the "glorious African past" (1995, 43). He writes that "Nineteenth-century blacks needed to reclaim for themselves a civilized African past in order to refute the charge that they were inherently inferior" (Raboteau 1995, 43). According to university professor and the former historian of the NBC Wilson Fallin, "Millenial Ethiopianism, which flourished among many African American Christians around the turn of the 19th century, predicted a future golden age in which black people around the world would rise to a significant role in history" (2007, 99).

African-descended Christians at this time connected this "future golden age" for African peoples with biblical prophecy: "Princes shall come out of Egypt: Ethiopia shall soon stretch out her hands unto God" (Psalm 68:31, KJV). In biblical usage, "Ethiopia" represented more than the kingdom of Abyssinia, but according to the theological comprehension of African American and other African-descended Christians, it referred to all Africans. Christians of the African Diaspora viewed themselves as chosen by God to play a vital role in the fulfillment of this prophecy.

Though many African American clergy embraced Ethiopianism as the theological basis for African redemption, theologian Edward Wheeler labels them accommodationists. By this he means that these clergymen accepted the dominant view of American civilization as the norm. According to Wheeler, "They accepted prevailing American standards of moral and ethical behavior, adopted the American political and economic system" (1986, 1). For Wheeler, this meant that these men were also visionaries in that they envisioned the African American potential as living as "equals rather than subordinates" in American society (1986, 1). Owing to this vision, these clergymen employed pejorative language in describing Africans.

By the middle of the nineteenth century, Alexander Crummell and Edward Blyden were the major proponents of this theology. Since both men had ministerial careers that stretched into the late nineteenth century, their thought formed the immediate context for Jordan's Ethiopianism. After returning to the United States in 1877 after serving in Liberia for twenty-four years, Crummell preached a sermon in which he expressed the connection between Ethiopianism and civilization. In the sermon, Crummell noted that civilization had come to West Africa through Christianity. He stated:

> For civilization, at numerous places, as well in the interior as on the coast, has displaced ancestral heathenism; and the standard of the Cross, uplifted on the banks of its great rivers, at large and important cities, and in the great seats of commercial activity, shows that the Heralds of the Cross have begun the conquest of the conquest for their glorious King. (1992, 200–201)

In Crummell's mind, through the proclamation of the gospel by African Americans, West Africans would gladly receive civilization as they assume their rightful place with other peoples of the world. This implies that Christian evangelism in Africa had to promote notions of what Americans believed was civilized behavior. Such a view intimates African American superiority in relation to native-born Africans. Such sentiments viewed African cultures as deficient and in desperate need of reform. For African peoples to grasp their destined place of superiority it meant that they had to drape themselves in the garb of American civilization while casting off their native cultures.

The other major Ethiopianist who influenced African American Christians was the Danish West Indian-born Edward Blyden. A little less radical than Crummell, Blyden's Ethiopianism was just as optimistic and grounded in scripture. He definitely believed that during the middle of the 19th century the time was ripe for African American Christians to engage in missionary work in Africa. One speech published in Blyden's *Christianity, Islam, and the Negro Race* exemplifies this belief. In the speech entitled "Ethiopia Stretching Out Her Hands to God: or Africa's Service to the World," Blyden holds that the term Ethiopia as it appears in Holy Scripture means the whole continent of Africa. Blyden writes, "It is pretty well established now, however, that by Ethiopia, is meant the continent of Africa, and by Ethiopians, the great race who inhabit the country" (1994, 130). Blyden quotes from *Smith's Bible Dictionary* and Herodotus to assert that biblical references to Ethiopians referred to black peoples. He further contends that these Africans, whether from West Africa, or East Africa, had communication and contact with Asia. This contact went back to the days of Abraham and Moses (Blyden 1994, 130–1).

At the time of this speech, Blyden claimed that every ethnic group on the continent of Africa was "stretching out" its hands to God. From this, he states that all Africans even in their traditional and local religions recognized the existence of a "Supreme Being." This was a segment of Blyden's application of Psalm 68:31. He further identifies the task of the Christian missionary: it was "to declare to them that Being whom they ignorantly worship" (1994, 132). Though there is no hard evidence in which Jordan quotes Blyden's writings and published speeches, the tone of the latter resonates in the former's work. That should be no surprise since Jordan knew Blyden personally.

Though African American Baptists tended to adopt Ethiopianism, they were also firm in their Baptist faith. As evangelicals, they held to the authority and sufficiency of the Scriptures, orthodox beliefs in the Trinity, the incarnation, the substitutionary atonement of Christ, and the resurrection of Christ among other doctrines all summarized in the *New*

Hampshire Declaration of Faith written in 1833 also referred to as the "Articles of Faith." Jordan's editorial writings in the *Mission Herald*, the monthly organ of the Foreign Mission Board Jordan founded in 1897, reveal both his Ethiopianism and evangelicalism.

Lewis Garnet Jordan, the person who helped to establish the NBC on the various African mission fields, was born into slavery in Lauderdale County, Mississippi somewhere between the towns of Meridian and Enterprise in eastern Mississippi near the Alabama border according to his account in his autobiography. Though Jordan offered his readers no month or year for his birth, it was during the late antebellum period arguably in the mid-1850s. This is ascertained because Jordan describes his experience of accompanying his master who fought in the Civil War. Jordan performed menial tasks in the nearby Confederate camp. It was during the unrest of this time that Jordan and his mother made their escape out of the clutches of slavery taking advantage of the situation when Union troops came to occupy Meridian and the surrounding areas (Jordan n.d., 7–8, 11; see Harvey 1997, 188).

After becoming a freeperson and being harbored within a Union camp, Jordan began his education. He relates an interesting story regarding his name at this juncture. He writes that he had no name (at least one that he knew of or could recollect) before escaping slavery only answering to "Nig." When he began classes for "contrabands" led by Mary Reeves from Ohio, he had to name himself. He remembered that one kind solider who had given him a pair of pants was named Lewis so he chose that to be his first name. Later he added Garnet and Jordan as his other names (Jordan n.d., 12–13).

A bit later during this period of his young life, Jordan's life took a drastic and monumental turn. While attending a Baptist revival meeting, Jordan experienced the "new birth." He submitted to believer's baptism, and would remain a committed Baptist for the rest of his life. He began to preach the gospel at sixteen or seventeen, and received his preaching license in September 1873 at a Baptist church in Davis Bend. A little over a year later Jordan received ordination as a Baptist minister in November 1874 in Cottonwood, Louisiana near Lake Providence, Louisiana. The next year (1875) Jordan began his pastoral ministry serving a church in Yazoo City, Mississippi. Sensing the need to receive a formal religious education, Jordan enrolled in Roger Williams University in Nashville, Tennessee in 1879 (Jordan n.d., 18–19).

For southern African American Baptists the period of Reconstruction was a period of a nearly mass exodus from bi-racial churches. Historian Paul Harvey writes that the Civil War "revolutionized" church life
for African American Baptists with the fruit of this revolution being their
institutionalization (1997, 11–12). In the wake of emancipation, one of
the first steps African American Baptists made toward realizing their social freedom was to leave their bi-racial churches and organize their own
independent churches, district associations, and state conventions. The
1860s and 1870s witnessed a blossoming of African American Baptist
denominationalism with former slaves grasping on to church offices and
powerful positions outside of the local church moderating district associations and presiding over state conventions. At the time of Jordan's
conversion and early ministry in African American Baptist churches, he
was part of a wave of independence consistent with the newly achieved
emancipation from slavery.[1]

The waning of African American civil rights in the South also began
to occur as Jordan assumed pastoral authority. Southern African Americans had begun to experience social and political backlash resulting from
betrayal by the Republican Party in specific and by the federal government in general in the aftermath of the Compromise of 1877. Logan assessed this betrayal by writing, "While all the Republicans uttered pious
platitudes about the denial to Negroes of rights guaranteed to them by
the Constitution and laws of the United States, they did virtually nothing to protect those rights" (1997, 12). The curtailing of civil rights to
southern African Americans caused a new type of nationalism to rise
among independent churches. Baptists sought to chart their own course
through efforts at national unity and sending missionaries to Africa. According to Montgomery, nineteenth-century African American nationalism "typically manifested itself either in a break away from the control
of external authority or in efforts to unify people who shared a common
culture but were disunited politically and economically" (Montgomery
1993, 224; Harvey 1997, 45). This description is apt in relation to the
activity of African American Baptist church leaders as they sought to

1. Much has been writing regarding the organization of independent African
American Baptist churches, district associations, and state conventions in the South
during Reconstruction. See Woodson, *The Negro Church*; Fitts, *History of Black Baptists*; Fallin, *Uplifting the People*; and William E. Montgomery, *Under Their Own Vine
and Fig Tree: The African American Church in the South 1865–1900* (Baton Rouge, LA:
Louisiana State University Press, 1993) 107–114; Harvey, *Redeeming the South*, 45.

clear themselves from any type of paternalistic relationship with white Baptists, both southern and northern. It is also appropriate when viewing the movement among African American Baptists to nationalize during the 1880s and 1890s as they organized three national conventions namely the Baptist Foreign Mission Convention, the American National Baptist Convention, and the National Baptist Educational Convention.[2]

African American nationalism during this period drew from what spokespersons understood about the African past. According to historian Edwin Redkey, African American spokespersons claimed a glorious African past as a collective sense of group consciousness; this was essential to African American nationalism, and when articulated by African American Christians, to Ethiopianism (1969, 11). Along with this nationalism there arose a renewed interest in African emigration, and southern African Americans were the ones spearheading this renewed interest with the African Methodist Bishop Henry M. Turner being the most prominent (Redkey 1969, 22–24; Montgomery 1993, 194–195; *see* Campbell 2006, ch. 3). Without doubt this harsh social and political climate influenced Jordan's thought as a young Baptist pastor in the South. Yet the nationalism and the resurgent call for emigration by southern African Americans also had a keen affect on young Jordan as would be seen in his leadership as corresponding secretary of the Foreign Mission Board of the NBC during the 1890s and beyond.

In February 1885, Jordan's life and ministry took a dramatic change. As the pastor of a Baptist church in Waco, Texas, Jordan had opportunity to travel to Africa. He formed the idea to make the voyage through the influence of some of his members who were interested in emigrating from the US to West Africa. Those potential emigrants decided to send Jordan to Liberia to scout out the land. He left for Liberia in February 1885 as an advanced scout for members of his flock. While there, he was a short-term missionary of sorts, according to historian Walter Williams (1982, 68). Though Jordan used his time in Liberia wisely by preaching and fellowshipping with African American Baptist missionaries on the

---

2. During this decade African American Baptists organized three separate "national" conventions: the Baptist Foreign Mission Convention (1880) the American National Baptist Convention (1886) and the National Baptist Educational Association (1893). For the founding of these conventions see Lewis Garnett Jordan, *Negro Baptist History USA 1750–1930* (Nashville, TN: Townsend Press, 1995) 153ff; E. A. Freeman, *The Epoch of Negro Baptists and the Foreign Mission Board* (Kansas City, KS: The Central Seminary Press, 1953) 75–79; LeRoy Fitts, *History of Black Baptists* (Nashville, TN: Boardman Press, 1985) 73–79.

ground, he had to return unexpectedly owing to illness (Jordan 1980, 19). This trip impressed upon Jordan the great possibility of African American Baptists planting more churches in Liberia particularly, but also throughout Africa (Jordan n.d., 24–26). Jordan wrote of the magnitude of this trip stating: "I was thus imbued with an enthusiasm for the missionary project" (Jordan n.d., 26). Though there was emigration fever in his church, Jordan at this time possessed a strong interest in the extension of African American Baptist missions in Africa rather than emigration and colonization.

From this first stirring of his missionary spirit upon his initial voyage to Africa and upon meeting prominent men such as Blyden on subsequent journeys to West Africa, Jordan would assume one of the most important positions within African American Baptist denominationalism just over a decade later. While he was the pastor of Union Baptist Church in Philadelphia in 1896, Jordan became the second corresponding secretary of the Foreign Mission Board of the National Baptist Convention organized in September 1895. His election in February 1896 came in the wake of L. M. Luke's death in December 1895. This was the beginning of a brilliant twenty-five year career in which Jordan built upon a shaky foundation of African American Baptist missionary work in Africa, establishing it as a viable enterprise with missionaries in West, Central, and Southern Africa at the end of his tenure in 1921 (Jordan n.d., 26).

Having been corresponding secretary for only five years, Jordan published his first book *Up the Ladder in Foreign Missions* in 1903. Probably written in 1901, this book was meant to inform African American Baptists about the history of Christian missions from the apostolic era to contemporary times. By no means is this work exhaustive: that was never Jordan's intention. His real emphasis in this history was to include the contributions African American Baptists had made in the history of American missions. By publishing this book, Jordan hoped to arouse the attention of young African American Baptists so that many would accept the challenge and heed the call to serve as missionaries in Africa (Jordan 1980, vi).

During the course of the book, Jordan broached the topic of Europe's "Scramble for Africa." In this section, Jordan revealed his accomodationism. In this brief discussion of European imperialism, Jordan failed to criticize European nations slicing up his dear Africa like a wedding cake. Rather than give explicit criticism to European imperial aggression, Jordan extols American and European travelers such as Henry M. Stanley and David Livingstone for opening roads for evangelism in different parts of Africa. Possibly Jordan hides his criticism of imperialism in his platitudes for the aforementioned explorers. Jordan's rhetoric in this section also evinces his accommodation to the dominant American cultural norms and the sense of superiority white Americans exuded. In praising Livingstone, Jordan writes: "After thirty years of toil he fell a victim to fever and died. Then it was that the dark sons of Africa showed their devotion" (1980, 85). His use of "dark sons" is the troublesome phrase. Coming from the pen of an African American, it oozes a sense of superiority and ethnocentricism. As Jordan ended this section, once again he demonstrates his accommodation to the rhetoric used by whites in describing Africa: "No people so anxious for the knowledge of the Gospel are neglected and left to plod their way in darkness as are the millions in darkest Africa" (1980, 86). Even as Jordan and other National Baptist leaders desired to be treated as equals by their white Baptist counterparts, Jordan employs pejorative language in describing his "Motherland."

Jordan's sense of African American exceptionalism is evident further in the text. He writes that "the Negroes of the United States are more intelligent, prosperous and better conditioned than a corresponding number anywhere else in the world" (1980, 87). He bases this assertion on "good authority"; what "good authority" he never reveals. Jordan's assertion, however, is nearly identical to that of the foremost recognized leader of African Americans at this time and Baptist, Booker T. Washington. Washington may be Jordan's "good authority" owing to the 1901 publication of his landmark *Up From Slavery*. In this autobiography, Washington pens these words: "the ten million Negroes inhabiting this country, who themselves or whose ancestors went through the school of American slavery, are in a stronger and more hopeful condition, materially, intellectually, morally, and religiously, than is true of an equal number of black people in any other portion of the globe" (2003, 47).[3] To offer more potency to this statement, Washington observes that many African Americans had returned to Africa as missionaries "to enlighten" Africans owing to the knowledge gained through their American experience (2003, 47).[4] From this observation, Jordan insists that since African

3. This statement by Washington demonstrates how pervasive this type of thought was at the turn of the 20th century.

4. From this passage, it is clear that Washington was an Ethiopianist as he attributed the African American missionary movement to Africa to God's Providence while at the same time condemning American slavery.

Americans are the leaders of the "Negro world" and since most African American Christians are Baptists then "much depends" on African American Baptists pertaining to evangelization and civilization in Africa (Jordan 1980, 87; *see* Montgomery 1993, 105).[5] Some white Baptist ministers had made similar claims about African American exceptionalism. As early as 1847, D. L. Carroll preached that "The Africans already look upon the white man as their superior, and hence desire to imitate him. The very ability to read and write gives dignity and importance to a colored man among them, and they express their admiration by calling him a white man" (1847, 333). Whatever problems one may have with Jordan's logic here the implication is clear: Jordan believed that African American Baptists were special instruments in the hands of God for the redemption of Africa. Jordan articulated a type of double exceptionalism: African American and African American Baptist.

In 1918, Jordan published his second book *Pebbles from an African Beach*. This is a book about Liberia written for missionary societies and other church study groups among National Baptist churches. At the time of this writing Jordan had visited Africa three times. For twenty-five years he had studied Africa. Based on this experience and his studies, he decided to write on Africa to correct what he called an "one-sided way" that writers on Africa treated it. Assumingly, Jordan meant white American or European writers. Because of this, Jordan's aim was to educate African Americans about Liberia. He wrote that Liberia "is the only Negro Republic in Africa, and ten million citizens of this great Republic [America] know almost nothing of the sister Republic, and care less" (Jordan 1918, 5). He also wrote to influence African Americans to serve Liberia, and possibly to relocate there. For any African American who was disappointed with life in America, Jordan declared: "There is an open door and a welcome hand to the Negro who wishes to return to the land of his fathers, not only to aid in its betterment with Bible, tool and farm implement, but to better himself in the open field of opportunity" (Jordan 1918, 5–6).

Portions of this text swell with the Ethiopian refrain of hope. Jordan became an unofficial ambassador for Liberia asserting that its future is bright and it is on the precipice of greatness while at the same time

---

5. According to Montgomery, African American Baptists were 54 percent of African American Christians in the South by 1890. In states such as Virginia, Louisiana, and Mississippi African American Baptists were 83, 62, and 61 percent of all African American Christians.

grounding this contention in the glorious African past in which he sees will be reclaimed by all persons of African descent. Jordan writes: "Who knows but that through the Republic of Liberia, the Negro is again coming into his own? What though he is down today, if only he is struggling up!" (Jordan 1918, 6). In mystical language, Jordan comments that the great African leaders of the past helped Africans and their descendants of his day toward progress. He remarks that the "spirits which are speaking to and acting through the Liberians today, and bidding them develop and perpetuate the Republic they have founded" (Jordan 1918, 8). For African Americans those spirits encouraged them to remember Africa and own their African identity and ancestry (Jordan 1918, 8). All of this comes from Jordan's preface and introduction. From the beginning, he clarifies that one of the designs of this study text was to cause a shift in the thinking of his audience: to make them more conscious of Africa, namely Liberia, in terms of how they could work to advance it. What is implicit here is Jordan's belief in an African American destiny as cultivators of a Christian civilization in Africa.

Part of Jordan's Ethiopian vision for Liberia was the expansion and development of Industrial Education. This thrust was quite common among African American intellectuals, Christians included. According to the text, Jordan observes that Liberia had great potential for agricultural production. Yet he indicates that the lack of technology in Liberia and the lack of African initiative in pursuing agricultural development were key impediments to overall agricultural production. Jordan notes, however, that this was a great opportunity for African American Baptists to contribute money to the Foreign Mission Board to initiate the requisite changes needed to improve the agricultural conditions in Liberia (Jordan 1918, 32–33).[6] Jordan mentions another bright spot: the arrival of African Americans coupled with the established Americo-Liberians who were hard at work improving agricultural production, which was a positive effect on other Liberians (Jordan 1918, 33–34).[7]

Though Jordan was a firm proponent of industrial education, he was still overall a Christian with a pastoral commitment to see the kingdom of Christ expanded. He understood that spiritual change was the most important change needed in Liberia (Jordan 1918, 40). In detailing the religious landscape of Liberia, Jordan's discourse assumes more of the standard tone

6. For example, Jordan stated that Liberians needed plows.

7. Agricultural products of Liberia included cotton, sugar cane, plantains, and bananas.

of American and European imperialistic-minded missionaries. Jordan registers complaints about the prevalence of traditional religion among Liberians. He even links the lack of industrial/agricultural progress with their devotion to their religion: "They neglect their homes, their farms, everything, and devote themselves to the observance of their barbarous rites" (Jordan 1918, 41). For an early-twentieth-century Baptist and an advocate of racial uplift, it would be easy for Jordan to conclude this since a non-Christian religion, especially on African soil, equated to backwardness.

At this point in his description, Jordan locates twin scapegoats. He finds Europeans and colonial rule as scapegoats. There are many theoretical problems with Jordan finding the locus of the problem in the phenomenon of European colonialism. It was too easy for Jordan to pounce upon in light of his target audience. Such pronouncements would ring loudly in the ears of his audience. Another problem was that Liberia was somewhat independent. It had its quasi-independence since 1847 so the Republic never had to fight off European imperialists during the late nineteenth century. It is obvious that Jordan complains of European colonialism in general in Africa. In the context of the lack of Christian presence in Liberia and elsewhere in West Africa by implication, Jordan uncovers the colonial practice of restricting Christian missions while preserving liberty to Islam. Within this particular grievance, Jordan never protests against colonialism. Jordan believes that colonization was needed to serve the interest of Christianity and civilization. In addition, he desires to see missions and colonial governments working together for mutual advancement (Jordan 1918, 42–43).

Though Jordan and the Foreign Mission Board could count on no support from colonial governments in other African mission fields, they had to chart their own course to dispel Africa's spiritual "darkness." This was through the aforementioned Industrial Education. For Jordan the time was ripe to press the action. In condescending language, Jordan writes: "the native is a splendid subject for evangelism. His simple, child-like faith, his docility, his sympathetic heart, like the fertile soil of his native heath, make virgin ground for Gospel seed" (Jordan 1918, 45). Jordan's goal was to build an African Christian culture, and this purpose carried the assumption that there was no indigenous culture to build from such as a body of literature, which was a mark of civilization. He asserts that to create such a civilization in Liberia "the Bible and the plow must go together" (Jordan 1918, 51). Such a statement reveals an undeveloped and limited view of Africans wrapped in paternalism. Jordan's thought here also represents how chauvinistic Ethiopianism could be articulated. Yet such sentiments did have a history among African American missionaries. Hilary Teague, son of Colin Teague, advocated the very same position during his time as a missionary in Liberia during the 1840s (Martin 1982, 67).[8]

In summary of this text, this is the most emigrationist and colonizationist Jordan appears in his writings. This may be owed to Jordan's own prognosis of the nature of European colonial rule. Possibly, he, like many members of the African elite in West and southern Africa, recognized European colonialism was to remain for a long period of time. What the system needed was reform and the inclusion of educationally qualified Africans to assume higher positions in colonial government. Similarly, Jordan may have believed that he needed to prod African Americans to assume a greater role in the transformation of Liberia and other African fields through missions and Industrial Education. Judging solely from the text and in comparison with his other writings, there seems to be no real solid justification for his strong insistence on African American emigration to Liberia at this juncture (1918).

Yet Jordan's first African experience in 1885 came as a result of the emigrationist aspirations of some of the members of his church. Their aspirations occurred in the aftermath of the emigration of African American South Carolinians in 1878 aboard the *Azor*. Among those who were aboard was Rev. Harrison Bouey and members of the newly organized Shiloh Baptist Church sent by the Baptist Educational, Missionary, and Sunday-School Convention. This seemed to be a joint venture of a missionary pastor and Christian emigrationists (Montgomery 1993,197–198; Martin 1982, 45–46). Such was similar during the 1910s, as African Americans began to flee the poverty and racial segregation of the South only to find the North and West less than hospitable. Having lived through an earlier period of disappointment in the 1870s, Jordan must have sensed this renewal of disappointment among African Americans and decided to advocate emigration.

There was another influence on Jordan's thought: his connection with the Garvey movement. There is evidence that Jordan addressed an UNIA meeting at Liberty Hall in 1920 informing the group of the good prospects of the possibility of emigration to Liberia (Martin 1976, 123). In the July 1920 issue of the *Mission Herald*, the monthly organ

8. Collin Teague was a missionary-colonizationist who left America in 1821 for West Africa with Lott Carey.

of the Foreign Mission Board, Jordan advertised the purchase of shares in the Philadelphia-based "African Steamship and Sawmill Co." that had plans to carry African Americans to Liberia. Jordan was one of the major sponsors of this company and venture (*Mission Herald* 1920). It can only be conjectured that Jordan's association with the Garvey movement stretched back to Garvey's organization of his first United States branch of the UNIA in 1916 in New York City. This connection is important in terms of Jordan's place within African American intellectual history. Jordan represents a bridge to the Ethiopianism of Crummell and the nationalism of Marcus Garvey. With Crummell, Jordan believed that Christianization was the key to African redemption and would result in Africa's restoration as a continent of high civilizations. With Garvey, Jordan encouraged African Americans to return to Africa in order to flourish beyond the tentacles of American racism; but different from Garvey, Jordan desired for African Americans to emigrate to an already existing republic in Africa rather than found a new nation-state.

From August 1910 through September 1921 there is a wealth of editorials and reports from the pen of Lewis Jordan published in the *Mission Herald*. These editorials reveal that Secretary Jordan was both a committed Baptist and an Ethiopian, who can be labeled a Christian "race man" interested in the "redemption" and "uplift" of Africans. They also offer a glimpse into Jordan's pastoral heart in the pointed fashion in which he communicated his desires for his beloved Foreign Mission Board.

In the 1910 August-September issue of the *Mission Herald*, Jordan offers clear evidence of his Evangelicalism and Ethiopianism. In an editorial piece entitled, "Will Their Work Live?" Jordan gives a historical exposé on the formation of the BFMC. Jordan reminisces: "One bright day in November, in 1880, just thirty years ago, three hundred of the Fathers, some of the noblest men who ever filled Baptist pulpits, assembled to pray for the lost in other lands and to devise plans for sending missionaries to preach the gospel to their benighted brethren in Africa" (1910, 1). Jordan went on to state that what drove these leaders were the words of Jesus recorded in Mark 16:15–16, which is one of the Great Commission passages. This indicates that Jordan understood these leaders to have had both a biblical motive for missions and a racial one.

In the same editorial, Secretary Jordan wrote about the significance of Africa throughout Christian and church history. He notes that "Africa shielded the infant Christ from the murderous hand of Herod" (1910, 1). This incident is recorded in Matthew 2:13–14. Then he cites Simon of

Cyrene, who helped to carry Jesus' cross. In summarizing these incidents during the life of Christ, the writer stated, "For these favors, God blessed Africa" (Jordan 1910, 1). It is interesting to note how his audience received such a history lesson and application. Baptists would believe the biblical passage that God is no respecter of persons, but African American Baptists would have a sense of pride welling up in their breasts upon learning how God used Africa and Africans in executing his plan of redemption.

How did God bless Africa? According to Jordan, God blessed the continent with numerous churches led by eminent men like Origen, Clement, Tertullian, and Augustine over the 225 years after the resurrection of Christ. Based on this glorious history, Jordan states that many people in 1910 believed that the "time was now ripe" for the evangelization of Africa. What Jordan implied was that African American Baptists needed to resume the work of evangelizing the continent. By doing this, they would also help to secure a place of stability for their institution, and it would also serve their belief that God had placed them in the prime position for redeeming Africa (Jordan 1910, 1–2).

Jordan offers a history lesson on the African Church and Africans in order to impress upon his readers the urgency of this matter. Jordan indicates that the African Church waned as a judgment from God brought on by the Church's neglect of evangelization, and its selfishness. By 1025 AD the once-thriving African Church had been reduced to nothing. Jordan picks up the story in 1620 with the first Africans arriving in the British American colonies, and then he catapults to 1865 and the end of slavery without detail. There is an evident belief in Providential Design here as Jordan explains: "He led us out with thousands of us Christians—a few ready for service at home, and here and there one ready for service in regions beyond" (1910, 2). All of this illustrates that Jordan possessed a strident race-consciousness, and a type of Ethiopianism that viewed the interconnectedness between Africans and African Americans.

In the August 1912 edition of the *Herald*, there is a strong editorial that attempted to stir the members of the National Baptist Convention to give more money for foreign missions. In the article "Human Need: The Beckoning Finger of God to Service," Jordan makes an urgent appeal for "One Million Souls" to serve Christ. He uses 1 John 3:17 as his biblical exhortation: "But whoso hath this world's goods, and seeth his brother have need, and shutteh up his bowels of compassion from him, how dwelleth the love of God in him?" (1 John 3:17, KJV). Jordan appeals to the racial pride of his audience urging young people to involve themselves in the missions, possibly by entering into the African mission field. He states that if Africa is to be redeemed it will be "through her own," meaning African Americans (Jordan 1912, 1).

There is a fervent Ethiopian element and appeal present in this editorial. In one section of the piece, Jordan exclaims, "how few of our young people are interested in their own blood, their brothers and sisters, who are sitting in darkness with no chance of gaining light unless their own of America bring the light of the Gospel to them" (1912, 1). This statement assumes a couple of things: first, it assumes that African Americans had a special duty to bring the gospel to Africans, which is an assertion that Jordan had already publicized in *Up the Ladder*; second, it assumes that no other group of Americans had the right spirit to undertake such. These assumptions display once again the sense of African American exceptionalism among African-descended peoples; such a notion was an essential component of Jordan's Ethiopianism.

Jordan equates love for God with Christian service, especially for young Christians to enter the mission field. He utilizes military imagery: "Wanted to enlist in the army of the Lord, to carry the story of the Redeemer and His Saving grace to all parts of the earth" (1912, 1). The tone of this statement is grave befitting the urgency of spreading the gospel to Africa during this time. It is almost a desperate call for a fresh crop of missionaries take up the mantle left by the older generation.

Also in this editorial is the notion that all Christians are fit for this type of service; and that all Christians are missionaries. Jordan writes, "You are under Marching Orders. You must not let the other races beat you to the goal and report their victory with Africa in darkness" (1912, 1). He states also that millions of young people of other races entered the mission field to give the gospel to their people. Here is an inducement that Jordan believed would compel more young people to involve themselves in missions. It points to a general motivation African Americans used during this day: older African Americans implored the younger generation that it had to be better than its white counterpart in order to succeed in this world. This emerged from the constant struggle of African Americans in a segregated society that relegated them to second class status.

In "The Sin of Neglecting to Evangelize the World," published in August 1913 Jordan wrote a scathing editorial highly critical of the convention's lack of financing the board's missions. Assumed in this article is his biblical understanding of the Great Commission; it is a command given to the whole Church along with individual Christians. Once again,

Jordan hinted at millenarianism in this article: to spread the gospel throughout the world will hasten Christ's return. In these types of articles, Jordan's theology has remained consistent (Jordan 1913, 1).

Regarding the sin committed by the NBC, Jordan listed eight points. First, it was open disobedience to Christ's command. Second, it was "a terrible breach of trust" (Jordan 1913, 4). Third, it was disloyalty. Fourth, it was "cruel." Fifth, it was "selfish." Sixth, it was "ungrateful." Seventh, it was avaricious. Eight, it was "to have the blood of souls upon us at last" (Jordan 1913, 4). Jordan combines a call for more financial help with a call to be faithful to the biblical commandment of Christ Jesus. In an interesting explanation of cruelty, Jordan asserts: "Every Christian knows that the Gospel is [the] only thing that drives out the awful practices and overcomes the terrible conditions of heathenism, and to neglect sending them the Gospel is to be guilty of cruelty" (1913, 4). Even with the various appeals through Ethiopian language in this article, Jordan's plea is solidly evangelical. Jordan's pastoral experience emerges here like never before as he employs the straightforward entreaty of the urgency of the gospel and obedience to Christ to make his point.

In the August 1919 issue of the *Herald*, Jordan noted the historical importance of African Christians in order to motivate contemporary African American Baptists. The article "Did You Know?" contains an Ethiopian element as it relates some of the major Africans who contributed to the Christian church—the early church. Jordan cites Tertullian, Origen, Augustine, and Cyprian as major theologians from Africa during this period. Jordan then advances an argument for why the churches of North Africa died, claiming that there were nine hundred churches, but they withered because they neglected the Great Commission. Here is a link between the historical church from an African perspective and Evangelical truth. It also serves as a warning to African American Baptists to remain obedient to their Christ and his commandments (Jordan 1919).

In the February 1921 edition of the *Herald*, Secretary Jordan celebrated his twenty-fifth anniversary as the corresponding secretary; it was the final anniversary celebrated in this position. In "The Quarto-Centennial of Our Secretary" Jordan reflects upon the last twenty-five years of his service to the NBC and to Africa. Jordan recollects:

> For the first few years I hoped to return to the pastorate, but the thought of Africa and Africa's needs and then the big non-Christian world grew on me until, in glad surrender, I finally decided to stick to it and prayed to be spared to travel many years,

up and down our favored country and plead for men, women
and money to be used in the uplift of the neglected. (1921, 2)

Jordan gives a brief overview of the current work. He writes that there
were sixty American and International ordained missionaries along with
three women who were workers, and 105 African workers; this was the
grand total of workers in the African field. He admits he was tired physically and the board needed to find a younger man to assume this work
to which he had given the last twenty-five years of his life. Regarding his
plans for the future, Jordan remarks that "I have no plans for the future
further than to be allowed to work with a yoke-fellow for the good of
Africa" (1921, 2).

The words from one of Jordan's successors as corresponding secretary of the Foreign Mission Board capture the significance of Jordan's
leadership. William Harvey states, "With the election of Rev. L. G. Jordan
as the Corresponding Secretary of the Foreign Mission Board, a new day
dawned for Black Baptists and the missionary enterprise" (1989, 32). In
viewing this time of the Foreign Mission Board's history, Harvey also
remarks on the motivation of National Baptist missions as "sending the
Christian message of spiritual, social and physical uplift to Africa" (1989,
31). In this statement, Harvey calls attention to the dynamism of the
Board's intentions. Harvey clearly asserts that uplift is the key in every
area of the Board's endeavors, though he gives prominence to spiritual
uplift. Fitts also has glowing words for the Jordan legacy: "He proved to
be the right leader to establish a more aggressive and effective missionary
program in Africa" (1985, 117). Fitts points to the initiative and energy
Jordan brought to this post by stating that in the first sixteen years of
Jordan's tenure the Foreign Mission Board commissioned twenty-six
missionaries overseas to Africa and South America (1985, 117).

Jordan was much more than an able corresponding secretary and
leader of a missionary board. Jordan was also an African American
Protestant intellectual who inherited and continued the Ethiopianism of
Crummell and Blyden. What is important regarding Jordan is that he
emerged as such despite his slave birth and his family instability post-
Emancipation. Both of these militated against him becoming a Christian
intellectual. Whatever theoretical problems contemporary readers may
have with Jordan's formulations regarding African American exceptionalism, paternalistic attitudes toward Africans, and his lack of questioning European colonialism in Africa, Jordan did self-identify with being

a person of African descent and desired this to be pervasive among all African Americans. He lived and thought from a theology that bubbled up from his experiences as a slave and his knowledge of God's inclusive plan for all nations and God's sovereignty in executing his plan.

9

What Do These Stones Mean?
Civil Rights Movement Tourism as an Act of Remembrance

Dr. Todd Allen, Grove City College

"In the future, when your children ask you, 'What do these stones mean?' tell them that the flow of the Jordan was cut off before the ark of the covenant of the Lord. When it crossed the Jordan, the waters were cut off. These stones are to be a memorial to the people of Israel forever" (Josh 4:6–7).

THESE WORDS, RECORDED IN the book of Joshua, tell the story of the people of Israel and how God intervened in the midst of their oppression and delivered them out of the bondage of slavery. So that future generations would remember what God had done, the people were instructed to erect a memorial in remembrance. Engaging in such symbolic acts was a frequent part of ancient biblical history and has remained a part of society throughout the ages down to the present day. Whether it is through the building of memorials, monuments, museums, or participation in rituals and ceremonies, as human beings we have a desire to remember and preserve the past. One such past that has been receiving increasing attention over the past several years has been the American civil rights movement.

This chapter will address the implications and relevance of commemorative practices related to the civil rights movement. While exploring the civil rights movement in general, particular emphasis will be given to civil rights movement tourism as a pedagogical tool for accessing the past. Presenting civil rights tourism as a specialized field, this chapter will discuss the relationship between the civil rights movement and public memory, explore the growth of commemorative practices related to the civil rights movement and resulting tourism, and the benefits and challenges of such tourism for social engagement and racial reconciliation. To remember these old landmarks of the African American freedom struggle reveals not only their pedagogical value, but their spiritual role in teaching lessons on the importance of honestly confronting the past, while promoting healing, forgiveness, and reconciliation in the present.

Public Memory: An Overview

Memory studies, most commonly referred to as collective or public memory, is a rapidly growing area of inquiry that encompasses such diverse disciplines as sociology, psychology, history, anthropology, architecture, and communication. In his groundbreaking work, *On Collective Memory*, sociologist Maurice Halbwachs differentiates between individual memory and those memories that are constructed and disseminated by a collective (i.e., public). According to Halbwachs, "it is in society that people normally acquire their memories. It is also in society that they recall, recognize, and localize their memories" (1992, 38). While acknowledging the place of individual memory, he concludes that human memory is perhaps better understood in a collective context. Societies promote collective memory for a variety of reasons, including the need to explain their past, to educate future generations, and to promote a sense of shared identity. In some instances, events of the past are also remembered in an effort to right past wrongs or to extol a society's greatness.

In *Framing Public Memory*, Kendall Phillips and other leading scholars in the field of memory studies provide critical insight into the dynamics of memory formation, loss, and expression in a shared context. Advocating for the use of the term public memory in place of collective memory, Phillips argues that "to speak of public memory as the memory of publics is to speak of more than many individuals remembering the same thing. It is to speak of a remembrance together as a crucial aspect of our togetherness, our existence as a public" (2004, 4). The focus of this chapter will be placed on the "public" aspect of memory as represented on the commemorative landscape. The choice of the term public versus collective or social memory is more than a semantic one. In speaking of the "public-ness" of memory, Edward Casey argues that "public memory in turn gathers place, people, and topics in its encompassing embrace by acting as the external horizon that encircles the situation" (2004, 37).

Collective memory may mistakenly imply that memory is merely the sum total of individual memories, which is not the case. Public memory on the other hand better emphasizes the dynamic and contested qualities of memory, as well as the performative nature of memory as it is presented in a public fashion on the commemorative landscape.

Memories are not perfect recollections of the past, but rather social constructions of the past. David Lowenthal makes this case in *The Past is a Foreign County* when he argues that "memories are not ready-made reflections of the past, but eclectic, selective reconstructions based on the subsequent actions and perceptions and on the ever-changing codes by which we delineate, symbolize, and classify the world around us" (1986, 210). As a result, memories of the past are often quite contested, resulting in the dialectical tension of remembering and forgetting, which in turn influences what is or is not present on the commemorative landscape.[1] Commenting on this aspect of memory, Arthur Neal states that "events are fashioned through a filtering of experiences. Some experiences are dismissed, while others are elaborated and given high levels of significance" (2005, 198). Those experiences that are labeled as significant more often than not find themselves as part of a society's set of commemorative practices, whereas as those that are dismissed gradually disappear.

Civil Rights Movement and Public Memory

Commemorative practices related to the civil rights movement of the 1950s–60s have been gaining popularity over the past decade (Romano and Raiford 2006). Much of this interest has centered around the life and legacy of Dr. Martin Luther King, Jr. Almost immediately following his assassination, acts of commemoration to his legacy were begun, most notable of which was the founding of the Martin Luther King, Jr. Center for Nonviolent Social Change in Atlanta, Georgia. Started by his widow, the late Coretta Scott King, the site has grown to include the gravesites of Dr. and Mrs. King, Dr. King's childhood home, historic Ebenezer Baptist Church, a museum of personal artifacts and archives, and a multi-media visitor's center operated by the National Park Service. In 1983, then President Ronald Reagan signed a bill designating Dr. King's birthday

---

1. For a more detailed examination of the politics of memory and how these politics shape the commemorative landscape see: Kenneth Foote, *Shadowed Ground: America's Landscapes of Violence and Tragedy* (Austin: University of Texas Press, 2003).

a national holiday. Perhaps more than any other civil rights figure, with the exception of Mrs. Rosa Parks, the name of Dr. Martin Luther King, Jr. has become synonymous with the cause of civil rights as presented on the commemorative landscape.

While this public acknowledgement of Dr. King and his contribution to the freedom struggle is well deserved and in some people's opinion long overdue, these acts of commemorative practice are not without limits. Owen Dwyer argues that while these commemorative sites do a good job of opening up the commemorative landscape to previously absent and marginalized voices, by focusing primarily and in some cases exclusively on Dr. King, these sites "re-inscribe certain hegemonic narratives" (Dwyer 2000, 661) that exclude the voices of women, youth, and local activists who were key to the movement's success.

Several museums dedicated to remembering the civil rights movement have opened since the early 1990's including the Birmingham Civil Rights Institute (Birmingham, Alabama) the National Civil Rights Museum (Memphis, Tennessee) the Rosa Parks Museum (Montgomery, Alabama) and the International Civil Rights Center and Museum (Greensboro, North Carolina).[2] Alongside these museums are a diverse set of memorials to veterans of the movement. Included in this group are the Civil Rights Memorial (Montgomery, Alabama) the Viola Liuzzo Memorial (Lowndes County, Alabama) and statues in honor of the Little Rock Nine (Little Rock, Arkansas) James Meredith (Oxford, Mississippi) Medgar Evers (Jackson, Mississippi) and the Dr. Martin Luther King, Jr. Memorial (Washington, D.C.). Likewise, numerous streets, roads, and highways have been named after veterans of the movement. The past few years have also witnessed an increase in commemorative celebrations marking key moments in civil rights movement history such as the 50th anniversaries of Brown v. Board of Education (1954) the Montgomery Bus Boycott (1955) the integration of Central High School (1957) the Freedom Rides (1961) and the March on Washington (1963).[3]

Despite this increase in commemorative activity, knowledge of the civil rights movement and its relevance for today's generation appears to be somewhat lacking. James Loewen, in his 1995 best-selling book

2. There are several museums currently in various phases of construction, most notably the National Museum of African American History and Culture on the National Mall in Washington D.C. scheduled to open in the Fall of 2015.

3. These and other milestones of the civil rights movement were commemorated in a 2005 postage stamp series entitled "To Form a More Perfect Union."

Lies My Teacher Told Me: Everything Your American History Textbook Got Wrong convincingly documents how students are often "handicapped by history" (1995, 11) as a result of the failure to teach the lessons of history in ways that are truthful and applicable to the lives of students. As a result, students are graduating from high school and entering the larger society knowing very little about the history that has shaped the nation in which they live. According to a 2008 report *Still at Risk: What Students Don't Know Even Now* published by Common Core, many of today's teenagers are losing touch with historical references, including those related to the civil rights movement (Hess 2008). Natalie Davis, a political science professor at Birmingham-Southern College laments that students "are absolutely ahistorical. It's about them—the world that surrounds them at the moment. And there's no looking back because they don't know what to be looking for" (Anthony 2008, 1A+). Despite Davis's rather strong conclusion, the decline in knowledge of the past is not one that solely plagues the nation's youth. According to movement veteran Mrs. Juanita Abernathy, widow of Rev. Ralph David Abernathy, "the reason many of our young people don't know this history is because their parents don't know this history" (personal interview, June 11, 2006). In many instances, historical myths have overshadowed historical reality. According to Maureen Costello, Director of the Southern Poverty Law Center's *Teaching Tolerance* initiative, "students learn two people and one word. They know Rosa Parks and Martin Luther King, Jr. and they know he had a dream" (Bonvillian 2011). Such a limited narrative reduces the teaching of the movement by obscuring the personal sacrifices of those who engaged in the struggle and the breadth of the social and institutional changes they wrought. According to a 2014 report, *Teaching the Movement 2014: The State of Civil Rights Education in the United States* published by the Southern Poverty Law Center, when it comes to civil rights education in the K-12 system most states are failing their students by not requiring that this defining moment in United States history be taught (Shuster 2014). The report concluded that "most states still pay little attention to the civil rights movement" and that "twenty states whose coverage is minimal received grades of F" while "fourteen states earned grades of D" (8–9).

Growth of Civil Rights Movement Tourism

One of the most powerful means for engaging sites of public memory is to visit them—to walk on sacred ground. Historian James Horton believes that "few experiences can connect us with our past more completely than walking the ground where our history happened" (Horton 2005, 8–9). Adds Edward Linenthal, "the conviction is that somehow places speak" (2006, 222) thus it is through the public's engagement with the rhetoric of the commemorative landscape that one can come to understand the past. Tourism is one such vehicle for accessing the meaning of the past.

The increase in the number of commemorative sites of the civil rights movement has resulted in the rapid growth of tourism geared towards these sites. Travel guides such as Townsend Davis's *Weary Feet, Rested Souls* (1998) James Carrier's *A Traveler's Guide to the Civil Rights Movement* (2004) and Charles Cobb's *On the Road to Freedom* (2008) have become popular sellers among those interested in civil rights related tourism. Likewise, states that once sought to deter those advocating for civil rights are now embracing their civil rights past as a cornerstone to regional economic growth. While it is difficult to pinpoint the precise origin of the birth of civil rights tourism, the preservation and commemoration of sites related to the movement gained considerable momentum in the 1980s–1990s. Ironically, it was the state of Alabama under the direction of former governor George Wallace that led the way in the promotion of this emerging field of tourism. In 1983, the Alabama Bureau of Tourism published a black heritage guide, the first state-wide brochure aimed at African Americans. This guide, which is still in print as the "Alabama Civil Rights Museum Trail" remains one of the premier state-wide publications for civil rights tourism.

Acknowledging that the promotion of this heritage is driven by historical as well as educational and economic motives, Lee Sentell, Alabama Tourism Director, says what makes Alabama a leader in this area is the fact that "no other state has the quality or quantity of destinations of what was a battlefield in the '60s" (Rawls 2004, 11A). While some people may see the promotion of the public memory of the Civil War and the civil rights movement narratives as contradictory, Sentell contends that "they are bookends of the same conflict" (ibid.). One outcome of this blending of contested public memories is that cities such as Montgomery now promote themselves as being home to both "The Cradle of the Confederacy" and "The Birthplace of Civil Rights."

Despite the potential for economic gain, many people throughout the south have been reluctant to publicly embrace their civil rights past. Jim Carrier, author of *A Traveler's Guide to the Civil Rights Movement* believes that "tourism has been forced on these places. It's not like they put out a sign one day and said, 'Come on down and see our civil rights history.' It's in response to people coming down here, lugging big history books, looking for these places" (Dewan 2004). Regardless of the economic potential that addressing these public memories holds, some resistance persists among people who see no need to discuss this shameful and painful past.

In a so-called post-racial and post-civil rights society, some have questioned the wisdom of expending resources for the commemoration of the civil rights movement and for travel to such sites. There are those who feel that the issues raised by the movement are all in the past and that if the country is to move ahead, we need to forget the past and focus on the present. For some, to remember and talk about the past is seen as too painful, too divisive, and thought to be counterproductive to living and working in community. These responses often cross boundaries of ethnicity, age, and geography. In response, movement veterans such as Congressman John Lewis have countered that society must do all it can to preserve the past "so that we understand where we are going as a people, as a nation" (Lewis 1994, 61). More will be said about this later in exploring the benefits and challenges to promoting civil rights tourism.

In spite of moments of resistance, civil rights tourism has continued to evolve as people increasingly wish to experience history through travel. There exist a variety of tours that are led by anyone from private tour promoters, to educators, to civil rights veterans themselves.[4] While the list of civil rights tours is endless, each in their own way shares the commonality of theme (freedom, justice, social action) context (i.e., visiting sites where the movement occurred) and characters, engaging the testimony, either directly or indirectly, the veterans of the civil rights movement to tell their stories of the freedom struggle. Where these tours have a tendency to vary is in their particular logistical details (i.e., number of sites visited, length of travel, target audience, etc.). In the case of civil rights movement tourism, each tour privileges an interpretation of

4. Tours that at one time or another have been led by veterans of the civil rights movement include the following: Pathways to Freedom (Rosa Parks) Civil Rights Heritage Educational Tour (Evelyn G. Lowery) Civil Rights Pilgrimage (John Lewis) Journeys for the Soul (Joanne Bland) and Civil Rights South (Julian Bond).

the past that shapes communicative memory from generation to generation. The meaning of the civil rights struggle as a social movement is translated through the narratives told by veterans of the movement, as well as through the various forms of commemorative practice (i.e., monuments, memorials, markers, etc.) constructed at each site. Whether conducted formally by an organized group or as personal family travel, there are many benefits to engaging sites dedicated to the past.

Benefits of Civil Rights Tourism

Congressman John Lewis, a long-time advocate for the preservation of sites related to the civil rights movement argues that "our history is a precious resource [and] we must do all we can to preserve it and insure its accuracy" (2006, 66). The primary means by which this preservation occurs is through the creation of "a rich, multi-layered landscape consisting of traditional expressions of civic memory (e.g., monuments and museums, murals, and historic plaques) as well as more mundane elements such as street signs and community centers" (Dwyer 2000, 661).

Encounters of sites related to the civil rights movement are often spoken of in religious terms as a sacred journey or pilgrimage. Visitors to these sites have been known to find themselves transformed through experiencing the civil rights movement from mere tourists to pilgrims undergoing a "physical and spiritual journey to a place of power" (Linenthal 2006, 223). While people's experiences are as varied as the persons who attend to these sites, at least two benefits of tourism related to the civil rights movement emerge. First, the rhetorical power of being in places where significant events of the civil rights movement occurred and second, the potential that visits to such sites yield for civic engagement and social action.

Historian James Loewen contends that "being at the place where history was made has a certain power" (1999, 27). The rhetorical impact of being physically present at places where history happened, and in some cases, with the very people who were participants in the making of history, provides one with an opportunity to directly engage what Vincent Harding refers to as the "human bridges between the past and the future" (1981, xiv). Visiting the places where this struggle for freedom took place allows for a form of immediacy and connection with the past that reading a book or viewing a film cannot capture. Said one participant in a civil rights tour:

> One of the most profound things for me on this trip was to be physically present in places where events of the civil rights movement happened. There is something mysterious about being in a place and meeting people who were there that touched me deeper than I could have expected. I was able to take in, literally, into my body, the smells, sounds, and tastes of the civil rights movement. (Westerlund 2001)

Another visitor added, "Coming to the places where these real things happened and seeing it in contemporary American eyes makes all the difference" (DeMillo 2007, 8AA) in understanding history as a social experience. Civil rights tourism, while not guaranteeing that one will become more civically engaged, places one in the rhetorical context of a figurative and literal struggle for freedom wherein one is brought face to face with social lessons that are applicable to the contemporary moment.

According to Edward Linenthal, while "we are not responsible for events long past, we are responsible for the preservation and presentation of them to coming generations. Conscientious remembrance is more than a necessary expansion of the nation's narrative. It is an act of moral engagement" (2006, 224).

For many, engagement with this history reveals a newfound awareness of the relevance of past historic struggles to current sociopolitical situations. The pedagogical value of such experiences has proven to be invaluable. A young high school student, reflecting upon their participation in such a tour, discovered that before visiting these sites, "I didn't realize how big of an issue segregation was and still is. I want to go back home and share the knowledge I learned here in order to make things better" (Konz 2007, 3A). Speaking on the personal transformation which resulted from participating in a tour, another student added, "I've stopped using the N-word and the B-word and other words that degrade people" (ibid.). College students have also talked about how these experiences have changed the way they view the world around them. According to one college sophomore, "I learned about history, but it was something more. I learned about reality. Not just the reality of the past, but the reality of the present and the future" (Yergeau 2004, 6–7). Concluded another, "after this trip I don't think I will ever take the right to vote for granted again" (Spruill 2006).

One specific area of civic engagement and social action that civil rights tourism can facilitate is that of racial reconciliation. Civil rights tourism, while not a cure all, can provide a unique forum for discussing issues of race. In *Lessons From Little Rock*, Terrence Roberts, a member of the Little Rock Nine, contends:

> If a dialogue begins, we will need to know as much as possible about what is going on. Each one of us needs to have a firm grasp of the essential elements involved. We need to have an informed historical perspective, some sense of the dynamics of racism as it is manifested today, and more importantly, where we are in our own thinking about these things (2009, 155).

Civil rights tourism can serve to promote this informed historical perspective which many seem to be lacking when it comes to knowledge of the civil rights movement.

According to Georgette Norman, director of the Rosa Parks Library and Museum in Montgomery stated, "Ten years ago in Alabama, blacks and whites had just started to socialize together. Now we're beginning to do the hard work of talking about the way things were back then and why they were that way" (Vestal 2008). James Waller, author of *Prejudice Across America* agrees that these commemorative sites can provide an impetus for dialogue and healing:

> Race is and always has been our most divisive issue. Finding our way toward racial reconciliation is the crucial social challenge of the new millennium. Our success in meeting this challenge depends, in large part, on our appreciation and understanding of people who are different from us—our ability to see with the other's eyes. (2000, xiv)

James Loewen affirms this perspective stating that "Americans share a common history that unites us. But we also share some more difficult events—a common history that divides us. These things too we must remember, for only then can we understand our divisions and work to reduce them" (1999, 22). Civil rights tourism, while perhaps not the ultimate solution to this dilemma, does provide a way forward through the creation of spaces for the discussion of issues of past and present racial discrimination, as well as presenting tools for the restoration of a spirit of civic engagement. However, while there are benefits to civil rights tourism, there are some challenges that must be addressed if this forum for civic engagement and social action is to continue.

Challenges to Civil Rights Tourism

Despite the benefits related to civil rights movement tourism, there are a few challenges to this form of heritage tourism as a means of tracing public memory. Among these challenges are the following: first, the tension between remembering and forgetting that is an inherent struggle in public memory; second, the loss of authentic voice through the passing of many of the veterans of this historic struggle, in some instances before their testimonies of history could be recorded; and third, the potential commercialization of the past that can occur when sites of the movement are more concerned about revenue than historical accuracy and authenticity. Added to these challenges is a general feeling by some in society that not every site on the public landscape is deemed worthy of being remembered, particularly sites that have a contested past. As a result, many are left feeling that the civil rights movement is a time period best left in the past and that for the nation to move forward in terms of racial progress, a complete break with this past is in order.

Speaking specifically of the state of Alabama, Georgette Norman believes that part of the desire to forget stems from a feeling that "Alabamans have had their dirty laundry aired under a national spotlight long enough. The old guard doesn't want any more of this kind of attention drawn to the state" (Vestal 2008). While these feeling are perhaps most prevalent in the southern part of the United States where a majority of movement activity occurred, these sentiments are hardly a regional phenomenon. What this means for commemorative practices related to the civil rights movement, including tourism, is that some would prefer that sites of the civil rights movement be left unmarked or even eliminated from the commemorative landscape, thus removing them from public memory.

For example, there is a debate waging in the state of Mississippi over the future of the Bryant Grocery Store in Money Mississippi. The store is the site of events that led to the murder of Emmett Till in August 1955, a murder that many consider to be one of the most brutal acts of violence in the nation and a catalyst for the civil rights movement.[5] The site, which

5. For further reading on the case of Emmett Till see: Christopher Mettress, *The Lynching of Emmett Till: a Documentary Narrative* (Charlottesville, VA: University of Virginia, 2002); Mamie Till-Mobley and Christopher Benson, *Death of Innocence: The Story of a Hate Crime That Changed America* (New York: Random House, 2003); and Simeo Wright, *Simeon's Story: An Eyewitness Account of the Kidnapping of Emmett Till* (Chicago: Lawrence Hill, 2010). Filmmaker Keith Beauchamp has also released an award winning documentary *The Untold Story of Emmett Louis Till*. New York: ThinkFilm, 2005.

has been placed on the Mississippi Heritage Trust's "10 Most Endangered Historic Places," is literally on the verge of collapse. While there are some who wish to preserve this site, perhaps converting the store into some sort of a museum, others, including the site's owner, appear to be less enthusiastic and supportive of such commemorative efforts (Mitchell 2007, 3A). In addition to the slow and gradual disappearance of this site, over the years there have been repeated acts of vandalism against a historic marker located on the spot where Till's mutilated body was pulled from the Tallahatchie River. Unfortunately this site is not alone in having such acts of destruction and desecration committed against it. Throughout the south, from Jimmie Lee Jackson's gravesite in Marion, Alabama to the Viola Liuzzo marker in Lowndes County, Alabama, civil rights sites have been targeted by persons opposed to any and all forms of public commemoration. However, despite such attempts to erase the act of violence committed against Till and others from the commemorative landscape, those persons who are committed to commemoration and remembrance have vowed to remain vigilant in their efforts to preserve these events in the public memory.

Closely related to the tension between remembering and forgetting this history is the problem of dealing with the loss of authentic witnesses to the movement. One of the benefits of civil rights tourism is that it holds the potential for visitors to directly engage not only the places of the movement, but in many instances, the people who participated in the making of this history. As representatives of authentic voices of the civil rights movement, these veterans serve to provide a vital link to the past. The past several years have witnessed the passing of many of the veterans of this historic freedom struggle. One can only wonder what will happen when those who lived this history are no longer alive or physically able to share their experiences. Such a state of affairs will definitely change the nature of civil rights movement tourism providing a challenge to maintaining the authenticity of their lived experiences.

As has been previously stated, there are many persons who feel that commemorative practices related to the civil rights movement of the past are a distraction from the civil rights issues and concerns of the present historical moment. Even within the African American community, there are voices emerging which feel that perhaps too much attention is being paid to the past and that "modern activism is being overshadowed by a near constant string of commemorations for bygone victories" (Texeira 2006, A3). Ben Gordon, former President of the NAACP warns that in honoring those who have passed away, "We should be very respectful of—and encouraged by the substantial progress that has been made. But in no way, shape, or form should we conclude that the civil rights mission is complete" (ibid., A3). How best to commemorate and present the past, while remaining vigilant in the present, seems to be an ongoing struggle in commemorative efforts related to the presentation of public memory related to the civil rights movement.

Connected to these concerns over remembering and forgetting, as well as authenticity, are the tensions between competing narratives of the past as presented by official and vernacular cultures. Michael Kammen distinguishes between these two forms of cultural memory with official cultural memory being "what is remembered by the dominant civic culture" of the power elites, while vernacular cultural memory is created by "ordinary folks" (1991, 10). The central point of tension between these two forms of cultural memory resides in the question, who has the authority to define the past? For example, speaking specifically of the tensions between the National Park Service's (i.e. official cultural memory) commemoration of the 1965 Selma to Montgomery March as compared to those of the National Voting Rights Museum and Institute (i.e. vernacular cultural memory) a local grassroots initiative based in Selma, Alabama, Reverend C.T. Vivian warns that when "they [official culture] begin to define your past, they are defining you and that it will not be long before they begin to re-define you" (personal interview, July 27, 2007). Yet again, given the increase I commemorative practices related to the civil rights movement on the national and local stage, the tensions between narratives as presented by official and vernacular cultures are certain to escalate.

One final challenge related to civil rights tourism pertains to the potential for the commercialization and trivialization of the meaning of the movement. Some scholars have argued that the industry that has arisen around the commemoration of the civil rights movement, be it in popular media such as film or through civil rights tourism, has denigrated rather than honored the movement. Owen Dwyer argues that one of the problems related to the marketing of civil rights sites is that in their attempts to appeal to mainstream audiences, "treatment of contemporary racism and racial politics is conspicuously absent" (Dwyer 2000, 666). While economic development is one of the benefits of civil rights tourism, one wonders at what cost to public memory are sites being constructed and narratives presented. For example, Bernard Armada provides an insightful discussion of the tension between commemoration and commercialization in his analysis of the National Civil Rights Museum in Memphis, Tennessee (1998, 235–243). Following the assassination of Dr. Martin Luther King, Jr. the Lorraine Motel, now the site of the museum, began to experience a steady economic decline. What was once a site of lodging for civil rights leaders, entertainers, and athletes had by the 1980s become a low-income, drug-infested dwelling. In an attempt to save the site for commemoration, residents of the motel were evicted to make way for the construction of a museum. Since March of 1988, Jacqueline Smith, a former resident of the Lorraine, has staged a one-woman boycott against what she calls the "National Civil Wrongs Museum." The official memory presented by the museum is of a site where "visitors can walk through virtually the entire history of the civil rights struggle in the United States" (Cobb 2008, 338) culminating in reflection on the assassination of Dr. King and the legacy of the movement. Smith's counter-narrative, based on an interpretation of the site as evidence of gentrification and neglect of the poor, presents a site that instead of honoring Dr. King and the movement represents the very antitheses of Dr. King's philosophy. While careful not to take sides in this controversy, Armada keenly points out the need for visitors to such commemorative sites to challenge themselves to become what he terms memory workers who are "active co-creators of public memory" through discourse seeking to "embody and enact the civil rights movement ideals of brotherhood, equality, and community" in social action, as opposed to memory tourists who represent "passive consumers of history" (2002, 27).

Further Research

The study of public memory and the civil rights movement is an emerging field. Within this area of research, there are at least three areas where communication scholars can make significant contributions.

First, while there has been significant analysis of major civil rights sites such as the National Civil Rights Museum, the Birmingham Civil Rights Institute, and the Dr. Martin Luther King, Jr. Center for Nonviolent Social Change, there are many other commemorative sites and forms of commemorative practice that have received very little, if any, scholarly attention. As the commemorative landscape discussed in this chapter illustrates, public memory related to such sites is never fixed, but rather is constantly evolving and being re-negotiated and re-interpreted. Scholarly analysis of this process could prove invaluable to better understanding the meaning of this past and its implications for public memory in the present and future.

Second, civil rights tourism as a genre of cultural heritage tourism, represents a unique coming together of place, memory, and narrative. In the choice of destinations, speakers, and participants, each tour selectively represents the construction and presentation of particular narratives about the movement. As James Loewen reminds us, "Historic sites don't just tell stories about the past; they also tell visitors what to think about the stories they tell" (1999, 22). Not only do these commemorative sites present particular narratives of the past, so too do the tours which develop around these sites. While civil rights tourism as an industry has grown, there has been very little in-depth analysis of the impact of such tours on public memory and discussions of social history.

Finally, the Civil War and the civil rights movement represent an interesting coming together of contested pasts that sometimes can leave the visitor encountering "parallel histories that do not speak to each other" (ibid., 449). As was previously noted, many of the sites that were once regarded for the confederacy have been re-inscribed with narratives related to the history of the civil rights movement. Thus, on the commemorative landscape it is not uncommon to see Civil War memory and civil rights memory intersect, literally as well as figuratively. In many of these places, city and tourism officials have sought to reconcile these pasts in varied ways. However, the process of reconciling such conflicting past has proven to be more difficult than the modification of travel brochures, street signs, and city mottos suggests. The similarities and differences between these contested pasts are more than geographical in nature. As two of the most influential events in the history of the United States, the Civil War and the civil rights movement resulted in significant transformations of the social order. Likewise, each has resulted in the development of commemorative practices that have greatly shaped public memory of the past. Therefore, there is much to be gained in better understanding how these pasts work in constructing narratives of race in the past, present, and future.

James Loewen has argued that "truth in the past can lead to justice in the present" (2005). Adds Gary Selby, "If racial healing is ever to come to our society, it will mean remembering and retelling our story of racial injustice and honoring the voices and the actions of those who stood against it" (2008, xi). In 2005 during the fiftieth anniversary celebration of the Montgomery Bus Boycott, the Montgomery Improvement Association had as its theme "Eyes Forward, Looking Back." Upon initially encountering this theme one may be a bit perplexed wondering how one could look for forward and backward at the same time. Upon closer reflection however one soon realizes that the beauty of this theme lies in its call to remember the past by looking back not merely in a nostalgic sort of way, but as a guide with one's eyes forward engaging contemporary issues in light of lessons gleaned from the past. Civil rights tourism provides a rather unique and engaging opportunity to step back and revisit the past, while keeping a foot in the present, in order to be challenged to move forward to the future.

This chapter began with words recorded in the book of Joshua admonishing the people of God to never forget the past, but to leave signs of remembrance for the generations yet unborn so that they would know from whence they came. Perhaps it is Dr. Martin Luther King, Jr., a man who is the most commemorated of all veterans of the civil rights movement, who best sums up what the true meaning and memory of this past ought to be. In his now famous "Letter From a Birmingham Jail" Dr. King said:

> One day the South will recognize its real heroes. They will be the James Merediths, with the noble sense of purpose that enables them to face jeering and hostile mobs, and with the agonizing loneliness that characterizes the life of the pioneer. They will be the old, oppressed, battered Negro women, symbolized in a seventy two year old woman in Montgomery, Alabama, who rose up with a sense of dignity and with her people decided not to ride segregated buses, and who responded with ungrammatical profundity. . . . "My feets is tired, but my soul is rested. They will be the young high school and college students, the young ministers of the gospel and a host of their elders, courageously and nonviolently sitting in at lunch counters and willing to go to jail for conscience's sake. One day the South will know that when these disinherited children of God sat down at lunch counters, they were really standing up for what is best in the American dream and for the most sacred values in our Judeo Christian heritage. (1963)

In the future when our children ask us "what means this movement for civil rights?" let us be ready to give an account of how in the midst of the oppression of racial segregation, the Lord carried his children over the Jordan into the promised land.

10

Affirmative Action and Conceptions of Fairness: Jonathan Haidt and the Righteous Black Community

Dr. Anthony Bradley, The King's College

Introduction

Race-based preferential policies as a means of rectifying past injustice and preventing future discrimination continue to arouse much emotion and debate in the United States. The African American experience of both formal and informal racial oppression has encouraged lawmakers to seek ways to level the playing field given the fact that whites have enjoyed hegemonic advantages. Affirmative action emerged a few decades ago as an intervention into the systemic realities of white privilege. The debate about affirmative action progressed with great controversy because of the complexities and uncertainties about the effectiveness of these programs as a remedy for past injustice. One central question in this context is this: "Is affirmative action fair?" The answer to this question is perspectival. That is, fair with respect to whom? For example, is affirmative action fair with respect to African Americans or is it fair to have preferential policies limit opportunities for whites for the sake of blacks, especially if individual whites or blacks were neither direct victims nor perpetrators of harm? This paper seeks to explore the contours of these questions. What is missing in the debate is the realization that advocates and opponents of this issue are relying on the same moral foundation of fairness to make their respective cases but in completely different ways. If this is not understood clearly there will be little to no progress in the discourse about affirmative action. In framing this discussion, this paper uses the moral foundation theory of Jonathan Haidt to provide the conceptual origins of the disagreement over affirmative action policy. Haidt's research can provide helpful and needed categories in the discussion of racial justice as it relates to opportunities for African Americans.

What is Affirmative Action?

Affirmative action consists of a set of anti-discrimination measures intended to provide access to preferred positions in a society for members of groups that would otherwise be excluded or underrepresented. It provides a mechanism to address contemporary exclusion, particularly a mechanism to desegregate elites. Affirmative action can be utilized to change the demography of elite position holders, making those positions more representative of the ethnic/racial/caste/gender composition of the society as a whole (Arity, Deshpande, and Weiskoff 2011).

The Role of Moral Reasoning

As a moral psychologist, Jonathan Haidt is interested in the origins and applications of moral reasoning. Haidt began his career challenging the rationalist approach championed by psychologist Lawrence Kohlberg in the long-standing debate about the moral development of children. Kolhberg extended the insights of Piaget's cognitive-developmental view quantifying a six-stage progression in children's moral reasoning (Haidt 2012, 7). Haidt disagrees with the Kolhbergian approach which locates morality as derivative for moral reasoning instead of locating it in a primary role compared to other forms of reasoning. Contrarily, Haidt believes that moral reasoning is generally a *post hoc* manifestation. Morality, then, can be innate as a set of evolved intuitions and learned as children and formed by the cultures in which they are immersed (Haidt 2012, 26). Moral reasoning is mostly a *post hoc* search for reasons to justify the judgments people have already made (Haidt 2012, 40). We do not use our moral reasoning to reconstruct the actual reasons why we came to certain judgments. In fact, according to Haidt, we reason to find the best possible arguments for why someone else ought to join us in our judgments and intuitions (Haidt 2012, 44). These intuitions need to be explored within the context of civil discourse about public policy because it is often the case that we assume our arguments are accomplishing more than they may be capable of doing. In public discourse opponents could have opposing moral intuitions about certain policy initiatives while not realizing the true basis of their disagreement. Haidt explains the potential impasse this way when we are in "combat mode" regarding policy prescriptions:

> The performance may impress our friends and show allies that we are committed members of the team, but no matter how good our logic, it's not going to change the minds of our opponents if they are in combat mode too. If you really want to change someone's mind on a moral or political matter, you'll need to see things from that person's angle as well as your own. (Haidt 2012, 49)

When it comes to issues like affirmative action, then, it is possible that advocates and dissenters have not done the conceptual work to understand the moral intuitions of the other side in an attempt to see things from a different point of view. Instead, interlocutors often demonize their opposition and charge others with being irrational, non-caring, or even racist. Perhaps there could be a more productive discourse if the first step in the art of persuasion was articulating the reasoning and intuitions behind the conclusion of one's opponent before evaluating the merits of the argument. Haidt adds that "if you ask people to believe something that violates their intuitions, they will devote their efforts to finding an escape hatch—a reason to doubt your argument or conclusion" (2012, 50). Haidt concludes this by articulating what he calls the first principle of moral psychology, namely that intuitions come first and our moral reasoning comes second (Haidt 2012, 52). We show our like or dislike for some things the instant we encounter them, often before we can explain why. What is true about all of us is that we come to discussions on social justice with prejudgments about the narrative surrounding people who could potentially be harmed or benefit from the long-term consequences of certain policies.

In America's storied racial history we find that most people "turn out to have negative implicit association with many social groups, such as black people, immigrants, obese people, and the elderly" (Haidt 2012, 58). In terms of affirmative action, we can also have implicit positive associations with the social groups and classes of people that are used to establish various preferential public policies. When it comes to policies that treat some groups preferentially, these associations, supported by *post hoc* moral reasoning, can prevent us from understanding why it is that others might disagree. Haidt's research indicates that our implicit associations and conclusions about moral issues are changed primarily by interacting with other people especially those with whom we disagree. Unfortunately the understanding for preferential policies tends to happen in closed ideological communities and networks.

Most of us do not seek evidence that challenges our own beliefs, but if there is "affection, admiration, or a desire to please the other person," argues Haidt, we are much more willing to try to find the truth in the other person's argument (Haidt 2012, 68). However, policy advocates and theorists are riddled with what Haidt calls "confirmation bias." Haidt describes this as "the tendency to seek out and interpret new evidence in ways that confirm what you already think" (Haidt 2012, 80). In general, according to Haidt, we are good at challenging statements made by other people but when it comes to one's own presuppositions facing opposition the tendency is to protect them and keep them. Policy advocates tend to approach issues by saying something like, "Here is some evidence I can point to as supporting my theory, and, therefore, the theory is right and should be acted on accordingly" (Haidt 2012, 80). Haidt is concerned with this important question: "If thinking is confirmatory rather than explanatory . . . what chance is there that people will think in an open-minded, explanatory way when self-interest, social identity, and strong emotions make them want or even need to reach a preordained conclusion?" (2012, 81). The implications of this insight cannot be overstated in the affirmative action debate. It is possible, if not likely, that the analysis of affirmative action as an act of justice may be muddled in a host of psycho-social influences that may not be related to whether or not a chosen course of action is effective in the long term. Moreover, because of our groupish nature and presuppositions, we can believe just about anything that supports our team and the conclusions we have already decided to be true. Haidt explains this phenomenon:

> People care about their groups, whether those be racial, region, religious, or political. The political scientist Don Kindler summarizes the findings like this: "In matters of public opinion, citizens seem to be asking themselves not 'What's in it for me?' but rather 'What's in it for my group?' Political opinions function as 'badges of social membership.' They're like an array of bumper stickers people put on their cars showing that political

causes, universities, and sports teams they support. Our politics
is groupish, not selfish. (2012, 86)

Haidt's work highlights the challenge of dialogue about preferential
racial policies in light of the complexities of navigating implicit associations, confirmation bias, and groupishness. These are the types of issues
that redirect our attention away from the particularities of policy application to their theoretical and moral justifications. The most effective long-
term strategy may not be the one we prefer, and our preferences may be
associated more with our biases than with evidence and data.

Moral Foundations and Fairness

Our presuppositions and moral foundations ultimately construct social
theories that later become public policy. According to Haidt, as Western-
ers we tend to individualize conceptions of justice by viewing the world
full of individuals and their particular rights, a tendency that leads us
to think about justice in terms of negotiating the relationship between
harm and fairness (Haidt 2012, 99). In reality, as Haidt establishes in his
second principle of moral psychology, "there is more to morality than
harm and fairness" (Haidt 2012, 98). In the West ethics is about the
pursuit of freedom because people are first and foremost "autonomous
individuals with wants, needs, and preferences," and, therefore, "should
be free to satisfy these wants, needs, and preferences as they see fit, and
so societies develop moral concepts such as rights, liberty, and justice" to
allow people to coexist without interfering in the free choices of others
(Haidt 2012, 99). Policies like affirmative action introduce new burdens
when treating classes of people as individuals causes the larger society
to rewrite policies for the sake of serving small, sacralized groups (Haidt
2012, 166–167). If public policy is reduced to the pursuit of individual
(or sacralized group) autonomy in the short term there may be missed
opportunities to develop policies that provide the scaffolding for equal
justice for all in the long term.

Haidt is additionally concerned with attempts to reduce morality to
one single principle, say for example Immanuel Kant's "categorical imperative" or John Rawls' notion of "justice as fairness." Haidt believes that
when we attempt to ground all of morality on a single principle, known
as monism, it "leads to societies that are unsatisfying to most people and
at high risk of becoming inhumane because they ignore so many other

moral principles" (Haidt 2012, 113). It is precisely a discussion of the complexities of other moral principles that is often missing in the debate about affirmative action. Haidt simply wants to broaden the discussions of morality beyond harm and fairness. Haidt and his colleagues developed the "Moral Foundations Theory" as way to describe the cognitive modules upon which cultures construct their sense of what ought to be done in response to any given state of affairs. Haidt defines the six moral foundations this way:

> 1) Care/harm: This foundation is related to our long evolution as mammals with attachment systems and an ability to feel (and dislike) the pain of others. It underlies virtues of kindness, gentleness, and nurturance.

> 2) Fairness/cheating: This foundation is related to the evolutionary process of reciprocal altruism. It generates ideas of justice, rights, and autonomy. [Note: In our original conception, fairness included concerns about equality, which are more strongly endorsed by political liberals. However, as we reformulated the theory in 2011 based on new data, we emphasize proportionality, which is endorsed by everyone, but is more strongly endorsed by conservatives.]

> 3) Liberty/oppression: This foundation is about the feelings of reactance and resentment people feel toward those who dominate them and restrict their liberty. Its intuitions are often in tension with those of the authority foundation. The hatred of bullies and dominators motivates people to come together, in solidarity, to oppose or take down the oppressor.

> 4) Loyalty/betrayal: This foundation is related to our long history as tribal creatures able to form shifting coalitions. It underlies virtues of patriotism and self-sacrifice for the group. It is active anytime people feel that it's "one for all, and all for one."

> 5) Authority/subversion: This foundation was shaped by our long primate history of hierarchical social interactions. It underlies virtues of leadership and followership, including deference to legitimate authority and respect for traditions.

> 6) Sanctity/degradation: This foundation was shaped by the psychology of disgust and contamination. It underlies religious notions of striving to live in an elevated, less carnal, nobler way. It underlies the widespread idea that the body is a temple which

can be desecrated by immoral activities and contaminants (an idea not unique to religious traditions). (Haidt 2013)

This list helps us see that for any given analysis a social theorist ought to rely on these moral foundations to determine public policy. By extension, then, there is more to policy-making than harm and fairness. The affirmative action debate, while not always explicit, tends to narrate the African American experience in terms of harm and fairness. In these debates disagreements about the justice of preferential policies simply represent competing trajectories that value, interpret, and apply Haidt's other moral foundations to the interpretations and evaluations of the past, present, and future.

Haidt's research finds that liberals (modern-day progressives) tend to conceptualize morality with an emphasis on the care, fairness, and liberty at the expense of the other three whereas conservatives tend to equally depend on all six foundations when creating policy prescriptions. The remainder of this paper will focus on role of the "fairness" moral foundation in the affirmative action debate. It could be said that what is at the root of the disagreement between supporters and opponents of affirmative action is that each side is ignorant to the fact that the other has a completely different conception of what fairness means. Each side may assume that the other side does not value fairness. They both appeal to fairness to refute the other side. Moreover, unless there is a robust discussion about these moral foundations, supporters and opponents will continue talking past and demonizing their respective opposition.

Using distinctions between liberals and conservatives, Haidt explains how fairness is conceptualized. Haidt notes that conservatives' notions of fairness primarily focus on proportionality, not equality (2012, 169). Moreover, conservatives tend to not believe that liberals care about fairness as proportionality. Liberals conceptualize equality as it relates to the issue of fairness. Haidt believes that their imbalance in moral foundations leads them "to sacralize equality, which is then pursued by fighting for civil rights and human rights" for particular groups or classes of people (Haidt 2012, 175). Liberals will tend to go beyond "the equality of rights to pursue equality of outcomes" which cannot be obtained in a country that pursues economic liberty for citizens. According to Haidt, this may explain why progressives usually favor "higher taxes on the rich, high levels of services provided to the poor, and sometimes guaranteed minimum income for everyone" (ibid.). By contrast, conservatives sacralize liberty, not equality, and are more concerned for fairness as it relates to people's freedom to not be coerced by government to pursue opportunities that are available to everyone by their free choice.

For conservatives, it is important to note that to question the equality of outcomes is not to advocate *for* inequality, as explained by someone like Thomas Sowell. Outcome disparities between groups call for other explanations that often fall outside of the realm of race, including income and wealth, performance, and merit at all levels of the individual performance (Sowell 1999, 55). Sowell would charge that progressives fail to account for the broad differences in individual performance within oppressed minorities when arbitrarily declaring that "whites" control the means of production, control the world's wealth, have conspired to keep blacks and other minorities down, and have been inherently racist in social orientation, and so on. When examined from a historical and international perspective, many of the pathologies and problems in black communities and poor communities around the world may be attributed to reasons other than oppression via individuals or social structures. Socioeconomic disparities, Sowell points out, have always been commonplace among peoples, nations, regions, and other groupings (Sowell 1999, 59). However, this fact should not imply, as many progressives maintain, that these disparities always have been—and continue to be—the result of oppression. For example, although it is true that discrimination and bias have resulted in inequalities, it is not always true that discrimination or bias can be inferred from statistical inequalities when applied to individuals (Sowell 1999, 62). For Sowell, the underlying false assumption of progressives is that "the world would be random or even, in the absence of discrimination or bias by individuals, institutions, or white 'society'" (Sowell 1999, 63). That is, since all people are created equal, in the absence of discrimination everyone would have equal socioeconomic outcomes. However, the truth is that people are created unequal with respect to gifts and abilities and this fact will yield unequal socioeconomic outcomes. Additionally, there are other factors working against equal social outcomes including such things as age and geography (Sowell 1999, 63–67).

Another way to conceptualize the fairness divide is this to frame it in terms of fair play versus fair shares (Ryan 1981). In the fair-play vision, inequalities are fair so long as the rules by which people compete for valued goods are fair (Wright and Rogers 2011, 187). In this framework there are winners and losers. When losers lose, as long as the rules are the same, the first assumption cannot be that they lost because of injustice and that, all things being equal, had they been equal from the start they would not have lost. That is, so long as there is equal opportunity, inequality of results is not a moral problem. Alternatively, in the fair-share vision everyone is entitled to a share of earnings of other individuals as their contribution to society's resources sufficient to live a dignified, flourishing life for all (Wright and Rogers 2011, 187). By "sufficient" Wright and Rogers mean "having enough to be able to participate fully in the exercise of rights and liberties, to be able to exercise personal freedom and develop one's talent" (ibid.). In the fair-share vision everyone has a human right to good healthcare, decent housing, adequate nutrition, and so on (ibid.). Everyone deserves a fair share of society's resources and "bounty." In the affirmative action debate, the central related question is this: "Does America's history of racial oppression prohibit African Americans today from getting their fair share of America's bounty?" If American history is taken seriously, then, some argue that only answer to that question is "yes" and, furthermore, affirmative action is the best way to deal with the past and ensure that the racial oppression of history is not allowed to prohibit African Americans from getting their fair share in the future. More broadly, affirmative action is seen as an essential weapon in the fight against racial oppression.

It is important to note Haidt's research indicates most adults do not favor social benefits being distributed equally if there are perceptions that recipients did not contribute equally (Haidt 2012, 180). The fairness foundation becomes more complex. Over the years Haidt revised an initial set of moral foundations to include a set of modules that "evolved in response to the adaptive challenge of reaping the rewards of cooperation" while protected from free loaders as well as the inclusion of looking "more closely at people's strong desires to protect their communities from cheaters, slackers, and free riders" who could undermine incentives for people to freely cooperate (Haidt 2012, 181). For conservatives the fairness foundation trigger is activated by the concern that a large social safety net or preferential policies will encourage abuse and decreased interest in making contributions to the whole of society. For example, affirmative action could introduce a sense of entitlement and desert that is disassociated from merit. Haidt concludes that liberals (modern-day progressives) have a three-foundation morality but are "willing to trade away fairness (as proportionality) when it conflicts with compassion or with their desire to fight oppression" (Haidt 2012, 184). Conservatives, on the other hand, have a six-foundation morality and are "more willing than liberals to sacrifice care and let some people get hurt in order to achieve their many other moral objectives" (Haidt 2012, 184). Another way of analyzing these polarities is to discuss them in terms of competing visions of what trade-offs are tolerable in society in order to make society work. By extension, then, the three-foundation morality will be less open to making social sacrifices. Recent discourse about affirmative action policy highlights Haidt's concerns as supporters and opponents of affirmative make the moral case for their position.

Affirmative Action and Fairness in Dialogue

As Haidt points out, confirmation bias affects the way one interprets data. In the affirmative action debate confirmation bias plays a significant role in the interpretation of America's racial history and its lingering effects on the ability of African Americans to receive their fair share of society's bounty. Perceptions, interpretations, and social visions determine whether or not affirmative action is viewed as an effective means to address the various forms of discrimination that exist today. Wright and Rogers are convinced that "no viable alternative to some form of affirmative action exists if we want to counter the pernicious effects of certain forms of discrimination" (Wright and Rogers 2011, 295). Preferential policies create good incentives for employers and schools to accept the additional costs needed to "overcome statistical discrimination based on race and actively seek out the best minority candidates they can find" (ibid.). In the end, Wright and Rogers argue, affirmative action undermines the perverse incentives that sustain discrimination based on group characteristics (ibid.).

The assumption that affirmative action is the only way to inoculate against racial discrimination has much to do how the African American experience is understood. For supporters of affirmative action, the point is made when evaluating for fair-play, as justice in history matters:

> The first African slaves were brought to the American colonies in 1619. Blacks have thus been part of what was to become the United States for four hundred years. During 245 of these years they were slaves, subordinated in brutal and dehumanizing ways. This period was followed by a century of legalized discrimination that ended less than fifty years ago. . . . It is hardly surprising that racial discrimination continues to operate and that economic inequalities associated with race have

not yet disappeared. The spontaneous action of actors in the
market will not be sufficient to eliminate these inequalities.
(Ibid.)

For supporters of affirmative action the only fair way to address this
history is to introduce race-based preferential programs and policies.
Otherwise, American society will not achieve equality between the races.

Fairness emerges as a central thread in the affirmative action debate
not only to have a fair society but as a means of pursuing equality, the
ultimate goal in much of the discourse. Crosby et al. explain the appeal of
affirmative action: many view it as a "proactive examination of whether
equal opportunity exists, and if does not, a plan can be implemented for
taking concrete measures to elimination the barriers and to establish true
equality" (Crosby et al. 2003, 95). The authors note that affirmative action
is integral to perceptions of how to increase diversity in the workplace
and in higher education. This, again, is key for battling and dismantling
covert and implicit forms of racial prejudice. Affirmative action can
come with certain trade-offs, the authors note, including a possibility of
undermining the self-confidence of those who benefit from preferential
programs, giving race too much weight in decision-making by organizations, dividing the black community by class, and wasting money
(Crosby et al. 2003, 107–8). Even with these costs in mind Crosby et al.
argue that affirmative action is the most effective way to reward merit on
the path to achieving true equality and diversity (ibid.). The assumption,
then, is that without affirmative action equality and diversity will never
be achieved. In the end affirmative action is fair primarily because of the
injustice it prevents now and in the future.

The emphasis on affirmative action as a means of achieving true
equality has shifted the debate away from one of its earlier justifications—namely, as a way to right past wrongs— to higher social aspirations for injustice prevention. Research shows that having perspective on
African American history affects how individuals consider the fairness of
affirmative action. For example, those who perceived a greater amount
of discrimination against a particular class of people were much more
likely to evaluate preferential treatment and costs of affirmative action
programs as fair (Linton and Christiansen 2006, 1632). Research by Aberson suggests that individuals who endorse the benefits of diversity and
recognize the prevalence of discrimination construct their own justifications for affirmative action policies (Aberson 2007, 2468). For example,

"if an individual does not believe that African Americans are targets of employment discrimination, then that individual would be unlikely to change his or her attitude about a policy based on justification focused on redressing discrimination" (Aberson 2007, 2468). Perceptions of fairness, then, are not constructed in the abstract for supporters. These perceptions remain tied to some form of past discrimination and injustice. Research by Katznelson is distinct because he does not focus on the legacy of slavery but how affirmative action initiatives function as a way of redressing the injustice from the FDR's "New Deal" and "Fair Deal" policies because they "constituted a massive transfer of privileges to white Americans" at the institutional level (Katznelson 2006, 565).

The emphasis shifted from preferential treatment of individuals in a class to the hopes, dreams, and goals for a future society at-large. Gary Massey argues, for example, that affirmative action achieves fairness in three ways: (1) by building into laws, procedures, guidelines, and organizational practices those behaviors and decisions that "explicitly prohibit consumer, worker, and statistical discrimination"; (2) by assuming the Rawlsian "veil of ignorance" in order to "counter" any "disadvantages of birth," remove all barriers to autonomy by "level the playing field" and "maximize the quality of life for everyone"; and (3) by socially engineering what we prefer, making "affirmative action a fair price to pay, a down payment of a better future" (Massey 2004, 792). McHugh further justifies affirmative action as fair because it takes seriously the historical memory of the black experience and is the best way for us as a community to pursue "shared being" by taking definite actions to achieve a collective promise to maintain equity of fair shares (McHugh 2005, 152–53).

For opponents of affirmative action the principal objection focuses on fairness as opportunity—i.e., fair play. Economists like Thomas Sowell object to the assumption that statistical disparities between races, in terms of income or education attainment, is a necessary and demonstrable result of racial discrimination. For Sowell, fair play requires that individuals be considered "*without regard* to race, sex, age, etc.," while affirmative action requires that people "be judged *with regard* to such group membership, receiving preferential or compensatory treatment" to achieve to a more desired representation in various institutions (1985, 38; emphasis in original). In this framework questions arise regarding the consistency of pursuing fairness and equality by using discriminatory, race-based preferential means. As Sowell argues, affirmative action is shifting the emphasis from "equality of prospective opportunity toward statistical parity of retrospective results" (1985, 39). Sowell charges that supporters of affirmative action wrongly assume that there must be equal results among groups presumed to have equal genetic potential as a law of nature. Inequality of opportunity becomes a *reductio ad absurdum* used to explain any and all disparities between whites and African Americans in those areas impacted by affirmative action policy. Sowell highlights the fact there are many other reasons tracing back to demographics, culture, geography, age, education, and so on that broaden out the explanations of disparities (Sowell 1985, 42). While affirmative action may seem to inform cosmic justice it cannot give any insight into whether or not any particular individual African American should receive preferential treatment and why any particular, individual white person should be passed over to provide an opportunity for someone who is black. The one-size-fits-all nature of affirmative action policy could lead to strange applications. For example, two 18-year-old men, one white and the other African American, apply for admission to Vanderbilt University. Both men graduated from the same public school district with the same grade point average and SAT scores. The difference is that the African American student has parents who are married and both second-generation lawyers and the white student is from a single-parent home with a mother who works two jobs. If Vanderbilt has an affirmative action policy in place in their admissions process the African American student will be given preferential treatment, but, of course, the question is, why should he? Is it fair to the white student? Affirmative action critics conclude that the notions that there could be no other explanation for disparities in college admissions rates, or that economic disparities between blacks and whites demand some sort of intervention, ignore other important possible mitigating factors. As a result, the pursuit of fair shares does not lead to the equality desired but creates new inequalities and injustice.

Some argue that it is difficult to know how the world would be without affirmative action, but advocates will not allow such a world to exist. When theorists on both sides of the debate rely on competing interpretations of the current effects of past events it leads to different evaluations of what affirmative action is intended to accomplish. While Sowell fully recognizes that African Americans in America's history experienced injustice, he demonstrates that blacks were making good progress without preferential policies. For example, in the late nineteenth century blacks had higher labor force participation rates and marriage rates than whites, numbers that remained high until the 1960s (Sowell 2004, 118). On what basis, then, are we to assume that blacks would not have the same incomes as whites in the absence of racial discrimination given the fact that various groups of American whites have had different incomes from one another at various periods in history? (Sowell 2004, 118). In other words, since there are profound disparities among whites as a race, why would we think there would be no disparities between races for similar reasons? Sowell argues that affirmative action supporters ignore that fact that the number of blacks rising in professional and other high level occupations was higher in the five years prior to the passage of the 1964 Civil Rights Act than in the five years following. To make matters worse, minority immigrants are eligible for affirmative action even though they have suffered no past discrimination in the United States on the scale of African Americans. As a result, more than four times as many businesses are owned by Hispanics than Asian Americans and thirteen times as many businesses are owned by women than African Americans (Sowell 2004, 121). In the end, questions must be raised about whether affirmative action is a fair way to achieve the equality that many want, given that fact that it assigns privileges to other races and groups (like women) that were intended for African Americans only.

What is true, says Sowell, is that affirmative action supporters seem to want it both ways. For Sowell fairness and true equality cannot both mean "(1) having the same performance receive the same evaluation or reward, regardless of the group from which the individual comes, and (2) equal outcomes or equal statistical probabilities of success for different groups" (Sowell 2004, 169). In this sense, supporters of affirmative action do not want individuals to be treated by equal rules but rather want to tilt, distort, and arbitrarily change the rules "to produce a preconceived equalizing of results" (ibid.). It is at this point where Haidt is helpful. Both supporters and critics make their cases for or against affirmative action by arguing for fair means to achieving equality. The difference is that affirmative action supporters tend to look at past discrimination as evidence that the only future intervention for material disparity between whites and African Americans of discriminatory preferential treatment. As mentioned earlier, affirmative action becomes the only way to produce a desired social vision for society. On the other hand, affirmative action critics view fairness as individuals being considered by the same rules without preferential treatment regardless of the result. Haidt is helpful in clarifying which moral foundations put a premium on fairness as means to equality with a focus on fair processes versus those that focus on fairness as a focus on true equality demonstrated by the elimination of disparities. While the affirmative action discourse remains trapped in pragmatic discussions about pros and cons, perceptions versus realities, and the like, what is needed for effective consensus policy is a more central discussion about the relationship between fairness and equality.

Discussion and Conclusion

The relationship between fairness and equality is a core discussion if we are to build social justice policy with any modicum of consensus and mutual compromise. We learned from Jonathan Haidt that that the six moral foundations of care, fairness, liberty, loyalty, authority, and sanctity must be considered in concert with one another when considering policies like these because intuitions determine whether or not people accept these policies as just or unjust. What is important to remember in the affirmative action debate is that the concept of fairness is actually a principle about the means of achieving something far weightier: *true equality*. Therefore, the answer to whether or not affirmative action is "fair" is procedural and conceptual and is derivative of whatever is meant by equality. What matters, then, is how we evaluate affirmative action as just according to its "with-respect-to-whatness." If our definition of equality means holding people to the same rules regardless of historical-social context then current policies will tend to be considered unfair because those policies are treating people unequally in the pursuit of equality. On the other hand, if equality means ensuring that various types of persons are equally distributed across certain sectors according to the vision of decision-makers then affirmative action will tend to be considered fair. In this view the emphasis is not on *how* we achieve true equality but rather, attempting to construct equality using whatever means also allow us to achieve ends that match the vision of the decision-makers.

For example, if the University of Theodore in Wacca, Montana (not a real university nor town) wanted to have "true equality" represented in their faculty hiring and student body, the school could pursue this is two ways: (1) become a famously competitive academic institution so that America's best students and faculty would want to be there, or (2) make whatever adjustments in admissions and hiring to engineer the equal community envisions by those in power making decisions. The results of the first approach would be truly equal in the sense that any student or potential faculty member could apply. However, the results of this process may give the appearance of unfairness and injustice if disparities result. That is, the school could easily remain predominantly white. This raises important questions about the assumption of injustice given the student and faculty demographics. Is the student body and faculty predominantly white because no black students or faculty desire to become a part of that community? Or, alternatively, is that school predominantly white among students and faculty because the school is preferring white over blacks? If everyone is held to the exact same standards and no one shows any favoritism whatsoever then the results might not be what society might hopes. Perhaps black students and potential faculty members have no interest in living Montana. Is it possible—for affirmative action advocates—there exists a certain confirmation bias that inevitably causes them to interpret any discrepancy between racial groups in the marketplace and education as evidence of discrimination? For conservatives, the decision here is whether or not society is willing to trade off a social vision about what the future should look like for sake of having all persons be held according to the same standards and rules no matter what. In this sense, what would constitute fairness in the pursuit of equality would be to treat all prospective students and faculty members according to the same respective standard. This would be fairness in the pursuit of equality.

On other hand, if equality is defined by pursuing a particular social vision then fairness will be pursued to produce a desired result. The rules will change as the desired social goals change. So, for example, if the university wants more women faculty and more Native American undergraduates it will change the rules of the game in order to create the desired social result on campus. In hiring, men will be passed over and, in recruiting, non-Native Americans will be considered in a different light. Is this fair? It depends. If the goal is to produce a social result by changing the process to render it preferential toward certain classes, then those whose definition of equality encompasses Native American students and more female faculty students will conceive of the process as fair. This affirmative action process is also discriminatory but will be justified by the higher goal of achieving true equality as understood by those in power in the university.

Until there is consensus about what it means to treat people equally, there will likely not be any agreement about the fairness of affirmative action. What is needed then is clarity about what equality is all about. Defining equality, however, introduces a symphony of new questions.[1] For example, does equal treatment imply equal shares or equal distributions? How do we prevent the pursuit of equality along one axis from creating inequality along another? For example, how do we pursue racial equality of African Americans without discriminating against whites? Do disparities between races always, generally, or necessarily include the presence of injustice? How does one account for social mobility disparities within racial classes? Are we treating people equally or unequally if we try to balance the unequal treatment they receive elsewhere or in the past? If so, as in the case of those who maintain that affirmative action staves off injustice, is this the right course of action and is it effective? If we understand that life is not a race we need to ask precisely what equality is for. Finally, we need to decide what is more important as an ideal: society doing all it can to foster people's ability to meet basic needs or society doing all it can to foster excellence? There are more questions to consider here, and the answers help determine under what conditions affirmative action can be considered fair or unfair.

The African American experience must be taken seriously if we are to have a society that is truly free and virtuous. Perhaps, moving forward, there can be some consensus that the morality of affirmative action cannot be determined unless trade-offs are assessed in light of multiple moral foundations. If intuitions come first and reasoning second, as Haidt suggests, perhaps America's affirmative action discussion started off on the wrong foot from the beginning—viz., rationalistically. Using our moral intuitions and being honest about the reality of confirmation bias, the contributions of Haidt help us see that the moral foundations of sanctity, authority, loyalty, liberty, fairness and care are necessary in the understanding the "ought" of affirmative action beyond considerations of fairness. Perhaps the current impasse between advocates and dissenters is a result of mutual moral monism that could be helped by understanding that just as there is more to morality than harm and fairness; there is more to understanding the African American experience than oppression and equality.

1. The questions that follow are variations of questions raised by David Schmidtz in *Elements of Justice* (Cambridge: Cambridge University Press, 2006) 107–57.

Bibliography

"10 Surprising Statistics on Women in the Workplace." *College Times*, February 15, 2010. http://collegetimes.us/10-surprising-statistics-on-women-in-the-workplace.

60620 Zip Code Income and Careers. USA.com. http://www.usa.com/60620-il-income-and-careers.htm

Aberson, Christopher. "Diversity, Merit, Fairness, and Discrimination Beliefs as Predictors of Support for Affirmative-Action Policy Actions." *Journal of Applied Social Psychology* 37:10 (2007) 2451–74.

Alex-Assenoh, Yvette M. et al. "Mentoring and African American Political Scientists." *Political Science and Politics* 38:2 (2005) 283–85.

Al-Tayyib, A. A. et al. "Effect of Low Medical Literacy on Health Survey Measurements." *American Journal of Public Health* 92:9 (2002) 1478–81.

Americans for Democratic Action. "Issues." http://www.adaaction.org/pages/issues. php.

Anthony, Ted. "America is Again at Edge of History." *Montgomery Advertiser*, June 8, 2008, section 1A.

Archdiocese of Chicago. "Facts & Figures for the Year Ending 2011." http://www. archchicago.org/about-us/statistics.shtm.

———. "Letter from Archdiocesan Representative for Anti-Violence Initiatives." http://www.archchicago.org.

Armada, Bernard. "Memorial Agon: An Interpretive Tour of the National Civil Rights Museum." *Southern Communication Journal* 63 (1998) 235–43.

———. "The Fierce Urgency of Now: Dr. Martin Luther King, Jr. and the Politics of Public Memory." *St. Thomas Magazine* 18:2 (2002) 34–37.

Arity, William, Jr., Ashwini Deshpande, and Thomas Weiskoff. "Who is Eligible? Should Affirmative Action be Group- or Class-Based?" *American Journal of Economics and Sociology* 70:1 (2011) 238–68.

Arozullah, A. M. et al. "The Roles of Low Literacy and Social Support in Predicting the Preventability of Hospital Admission." *Journal of General Internal Medicine* 21:2 (2006) 140–45.

Astin, Alexander W., and Helen S. Astin. *Meaning and Spirituality in the Lives of College Faculty: A Study of Values and Authenticity and Stress*. Los Angeles: Higher Education Research Institute, 1999.

Austin, Grace. "Past and Present Come Together at Spelman College." *Profiles in Diversity Journal* (March 2012). No pages. Online: http://www.diversityjournal. com/7832-past-present-come-together-at-spelman-college/.

Baker, D. W. et al. "Development of a Brief Test to Measure Functional Health Literacy." *Patient Education and Counseling* 38:1 (1999) 33–42.

Baker, D. W. et al. "The Relationship of Patient Reading Ability to Self-Reported Health and Use of Health Services." *American Journal of Public Health* 87:6 (1997) 1027–30.

Barber, M. N. et al. "Up to a Quarter of the Australian Population May Have Suboptimal Health Literacy Depending upon the Measurement Tool: Results From a Population-Based Survey." *Health Promotional International* 24:3 (2009) 252–61.

Barrett, Betty. "Is 'Safety' Dangerous? A Critical Examination of the Classroom as Safe Space." *The Canadian Journal for the Scholarship of Teaching and Learning* 1:1 (2010) article 9.

Bass, P. F. III, J. F. Wilson, and C. H. Griffith. "A Shortened Instrument for Literacy Screening." *Journal of General Internal Medicine* 18:12 (2003) 1036–38.

Baumgartner, Frank R., and Bryan D. Jones. *Agendas and Instability in American Politics*. Chicago: University of Chicago Press, 1993.

Benjamin, Lois, ed. *Black Women in the Academy: Promises and Perils*. Gainsville, FL: University Press of Florida, 1997.

Bensman, David. *Building School-Family Partnerships in a South-Bronx Neighborhood*. National Center for Restructuring Education, Schools, and Teaching. New York: Columbia University Press, 1999.

Beauchamp, Keith. *The Untold Story of Emmett Louis Till*. New York: ThinkFilm, 2005.

Bhargava, Divya. "Women and Negative Stereotypes: An End Before a Start." *CounterCurrents,* July 6, 2009. http://www.countercurrents.org/bhargava060709.htm.

Bird, Tammy S. "Blogging Through My Son's Incarceration: An Autoethnography Exploring Voice and Power in an Online Space." PhD dissertation, North Carolina State University, 2012.

Blyden, Edward. "Ethiopia Stretching Out Her Hands to God: Or Africa's Service to the World." In *Christianity, Islam, and the Negro Race*, edited by Edward Blyden, 130–49. Baltimore, MD: Black Classic, 1994. Collection of essays and speeches by Blyden originally published in 1888.

Bonner, Florence B., and Veronica G. Thomas. "Introduction and Overview: New and Continuing Challenges and Opportunities for Black Women in the Academy." *Journal of Negro Education* 70:3 (2001) 121–23. http://www.jstor.org/stable/3211204.

Bonner, Fred A., Aretha Marbley, and Mary F. Howard-Hamilton. *Diverse Millennial Students in College: Implications for Faculty and Student Affairs*. Sterling: Stylus, 2011.

Bonilla-Silva, Eduardo. "Colorblind Racism." In *Race, Class, and Gender in the U.S.*, edited by Paula S. Rothenberg, 131–37. New York: Worth, 2007.

Bonvillian, Crystal. "Alabama Best in the Nation at Teaching Children About the Civil Rights Movement, Report Says." *The Huntsville Times*, September 29, 2011. http://blog.al.com/breaking/2011/09/alabama_best_in_the_nation_at.html.

Bower, Beverly L. "Campus Life for Faculty of Color: Still Strangers After All These Years?" *New Directions for Community Colleges* 118 (2002) 79–88.

Bradley, Anthony. "Black Professors Have Credibility Obstacles at Predominantly White Universities." *The Institute*, June 16, 2011. http://bradley.chattablogs.com/archives/2011/06/black-professor.html.

Broido, Ellen. "Understanding Diversity in Millennial Students." *New Directions for Student Success* 106 (2004) 73–85.

Brown, J. I., V. V. Fishco, and G. Hanna. *The Nelson-Denny Reading Test*. Chicago: Riverside, 1993.

Butner, Bonita K., Hansel Burley, and Aretha Faye Marbley. "Coping with the Unexpected: Black Faculty at Predominantly White Institutions." *Journal of Black Studies* 30:3 (2000) 453–62.

Buying Influence, Inc. "The Wage Gap Continues to Exist in Corporate America." *Buying Influence*. http://thetask.com/~binfluence/wage_gap.html

Cade, Roshaunda D. "Mulatta Mama Performing Passing and Mimicking Minstrelsy in Mark Twain's *Pudd'nhead Wilson*." *Mothering, Race, Ethnicity, Culture and Class* 9:2 (2007) 230–39.

Campbell, James T. *Middle Passages: African American Journeys to Africa, 1787–2005*. New York: Penguin, 2006.

Campbell, Marci Kramish et al. "Church-Based Health Promotion Interventions: Evidence and Lessons Learned." *Annual Review of Public Health* 28 (2007) 213–34. http://www.ncbi.nlm.nih.gov/pubmed/17155879.

Campbell, Valencia. *Advice from the Top: What Minority Women Say about their Career Success*. Santa Barbara, CA: Praeger, 2009.

Carrier, James. *A Traveler's Guide to the Civil Rights Movement*. Orlando: Harcourt, 2004.

Carroll, D. L. "The Claims of Africa on the Christian World to Send Her the Gospel." *The African Repository and Colonial Journal* 23:11 (1847) 323–34.

Carter, J. Kameron. *Race: A Theological Account*. New York: Oxford University Press, 2008.

Casey, Edward. "Public Memory in Place and Time." In *Framing Public Memory*, edited by Kendall Phillips, 17–44. Tuscaloosa, AL: The University of Alabama Press, 2004.

Chamblee, Marquita T. "On Becoming Allies: Opportunities and Challenges in Creating Alliance Between White Women and Women of Color in the Academy." In *Unlikely Allies in the Academy: Women of Color and White Women in Conversation*, edited by Karen L. Dace, 54–64. New York: Routledge, 2012.

Chang, Heewon. *Autoethnography as Method*. Walnut Creek, CA: Left Coast, 2008.

Chang, Heewon, and Derick Boyd, eds. *Spirituality in Higher Education: Autoethnographies*. Walnut Creek, CA: Left Coast, 2011.

Chisolm, D. J., and L. Buchanan. "Measuring Adolescent Functional Health Literacy: A Pilot Validation of The Test of Functional Health Literacy in Adults." *Journal of Adolescent Health* 41:3 (2007) 312–14.

City Data. "Auburn Gresham Neighborhood in Chicago, Illinois, 60620 Detailed Profile." http://www.city-data.com/neighborhood/Auburn-Gresham-Chicago-IL.html.

Clayton, Dewey M. *The Presidential Campaign of Barack Obama: A Critical Analysis of a Racially Transcendent Strategy*. New York: Routledge, 2010.

Clinton, Robert J., and Richard W. Clinton. *The Mentor Handbook: Detailed Guidelines and Helps for Christian Mentors and Mentorees*. Altadena: Barnabas, 1991.

Clowney, Charmaine P. "Best Practices in Recruiting and Retaining Diverse Faculty." http://www.ewu.edu/groups/academicaffairs/BestPractices.ppt.

Cobb, Charles. *On the Road to Freedom: A Guided Tour of the Civil Rights Trail*. Chapel Hill, NC: Algonquin, 2008.

Cohen, Cathy J. *Boundaries of Blackness: AIDS and the Breakdown of Black Politics.* Chicago: University of Chicago Press, 1999.

———. "Millennials and the Myth of the Post-Racial Society: Black Youth, Intragenerational Divisions, and the Continuing Racial Divide in American Politics." *Journal of the American Academy of Arts and Sciences* 140:2 (2011) 1–9.

Cone, James H. *Black Theology and Black Power.* Maryknoll, NY: Orbis, 1969.

Confer, Chris, and Ketevan Mamiseishvili. "College Choice of Minority Students Admitted to Institutions in the Council for Christian Colleges and Universities." *Journal of College Admission* 217 (2012) 4–15.

Congressional Black Caucus. "About." http://cbc.fudge.house.gov/about/

Constantine, M., L. Smith, R. M. Redington, and D. Owens. "Racial Microaggressions Against Black Counseling and Counseling Psychology Faculty: A Central Challenge in the Multicultural Counseling Movement." *Journal of Counseling and Development* 86 (2008) 348–55.

Cook, Sarah Gibbard. "Help Women Academic Leaders Chart Their Courses." *Women in Higher Education Newsletter* 19:3 (2010) 21.

Council for Christian Colleges and Universities. Multi-Ethnic Leadership Development Institute Application. Available online at www.cccu.org during the application period in 2011.

Crawford, Kijana, and Danielle Smith. "The We and the Us: Mentoring African American Women." *Journal of Black Studies* 36:1 (2005) 52–67.

Crenshaw, Kimberlé. "Demarginalizing the Intersection of Race and Sex: a Black Feminist Critique of Antidiscrimination Doctrine, Feminist Theory, and Antiracist Politics." *University of Chicago Legal Forum* 140 (1989) 139–67.

Crosby, Faye J., Aarti Iyer, Susan Clayton, and Roberta A. Downing. "Affirmative Action: Psychological Data and the Policy Debates." *American Psychologist* 58:2 (2003) 93–153.

Cross, Theodore, and Robert Bruce Slater. "Black Enrollments at the Nation's Christian Colleges are on the Rise." *Christian Higher Education* 3:4 (2004) 391–99.

Crummell, Alexander. "The Destined Superiority of the Negro." In *Destiny and Race: Selected Writings 1840–1898*, edited by Wilson Jeremiah Moses, 194–205. Amherst, MA: The University of Massachusetts Press, 1992.

Cutilli, C. C., and I. M. Bennett. "Understanding the Health Literacy of America: Results of the National Assessment of Adult Literacy." *Orthopedic Nursing* 28:1 (2009) 27–33.

Dace, Karen L. "The Whiteness of Truth and the Presumption of Innocence." In *Unlikely Allies in the Academy: Women of Color and White Women in Conversation*, edited by Karen L. Dace, 42–53. New York: Routledge, 2012.

———. "What Do I Do With All of Your Tears?" In *Unlikely Allies in the Academy: Women of Color and White Women in Conversation*, edited by Karen L. Dace, 76–87. New York: Routledge, 2012.

Datatorch.com. 2009. "Carl Linnaeus's Classification of Human Being." http://www.datatorch.com/Science/Scientists_Stories.aspx?id=38

Davis, Danielle Joy. "Mentorship and the Socialization of Underrepresented Minorities into the Professorate: Examining Varied Influences." *Mentoring and Tutoring* 16:3 (2008) 278–93.

Davis, T. C. et al. "Rapid Estimate of Adult Literacy In Medicine: A Shortened Screening Instrument." *Family Medicine* 25:6 (1993) 391.

Davis, T. et al. "Literacy Testing in Health Care Research." In *Understanding Health Literacy: Implications for Medicine and Public Health*, edited by J. G. Schwartzberg, J. B. VanGeest, and C. C. Wang, 157–79. Chicago: American Medical Association, 2005.

Davis, Townsend. *Weary Feet, Rested Souls: A Guided History of the Civil Rights Movement*. New York: W. W. Norton, 1998.

Dawson, Michael C. *Behind the Mule: Race and Class in African-American Politics.* Princeton: Princeton University Press, 1994.

———. *Black Visions: The Roots of Contemporary African-American Political Ideologies.* Chicago: University of Chicago Press, 2003.

De Bard, Robert. "Millennials Coming to College." *New Directions for Student Success* 106 (2004) 33–45.

DeMillo, Andrew. "African Students Trace U.S. Civil Rights History." *Montgomery Advertiser*, July 29, 2007, section 8AA.

Dennis, Jessica M., Jean Phinney, and Lizette Chauteco. "The Role of Motivation, Parental Support, and Peer Support in the Academic Success of Ethnic Minority First-Generation College Students." *Journal of College Student Development* 46:3 (2005) 223–36.

DeWalt, D. A. et al. "Literacy and Health Outcomes." *Journal of General Internal Medicine* 19:12 (2004) 1228–39.

Dewan, Shaila. "Civil Rights Battleground Enters World of Tourism." *New York Times*, August 10, 2004. http://www.nytimes.com/2004/08/10/national/10tourism.html.

Dubois, W. E. B. *The Souls of Black Folk*. Mineola, NY: Dover, 1903.

Duncan, Margot. "Autoethnography: Critical Appreciation of an Emerging Art." *International Journal of Qualitative Methods* 3:4 (2004) article 3. http://www.ualberta.ca/~iiqm/backissues/3_4/pdf/duncan.pdf.

Dwyer, Owen. "Interpreting the Civil Rights Movement: Place, Memory, and Conflict." *Professional Geographer* 52:4 (2004) 660–71.

Ecklund, Kathryn. "First Generation Social and Ethnic Minority Students in Christian Universities: Student Recommendations for Successful Support of Diverse Students." *Christian Higher Education* 12:3 (2013) 159–80.

Ellison, Christopher G., and Darren E. Sherkat. "The 'Semi-involuntary Institution' Revisited: Regional Variations in Church Participation among Black Americans." *Social Forces* 73:4 (1995).

Emerson, Michael O., and Christian Smith. *Divided by Faith: Evangelical Religion and the Problem of Race in America.* New York: Oxford University Press, 2000.

The Faith Community of St. Sabina. "Safe Homes of St. Sabina." http://www.saintsabina.org/index.php/outreach/safe-homes-of-saint-sabina.

Fallin, Wilson Jr. *Uplifting the People: Three Centuries of Black Baptists in Alabama.* Tuscaloosa, AL: University of Alabama Press, 2007.

Feagin, Joe R. *The White Racial Frame: Centuries of Racial Framing and Counter-Framing.* New York: Routledge, 2010.

Fenton, Steve. *Ethnicity: Racism, Class and Culture.* Lanham, MD: Rowman and Littlefield, 1999.

Finke, Roger, and Patricia Wittberg. "Organizational Revival From Within: Explaining Revivalism and Reform in the Roman Catholic Church." *Journal for the Scientific Study of Religion* 39:2 (2000) 154–70.

Fitts, LeRoy. *History of Black Baptists*. Nashville: Boardman, 1985.

Friedman, D. B., S. J. Corwin, G. M. Dominick, and I. D. Rose. "African American Men's Understanding and Perceptions about Prostate Cancer: Why Multiple Dimensions of Health Literacy are Important in Cancer Communication." *Journal of Community Health: The Publication for Health Promotion and Disease Prevention* 34:5 (2009) 449–60.

Fong, Bobby. "Toto, I Think We're Still in Kansas." *Liberal Education* 86:4 (2007) 56.

Gilbreath, Ed. *Reconciliation Blues*. Downers Grove, IL: InterVarsity, 2008.

Glassman, Penny. "Health Literacy." *National Network of Libraries of Medicine.* http://nnlm.gov/outreach/consumer/hlthlit.html

Glaude, Eddie. *In a Shade of Blue: Pragmatism and the Politics of Black America*. Chicago: University of Chicago Press, 2008.

Goodson, Albert A. "We've Come This Far by Faith." Manna Music, Inc. 1963.

Graves, Jim. "Black and Catholic." *National Catholic Register,* January 16, 2012. http://ncregister.com/daily-news/black-and-catholic/

Gregory, Sheila T. *Black Women in the Academy: The Secrets to Success and Achievement*. New York: University Press of America, 1995.

———. "Black Faculty Women in the Academy: History, Status, and Future." *Journal of Negro Education* 70:3 (2001) 124–38.

Gutierrez, Kris D., and Barbara Rogoff. "Cultural Ways of Learning: Individual Traits or Repertoires of Practice." *Educational Researcher* 32:5 (2003) 19–25.

Haidt, Jonathan. *The Righteous Mind: Why Good People are Divided by Politics and Religion*. New York: Pantheon, 2012.

———. "Moral Foundations." MoralFoundations.org.

Halbwachs, Maurice. *On Collective Memory*. Translated by Lewis A. Coser. Chicago: University of Chicago Press, 1992.

Hamlet, J. D. "Giving the Sistuhs their Due: The Lived Experiences of African American Women in Academia." In *Nature of a Sistuh: Black Women in Contemporary Culture*, edited by Trevy A. McDonald and T. Ford-Ahmed, 11–26. Durham, NC: Carolina Academic, 1999.

Hanchate, A. D. et al. "The Demographic Assessment for Health Literacy (DAHL): A New Tool For Estimating Associations Between Health Literacy and Outcomes in National Surveys." *Journal of General Internal Medicine* 23:10 (2008) 1561–66.

Hancock, Ange-Marie. *The Politics of Disgust: The Public Identity of the Welfare Queen*. New York: New York University Press, 2004.

Harding, Vincent. *There is a River: The Black Struggle for Freedom in America*. New York: Harcourt Brace, 1981.

Harris, Fredrick C. *Something Within: Religion in African-American Political Activism*. New York: Oxford University Press, 1999.

Harris-Lacewell, Melissa Victoria. *Barbershops, Bibles, and BET: Everyday Talk and Black Political Thought*. Princeton: Princeton University Press, 2004.

Harrison, Nonna Verna. *God's Many-Splendored Image: Theological Anthropology for Christian Formation*. Grand Rapids: Baker Academic, 2010.

Harris-Perry, Melissa. "Cornel West v. Barack Obama." *The Nation* (blog), May 17, 2011. http://www.thenation.com/blog/160725/cornel-west-v-barack-obama#.

Harvey, Paul. *Redeeming the South: Religious Cultures and Racial Identities Among Southern Baptists 1865–1925*. Chapel Hill, NC: University of North Carolina Press, 1997.

Harvey, William J. *Bridges of Faith Across the Seas: The Story of the Foreign Mission Board National Baptist Convention, USA, Inc.* Philadelphia: Foreign Mission Board National Baptist Convention, 1989.

Hawkins, Larycia. "Framing the Faith-Based and Community Initiative: Black Church Elites and the Black Policy Agenda." PhD Dissertation, University of Oklahoma, 2009. http://udini.proquest.com/view/framing-the-faith-based-initiative-pqid:1903462191/

Haynie, Kerry L. *African American Legislators in the American States.* New York: Columbia University Press, 2001.

Henderson, Tammy L., Andrea G. Hunter, and Gladys J. Hildreth. "Outsiders within the Academy: Strategies for Resistance and Mentoring African American Women." Ann Arbor, MI: University of Michigan Press, 2010. http://hdl.handle.net/2027/spo.4919087.0014.105.

Hendrix, Katherine Grace. "She Must be Trippin': The Secret of Disrespect from Students of Color Toward Faculty of Color." *New Directions for Teaching and Learning* 110 (Summer 2007) 85–96.

Henry, Wilma J. "Black Female Millennial College Students: Dating Dilemmas and Identity Development." *Multicultural Education* 16:2 (2008) 17–21.

Henry, Wilma J., Nicole M. West, and Andrea Jackson. "Hip-Hop's Influence on the Identity Development of Black Female College Students: A Literature Review." *Journal of College Student Development* 51:3 (2010) 237–51.

Hess, Frederick. "Still at Risk: What Students Don't Know, Even Now." Washington, DC: Common Core, 2008.

Heyer, Kristin E. "Catholics and the Political Arena: How Faith Should Inform Catholic Voters and Politicians." In *Catholics and Politics: The Dynamic Tension between Faith and Power*, edited by Kristin E. Heyer and Mark J. Rozell, 61–74. Washington, DC: Georgetown University Press, 2008.

Higgins, Monica C., and Kathy E. Kram. "Reconceptualizing Mentoring at Work: A Developmental Network Perspective." *Academy of Management Review* 26:2 (2001) 264–88.

Hochschild, Jennifer. *Facing up to the American Dream: Race, Class, and the Soul of the Nation.* Princeton, NJ: Princeton University Press, 1996.

Horton, James, ed. Introduction to *Landmarks of African American History.* New York: Oxford University Press, 2005.

Howe, Neil, William Strauss, and R. J. Matson. *Millennials Rising: The Next Great Generation.* New York: Vintage, 2000.

Howell, Brian M. *Christianity in the Local Context: Southern Baptists in the Philippines.* New York: Palgrave McMillan, 2008.

Huston, Therese. *Research Report: Race and Gender Bias in Student Evaluations of Teaching.* Seattle, Seattle University Press, October 31, 2005.

Ickes, M. J., and R. Cottrell. "Health Literacy in College Students." *Journal of American College Health* 58:5 (2010) 491–98.

Irwin, Aisling. "Mothering with a Spot of Infanticide." *Times Higher Education.* http://www.timeshighereducation.co.uk.

Jackson, Cydney H., M. Kite, and N. Branscome. "African American Women's Mentoring Experiences." Paper presented at Annual Meeting of the American Psychological Association, Ontario, Canada, August 9–13, 1996.

Jackson, John P. Jr., and Nadine M. Weidman. *Race, Racism and Science: Social Impact and Interaction*. Santa Barbara, CA: ABC-CLIO, 2004.

Jencks, C., and M. Phillips. "America's Next Achievement Test: Closing the Black-White Test Score Gap." *American Prospect* 40 (1998) 44–53.

Johnson, Barbara J., and Pichon Henrietta. "The Status of African American Faculty in the Academy: Where Do We Go From Here?" In *Strengthening the African American Educational Pipeline: Informing Research, Policy, and Practice*, edited by Jerlando F. L. Jackson, 97–114. Albany, NY: State University of New York Press, 2007.

Jones, Lewis E. "There Is Power in the Blood." Public Domain. 1899.

Jones, Susan R., and Marylu K. McEwen. "A Conceptual Model of Multiple Dimensions of Identity." *Journal of College Student Development* 41:4 (2000) 405–14.

Jordan, Lewis G. "Will Their Work Live?" *Mission Herald*, August-September, 1910, 1. For documentation precision, these editorials list no writer, but since Jordan was the editor it is assumed that he wrote all of these editorials.

———. "Human Need: The Beckoning Finger of God to Service." *Mission Herald*, August 1, 1912.

———. "The Sin of Neglecting to Evangelize the World." *Mission Herald*, August 1, 1913.

———. "Did You Know?" *Mission Herald*, August, 1919.

———. "The Quarto-Centennial of Our Secretary." *Mission Herald*, February 2, 1921.

———. *Up the Ladder in Foreign Missions*. New York: Arno, 1980.

———. *Pebbles from an African Beach*. Philadelphia, PA: The Lisle-Carey, 1918.

———. *On Two Hemispheres: Bits from the Life Story of Lewis Jordan as Told By Himself*.

Kammen, Michael. *Mystic Chords of Memory: The Transformation of Tradition in American Culture*. New York: Vintage, 1991.

Katznelson, Ira. "When Is Affirmative Action Fair? On Grievous Harms and Public Remedies." *Social Research* 73:2 (2006) 541–68.

King, Martin Luther. "Letter From a Birmingham Jail." The King Papers Project. http://mlk-kpp01.stanford.edu.

Kodama, Corinne, and John Dugan. "Leveraging Leadership Efficacy for College Students: Disaggregating Data Examine Unique Predictors by Race." *Equity & Excellence In Education* 46:2 (2013) 184–201.

Konz, Antoinette. "Students Travel Into Civil Rights' Rich History." *USA Today*, February 23, 2007, section 3A.

Kutner, Mark et al. "Literacy in Everyday Life: Results from the 2003 National Assessment of Adult Literacy." *NCES 2007–490*: National Center for Education Statistics, 2007.

Kuyper, Abraham. "Common Grace." In *Abraham Kuyper: A Centennial Reader*, edited by James D. Bratt, 165–204. Grand Rapids: Eerdmans, 1998.

Ladson-Billings, Gloria. "Silences as Weapons: Challenges of a Black Professor Teaching White Students." *Theory into Practice* 35:2 (1996) 79–86.

Lee, J. "Racial and Ethnic Achievement Gap Trends: Reversing the Progress Toward Equity?" *Educational Researcher* 31:1 (2002) 3–12.

Leege, David C. "Catholics and the Civic Order: Parish Participation, Politics, and Civic Participation." *The Review of Politics* 50:4 (1988) 704–36.

Leonard, Bill. *God's Last and Only Hope: The Fragmentation of the Southern Baptist Convention*. Grand Rapids: Eerdmans, 1990. Quoted in Susan Lea Jennings,

"Women's Place: Women's Roles in Church and Society." MA thesis, Appalachian State University, 1998.

Lewis, Amanda, Mark Chesler, and Tyrone Forman. "The Impact of 'Color-blind' Ideologies on Students of Color: Intergroup Relations at a Predominantly White University." *The Journal of Negro Education* 69:1/2 (2000) 74–91.

Lewis, John. "The Power of Historic Places: My Civil Rights Experiences." In *African American Historic Places*, edited by Beth Savage, 61–66. New York: Preservation, 1994.

Lincoln, C. Eric, and Lawrence H. Mamiya. *The Black Church in the African-American Experience*. Durham, NC: Duke University Press, 1990.

Linenthal, Edward. "Epilogue." In *Slavery and Public History: The Tough Stuff of American Memory*, edited by James Oliver Horton and Lois E. Horton, 213–24. New York: The New Press, 2006.

Linton, Larissa L., and Neil Christiansen. "Restoring Equity or Introducing Bias? A Contingency Model of Attitudes Toward Affirmative Action Programs." *Journal of Applied Social Psychology* 36:7 (2006) 1617–39.

Lo, S., I. Sharif, and P. O. Ozuah. "Health Literacy among English-Speaking Parents in a Poor Urban Setting." *Journal of Health Care for the Poor and Underserved* 17:3 (2006) 504–11.

Logan, Rayford W. *The Betrayal of the Negro: From Rutherford B. Hayes to Woodrow Wilson*. Cambridge, MA: Da Capo, 1997.

López, María Pabón. "Attorneys, Female." In *Multimedia Encyclopedia of Women in Today's World*, 1st edition, edited by Mary Zeiss Stange, Carol K. Oyster, and Jane E. Sloan, 108–10. Thousand Oaks, CA: SAGE, 2011.

Loury, Alden. "If Chicago's West and South Sides Were Their Own Cities, They'd Be the Deadliest and Most Violent in America." *Chicago Now*, June 17, 2010. http://www.chicgaonow.com

Loewen, James. *Lies My Teacher Told Me: Everything Your American History Textbook Got Wrong*. New York: Touchstone, 1995.

———. *Lies Across America: What Our Historic Sites Get Wrong*. New York: Touchstone, 1999.

———. "What We Remember. What We Forget. What Difference it Makes." Contesting Public Memories Conference, Syracuse University, Syracuse, NY, October 8, 2005.

Love, Patrick, and Donna Talbot. "Defining Spiritual Development: A Missing Consideration for Student Affairs." *NASPA Journal* 37:1 (1999) 361–75.

Lowenthal, David. *The Past is a Foreign Country*. Cambridge: Cambridge University Press, 1986.

Loyd-Paige, Michelle R. *Lost and Found: The Anatomy of a Reconnected Life*. Unpublished intellectual autobiography, July 2007. Consultation for Afro-Christian Scholars in Higher Education Self-Reflective Writing Exercise.

———. Self-Reflective Writing Entry, June 20, 2011. Pre-ME-LDI survey answers.

———. Self-Reflective Writing Entry, June 24, 2011. Post-ME-LDI survey answers.

———. ME-LDI transcripts, 2011.

Manganello, J. A. "Health Literacy and Adolescents: A Framework and Agenda for Future Research." *Health Education Research* 23:5 (2008) 840–47.

Marbley, Aretha Faye. "Finding My Voice: An African-American Female Professor at a Predominantly White University." *Advancing Women in Leadership Online*

Journal 22 (Winter 2007). No pages. Online: http://www.advancingwomen.com/awl/winter2007/finding_my_voice.htm.

Martin, Sandy Dwayne. "Black Baptists, Foreign Missions, and African Colonization, 1814–1882." In *Black Americans and the Missionary Movement in Africa*, edited by Sylvia M. Jacobs, 63–76. Westport, CT: Greenwood, 1982.

Martin, Tony. *Race First: The Ideological and Organizational Struggles of Marcus Garvey and the Universal Negro Improvement Association*. Dover, MA: Majority, 1976.

Mason, Mary Ann. "Balancing Act: Role Models and Mentors." *Chronicle of Higher Education*, March 25, 2009. http://chronicle.com/jobs/news/2009/03/2009032501c.htm.

Massey, Garth. "Thinking about Affirmative Action: Arguments Supporting Preferential Policies." *Review of Social Policy Research* 21:6 (2004) 783–97.

Matthews, Kenneth A., and M. Sydney Park. *The Post-Racial Church: A Biblical Framework for Multiethnic Reconciliation*. Grand Rapids: Kregel, 2011.

Mayhew, David. *Congress: The Electoral Connection*. New Haven, CT: Yale University Press, 1974.

McAdam, Doug, John D. McCarthy, and Mayer N. Zald. *Comparative Perspectives on Social Movements: Political Opportunities, Mobilizing Structures, and Cultural Framings*. Cambridge: Cambridge University Press, 1996.

McClerking, Harwood K., and Eric L. McDaniel. "Belonging and Doing: Political Churches and Black Political Participation." *Political Psychology* 26:5 (2005) 721–53.

McDaniel, Eric L., and Christopher G. Ellison. "God's Party: Race, Religion, and Partisanship over Time." *Political Research Quarterly* 61:2 (June 2008) 180–91.

McGreevy, John T. *Parish Boundaries: The Catholic Encounter with Race in the Twentieth Century Urban North*. Chicago: University of Chicago Press, 1996.

Meneses, Eloise Hiebert. "Science and the Myth of Biological Race." In *This Side of Heaven: Race, Ethnicity, and Christian Faith*, edited by Robert J. Priest and Alvaro L. Nieves, 33–46. New York: Oxford University Press, 2007.

Miller, Will, Brinck Kerr, and Margaret Reid. "Descriptive Representation by Gender and Race/Ethnicity in Municipal Bureaucracies: Change in US Multiethnic Cities, 1987–2001." *Journal of Women, Politics & Policy* 31:3 (2010) 217–42.

Mission Herald. July 1920, n.p.

Mitchell, Jerry. "Big Piece of Civil Rights History is Falling Apart." *USA Today*, February 12, 2007, section 3A.

Montgomery, William E. *Under Their Own Vine and Fig Tree: The African-American Church in the South 1865–1900*. Baton Rouge, LA: Louisiana State University Press, 1993.

Moody, JoAnn. *Faculty Diversity: Problems and Solutions*. New York: Routledge, 2004.

Morris, Aldon. "Reflections on Social Movement Theory: Criticisms and Proposals." *Contemporary Sociology* 29:3 (2000) 445–54.

Moses, Wilson Jeremiah. *The Golden Age of Black Nationalism, 1850–1925*. New York: Oxford University Press, 1978.

Moses, Yolanda T. *Black Women in Academe: Issues and Strategies*. Washington, DC: Association of American Colleges and Universities, 1989.

Myers, David. *Social Psychology*. San Francisco: McGraw-Hill, 2005. Quoted in Melissa Diaz, "Social Bias: Sound Familiar?" *Yahoo! Voices*, August 12, 2011.

Nash, Jennifer C. "Re-thinking Intersectionality." *Feminist Review* 89 (2008) 1–15.

Neal, Arthur. *National Trauma and Collective Memory: Extraordinary Events in the American Experience.* New York: M. E. Sharpe, 2005.

Newlin, Kelly, Kathleen Knafl, and G. D'Eramo Melkus. "African-American Spirituality: A Concept Analysis." *Advances in Nursing Science* 25:2 (2002) 57–70.

O'Quinn, Doretha. "Formal and Informal Approaches to the Mentoring of Faculty and Professional People of Color in a Predominantly White Academic Setting." Presentation at Educating for Shalom Conference, Calvin College, November 5–7, 2010.

Osborn, C. Y. et al. "Measuring Adult Literacy in Health Care: Performance of the Newest Vital Sign." *American Journal of Health Behavior* 31:1 (2007) S36-S46.

Papi, Hector. "Pastor." In *The Catholic Encyclopedia* 11. New York: Robert Appleton Company, 1911. http://www.newadvent.org/cathen/11537b.htm.

Parker, R. M., D. W. Baker, M. V. Williams, and J. R. Nurss. "The Test of Functional Health Literacy in Adults: A New Instrument for Measuring Patients' Literacy Skills." *Journal General Internal Medicine* 10:10 (1995) 537–41.

Painter, Neil. *Sojourner Truth: A Life a Symbol.* New York: W. W. Norton, 1996.

Patton, Stacey. "Black Studies: 'Swaggering Into the Future': A New Generation of Ph.D.'s Advances the Discipline." *Chronicle of Higher Education* 28:33 (2012) A2–A6.

Pascarella, Ernest T., Christopher T. Pierson, Gregory C. Wolniak, and Patrick T. Terenzini. "First-Generation College Students: Additional Evidence on College Experiences and Outcomes." *Journal of Higher Education* 75:3 (2004) 249–84.

PBS. *Race: The Power of an Illusion.* PBS video, California Newsreel, 2003. http://www.pbs.org/race/000_General/000_00-Home.htm.

Petersen, C., J. A. Glover, and R. R. Ronning. "An Examination of Three Prose Learning Strategies on Reading Comprehension." *Journal of General Psychology* 102:1 (1980) 39–52.

Pew Forum. "A Religious Portrait of African-Americans." January 30, 2009. http://www.pewforum.org

Pew Research Center. U.S. Religious Landscape Survey, June 23, 2008. Washington, DC: Pew Forum on Religion and Public Life.

Phillips, Kendall, ed. *Framing Public Memory.* Tuscaloosa, AL: The University of Alabama Press, 2004.

Pittman, Chavella T. "Racial Microaggressions: The Narratives of African American Faculty at a Predominantly White University." *The Journal of Negro Education* 81:1 (2012) 83.

Pye, Yvette L. "Innovations in Mentoring: The Many Faces of Chosen to Achieve." In *Breaking the Mold of Education for Culturally and Linguistically Diverse Students,* edited by Andrea Honigsfeld and Audrey Cohan, 119–28. Lanham: Rowman and Littlefield Education, 2012.

Raboteau, Albert J. *A Fire in the Bones: Reflections on African-American Religious History.* Boston, MA: Beacon, 1995.

———. "Relating Race and Religion." In *Uncommon Faithfulness: The Black Catholic Experience,* edited by M. Shawn Copeland, 9–25. New York: Orbis, 2009.

Randolph, Laura B. "All I Really Need to Know I Learned From Black Women." *Ebony,* May 28, 1997.

Rawls, John. *Political Liberalism.* New York: Columbia University Press, 1996.

Rawls, Phillip. "Civil Rights Sites Vital to Alabama Tourism." *USA Today,* January 28, 2004, section 11A.

Redkey, Edwin. *Black Exodus: Black Nationalist and Back-to-Africa Movements, 1890–1910*. New Haven, CT: Yale University Press, 1969.

Reed Jr., Adolph L. *The Jesse Jackson Phenomenon: The Crisis of Purpose in Afro-American Politics*. New Haven: Yale University Press, 1986.

Roberts, Donna. "Qualitative vs. Quantitative Data." *Regents Exam Prep Center*, 1998–2012. http://regentsprep.org/Regents/math/ALGEBRA/AD1/qualquant.htm.

Roberts, Terrence. *Lessons From Little Rock*. Little Rock, AR: Butler Center, 2009.

Robertson, Dan, Simon Larose, Roland Roy and Frederic Legault. "Risk Factors and Success: Non-Intellectual Learning Factors as Determinants for Success in College." *Research in Higher Education* 39:3 (1998) 275–97.

Romano, Renee, and Leigh Raiford, eds. *The Civil Rights Movement in American Memory*. Athens, GA: The University of Georgia Press, 2006.

Rosenstone, Steven J., and John Mark Hansen. *Mobilization, Participation, and Democracy in America*. New York: Macmillan, 1993.

Rudd, R. E. "Health Literacy Skills of U.S. Adults." *American Journal of Health Behavior* 31:1 (2007) S8-SS18.

Ryan, William. *Equality*. New York: Pantheon, 1981.

Sabharwal, S., S. Badarudeen , and S. U. Kunju. "Readability of Online Patient Education Materials from the AAOS Web Site." *Clinical Orthopaedics and Related Research* 466:1 (1981) 1245–50.

Salkind, N. J., ed. *Encyclopedia of Educational Psychology* (1–2). Thousand Oaks, CA: SAGE, 2008.

Selby, Gary. *Martin Luther King and the Rhetoric of Freedom: The Exodus Narrative in America's Struggle for Civil Rights*. Waco, TX: Baylor University Press, 2008.

Sechrist, Linda. "The Power of Place." *Natural Awakenings*, September 1, 2012, 25.

Shea, J. A. et al. "Assessing Health Literacy in African American and Caucasian Adults: Disparities in Rapid Estimate of Adult Literacy in Medicine (REALM) Scores." *Family Medicine* 36:8 (2004) 575.

Shuster, Kate. *Teaching the Movement 2014: The State of Civil Rights Education in the United States*. Montgomery, AL: Southern Poverty Law Center, 2014.

Singh, Robert. *The Congressional Black Caucus: Racial Politics in the U.S. Congress*. Thousand Oaks, CA: Sage, 1997.

Smith, Gregory A. "One Church, Many Messages: The Politics of the U.S. Catholic Clergy." In *Catholics and Politics: The Dynamic Tension between Faith and Power* edited by Kristin E. Heyer and Mark J. Rozell, 43–60. Washington, DC: Georgetown University Press, 2008.

Smith, R. Drew, and Fredrick C. Harris. *Black Churches and Local Politics: Clergy Influence, Organizational Partnerships, and Civic Empowerment*. Lanham, MD: Rowman and Littlefield, 2005.

Smith, William, Walter R. Allen, and Lynette L. Danley. "Assume the Position. . . You Fit the Description." *American Behavioral Scientist* 51:4 (2007) 551–78.

Snow, C., M. Burns, and P. Griffin, eds. *Preventing Reading Difficulties in Young Children*. Washington, DC: National Academy Press, 1998.

Snyder, Thomas D., and Sally A. Dillow. 2011. "Digest of Education Statistics, 2010 (NCES 2011–2015)." National Center for Education Statistics, US Department of Education. Table 256.

Solorazano, Daniel G., and Tara J. Yasso. "Critical Race Methodology: Counter-Storytelling as an Analytic Framework for Education Research." *Qualitative Inquiry* 8:1 (2002) 23–44.

Sotello Viernes Turner, Caroline, Juan Carlos Gonzalez, and J. Luke Wood. "Faculty of Color in Academe: What 20 Years of Literature Tells Us." *Journal of Diversity in Higher Education* 1:3 (2008) 139–68.

Sotello Viernes Turner, Caroline. Executive Summary for *Keeping our Faculties: Addressing the Recruitment and Retention of Faculty of Color in Higher Education* Symposium, University of Minnesota, October 18–20, 1998. http://www.diversityweb.org.

Sowell, Thomas. *Affirmative Action Around the World: An Empirical Study*. New Haven, CT: Yale University Press, 2004.

———. *Civil Rights: Rhetoric or Reality?* 1st Quill Edition. New York: William Morrow, 1985.

———. *The Quest for Cosmic Justice*. New York: Free Press, 1999.

Spargo, E., and G. R. Williston. *Timed Readings*. Providence, RI: Jamestown, 1973.

Speck, Bruce, and Sherry L. Hoppe. *Searching for Spirituality in Higher Education*. New York: Peter Lang, 2007.

Spruill, Ken. "Civil Writings: Blogging the Civil Rights Bus Tour." CD-ROM. Pittsburgh: PNC Financial Services, 2006.

SPSS Inc. PASW Statistics for Windows, Version 18.0. Chicago: SPSS, 2009.

Stanley, Cristine A., and Yvonna S. Lincoln. "Cross Race Faculty Mentoring." *Change* 37:2 (2007) 46.

Stone, Deborah. *Policy Paradox: The Art of Political Decision Making*. New York: W. W. Norton, 2001.

Strauss, Anselm, and Juliet Corbin. *Basics of Qualitative Research: Techniques and Procedures for Developing Grounded Theory*. Thousand Oaks, CA: Sage, 1998.

Strayhorn, Terrell L. *The Evolving Challenges of Black College Students: New Insights for Policy, Practice, and Research*. Sterling: Stylus, 2010.

Tate, Katherine. *Black Faces in the Mirror: African Americans and their Representatives in the U.S. Congress*. Princeton: Princeton University Press, 2004.

Texeira, Erin. "Civil Rights Leaders Worry Focus on Past Hurts Movement." *New Pittsburgh Courier*, February 8–14, 2006, section A3.

This Far by Faith: An African American Resource for Worship. Minneapolis: Augsburg Fortress, 1999.

Thomas, Linda E. "Womanist Theology, Epistemology, and a New Anthropological Paradigm." *Cross Currents* 48:4 (1998). No pages. Online: http://www.crosscurrents.org/thomas.htm.

Tilly, Charles. "Survey Article: Power—Top Down and Bottom Up." *The Journal of Political Philosophy* 7:3 (1999) 330–52.

Torgesen, J. K., R. K. Wagner, and C. A. Rashotte. *Test of Word Reading Efficiency*. Austin, TX: Pro-Ed, 1997.

Touchton, Judy, and Caryn McTighe Musil, and Kathryn Peltier Campbell. "A Measure of Equity: Women's Progress in Higher Education." *Program on the Status and Education of Women*, Association of American Colleges and Universities, 2009.

Townsend-Johnson, Linda. *African-American Women Faculty Teaching at Institutions of Higher Learning in the Pacific Northwest: Challenges, Dilemmas, and Sustainability*. Corvallis, OR: Oregon State University, 2006.

Trotman, Frances K. "The Imposter Phenomenon Among African American Women in U.S. Institutions of Higher Education: Implications for Counseling." In *Compelling Counseling Interventions*, edited by G. R. Walz, J. C. Bleuer, and R. K. Yep, 77–86. Alexandria, VA: American Counseling Association, 2009.

United States Conference of Catholic Bishops. "Backgrounder: African American Catholics in the United States." Office of Media Relations. http://old.usccb.org/comm/backgrounders/african_americans.shtml

U.S. Congress. House. Donald Payne. Haiti Earthquake Relief. 2010. 111th Congress., 2nd session.

U.S. Congress. House. Barbara Lee. Haiti Earthquake Relief. 2010. 111th Congress., 2nd session.

U.S. Congress. House. Sheila Jackson. Haiti Earthquake Relief. 2010. 111th Congress., 2nd session.

U.S. Congress. House. Maxine Waters. Haiti Earthquake Relief. 2010. 111th Congress., 2nd session.

U.S. Congress. House. Bobby Rush. Haiti Earthquake Relief. 2010. 111th Congress., 2nd session.

U.S. Congress. House. John Conyers. Haiti Earthquake Relief and TPS. 2010. 111th Congress., 2nd session.

U.S. Congress. House. Nita Lowey. Haiti Earthquake Relief. 2010. 111th Congress., 2nd session.

U.S. Congress. House. Debbie Wasserman-Schultz. Haiti Earthquake Relief. 2010. 111th Congress., 2nd session.

U.S. Congress. House. Eliot Engel. Haiti Earthquake Relief. 2010. 111th Congress., 2nd session.

U.S. Congress. House. Ileana Ros-Letihen. Pre-Earthquake Commentary on Challenges in Haiti. 2009. 111th Congress., 1st session.

U.S. Congress. House. Ileana Ros-Letihen. Haiti Earthquake Relief. 2010. 111th Congress., 2nd session.

U.S. Congress. House. Jerry Moran. Haiti Earthquake Relief. 2010. 111th Congress., 2nd session.

U.S. Congress. House. Melvin Watt. Statements on Welfare Reform. 1995. 104th Congress., 1st session.

U.S. Congress. House. Lee Hamilton. Statements on Welfare Reform. 1996. 104th Congress., 2nd session.

Vargas, Lucilia, ed. *Women Faculty of Color in the White Classroom: Narratives on the Pedagogical Implications of Teacher Diversity*. New York: Peter Lang, 2002.

Verba, Schlozman, and Henry Brady. *Voice and Equality: Civic Voluntarism in America*. Cambridge: Harvard University Press, 1995.

Vestal, Christine. "Alabama Seeks Civil Rights Tourism, Racial Accord." Stateline.org, November 11, 2008. No pages. Online: http://www.stateline.org/live/details/story?contentId=354797.

Waller, James. *Prejudice Across America*. Jackson, MS: University Press of Mississippi, 2000.

Washington, Booker T. *Up From Slavery*. Edited by W. Fitzhugh Brundage. Boston: St. Martin's, 2003.

Washington, Patricia. "Narratives from Women of Color in the Halls of the Academe." Review of *Contesting the Terrain of the Ivory Tower: Spiritual Leadership of African-*

American Women in the Academy, by Rochelle Garner; *Building Bridges for Women of Color in Higher Education: A Practical Guide for Success*, edited by Conchita Y. Battle and Chontrese M. Doswell; and *From Oppression to Grace: Women of Color and Their Dilemmas Within the Academy*, edited by Theodorea Regina Berry and Nathalie D. Mizelle. *Feminist Collections* 28:1 (2006) 1.

Weisenfeld, Judith. *African American Women and Christian Activism: New York's Black YWCA, 1905–1945*. Cambridge, MA: Harvard University Press, 1997.

Weiss, B. D. et al. "Quick Assessment of Literacy in Primary Care: The Newest Vital Sign." *Annals of Family Medicine* 3:6 (2005) 514–22.

Westerlund, Dave. "Flesh and Blood History." Jubilee. http://www.ccojubilee.org/minex2001/dec2001/Westerlund_December01.html.

Wheeler, Edward L. *Uplifting the Race: The Black Minister in the New South 1865–1902*. Lanham, NY: University Press of America, 1986.

Williams, Rihana S., Omer Ari, and Cedrick Dortch. "The Relations Between Human Capital, Implicit Views of Intelligence, and Literacy Performance: Implications For The Obama Education Era." *Urban Education* 46:4 (2011) 563–87.

Williams, Rihana S., Omer Ari, and Carmen N. Santamaria. "Measuring College Students' Reading Comprehension Ability Using Cloze Tests." *Journal of Research in Reading* 34:2 (2011) 215–31.

Williams, Walter L. *Black Americans and the Evangelization of Africa 1877–1900*. Madison, WI: University of Wisconsin Press, 1982.

Wilson, Catherine E. *The Politics of Latino Faith: Religion, Identity, and Urban Community*. New York: New York University Press, 2008.

Wilson, J. Matthew, ed. *From Pews to Polling Places: Faith and Politics in the American Religious Mosaic*. Washington, DC: Georgetown University Press, 2007.

Wilson, Reginald. "Women of Color in Academic Administration: Trends, Progress, and Barriers." *Sex Roles* 21:1/2 (1989) 85.

Wright, Erik Olin, and Joel Rogers. *American Society: How it Really Works*. New York: W. W. Norton, 2011.

Wolf, M. S. et al. "Misunderstanding of Prescription Drug Warning Labels among Patients with Low Literacy." *American Journal of Health-System Pharmacy* 63:11 (2006) 1048–55.

Yancy, George. "Whiteness and the Return of the Black Body." *The Journal of Speculative Philosophy* 19 (2005) 230.

Yergeau, Melanie. "Beaver Falls to Birmingham." *Geneva Magazine* 85:1 (2004) 6–7.

Zangwill, Israel. *The Melting Pot*. Baltimore: Macmillan, 1914. http://www.gutenberg.org/files/23893/23893-h/23893-h.htm.

Contributors

Chizara Ahuama-Jonas (BA, Georgia State University) is a clinical graduate student at the University of Cinncinati who completed her undergraduate honors thesis under the direction of Rihana S. Mason.

Todd Allen (PhD, Duquesne University) is Professor of Communication Studies at Grove City College. In 2006 Dr. Allen founded The Common Ground Project, a community based non-profit dedicated to promoting an understanding of the Civil Rights Movement. Through this organization he conducts the "Returning to the Roots of Civil Rights Bus Tour," which visits many of the key sites of the movement. He has been the recipient of numerous awards including fellowships at the Gilder Lehrman Institute of American History and the National Endowment for the Humanities, New Pittsburgh Courier "50 Men of Excellence," and the YWCA of Greater Pittsburgh Racial Justice Award.

Vincent Bacote (PhD, Drew University) is Associate Professor of Theology and the Director of the Center for Applied Christian Ethics at Wheaton College in Wheaton, IL. Dr. Bacote has also contributed to books such as *Global Theology in Evangelical Perspective* (InterVarsity Press, 2012), *Prophetic Evangelicals: Envisioning a Just and Peaceable Kingdom* (Eerdmans, 2012), *Keep Your Head Up: America's New Black Christian Leaders, Social Consciousness, and the Cosby Conversation* (Crossway, 2012), *Not Just Science* (Zondervan, 2005), *The Dictionary for the Theological Interpretation of the Bible* (Baker, 2005), *What Does it Mean to be Saved?* (Baker, 2002), *Building Unity in the Church of the New Millennium* (Moody Press, 2002), and *The Best Christian Writing 2000* (Harper, 2000). He is a regular columnist for *Comment* and has also had articles appear in magazines such as *Christianity Today* and *Re:generation Quarterly* and journals such as *Urban Mission* and the *Journal for Christian Theological Research*. He has been President of the Christian Theological Research

Fellowship, and is a member of the Evangelical Theological Society, the Society of Christian Ethics and the American Academy of Religion.

Anthony B. Bradley (PhD, Westminster Theological Seminary; MA Fordham University) is Associate Professor of Theology and Ethics at The King's College in New York City and serves as a Research Fellow at the Acton Institute in Grand Rapids, Michigan. Dr. Bradley lectures at colleges, universities, business organizations, conferences, and churches throughout the US and abroad. His writings on religious and cultural issues have been published in a variety of journals, including the *Atlanta Journal-Constitution*, the *Detroit News*, and *World* magazine. Dr. Bradley is called upon by members of the broadcast media for comment on current issues and has appeared on C-SPAN, NPR, CNN/Headline News, Fox News, and Court TV Radio, among others. His books include: *Liberating Black Theology* (2010), *Black and Tired* (2011), *The Political Economy of Liberation* (2012), *Keep Your Head Up* (2012), and *Aliens In The Promised Land* (2013).

Deshonna Collier-Goubil (PhD, Howard University; MA, Fuller Theological Seminary) is an Assistant Professor of Sociology at Biola University. Her dissertation work used spatial analysis to look at the effects of economic strain (measured by home foreclosures) on domestic violence while controlling for characteristics of neighborhood deprivation. She's also completed research on youth violence in urban communities, researcher-practitioner community collaborations, and prisoner re-entry. Additionally, Dr. Collier-Goubil conducts research in hip hop, the urban church, and black theology, as well as womanist musings. In her current post, Dr. Collier-Goubil coordinates the criminology concentration, teaches classes on research methods, criminology, and race. In her spare time, Dr. Collier-Goubil developed a leadership development group for female students of color on Biola's campus and the program is flourishing.

Larycia A. Hawkins (PhD, University of Oklahoma) is Associate Professor of Politics and International Relations at Wheaton College in Wheaton, IL. In 2011, her co-edited book, *Religion and American Politics: Classic and Contemporary Perspectives,* was published by Pearson. Her active research agenda includes projects that explore how and whether black liberation theology frames contemporary black political rhetoric and how black liberation theology is reflected on black political agendas, like those of the Congressional Black Caucus and the NAACP. Prior to academia, Dr. Hawkins worked briefly in state government administering federal programs, including the Social Security Disability program and the Community Development Block Grant.

Michelle Loyd-Paige (PhD, Purdue University) is Executive Associate to the president for diversity and inclusion at Calvin College in Grand Rapids, Michigan. Dr. Loyd-Paige accepted the executive associate's position after seven years as the dean for multicultural affairs and twenty years as a faculty member in the department of sociology and social work at Calvin College in 2013. Dr. Loyd-Paige's primary role is to lead and promote campus-wide initiatives that help to facilitate systemic changes that inspire anti-racism, diversity, and equity as essential values in support of academic excellence. Dr. Loyd-Paige's research interests include: afro-Christian clergywomen, anti-racism, being black and reformed, and plant-based diets among African-Americans.

Rihana S. Mason (PhD, University of South Carolina) is an Assistant Professor of Psychology at Emmanuel College. Dr. Mason's research areas include: the time course of incidental vocabulary acquisition, the assessment of vocabulary and reading in children and adults from disadvantaged backgrounds, and the influences of cognitive factors like working memory on sentence comprehension. At Emmanuel College, Dr. Mason integrates her faith and scholarship through the teaching of undergraduate courses related to the areas of development, cognition, social psychology, statistics, assessment and research.

Yvonne RB-Banks (EdD, University of Minnesota) is a Professor in the department of education, and Dean of Academic Support Services at University of Northwestern-St. Paul, in St. Paul, Minnesota. Dr. RB-Banks' primary research focus relates to issues surrounding equity in the Pk-12 educational system. Specially, her research centers on special education placements and remediation strategies that impact African-American males' over-representation in EB/D settings and barriers to entering higher education. Dr. RB-Banks is an author and international presenter on a variety of topics related to culture, equity, and gender experiences in the classroom. She teaches in the core curriculum and uses her courses to promote educational equity through the development of pre-service teachers. She has a growing interest in equity research centered on African-American faculty evolving out of her experiences as the only African American female faculty/administrator at her institution after fifteen years.

Eric Michael Washington (PhD, Michigan State University) is Assistant Professor of African American and African History, and Director of African and African Diaspora Studies at Calvin College, Grand Rapids, Michigan. A native of New Orleans, Washington's interest is in nineteenth-century and early-twentieth-century African American Baptist missions to Africa focusing on the interrelation of evangelicalism and Ethiopianism as dual motivating ideals. His other research interests include the development of black Atlantic Calvinism during the late-eighteenth and early-nineteenth centuries primarily through the study and analysis of slave narratives.

Subject and Character Index

18433812R00134

Made in the USA
Middletown, DE
06 March 2015